The

SPA MANAGER'S ESSENTIAL GUIDE

MIKE WALLACE & MELANIE SMITH

(G) Goodfellow Publishers Ltd

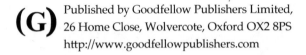

Published by Goodfellow Publishers Limited,
26 Home Close, Wolvercote, Oxford OX2 8PS
http://www.goodfellowpublishers.com

British Library Cataloguing in Publication Data: a catalogue record for this
title is available from the British Library.

Library of Congress Catalog Card Number: on file.

ISBN: 978-1-911635-20-8

Design and typesetting by P.K. McBride, www.macbride.org.uk

Cover design by Cylinder

Printed by Marston Book Services, www.marston.co.uk

Contents

Acknowledgements

Whilst the information in this book has been based on the experience and views of the authors, we are extremely grateful for the contributions sent to us and for those that took the time to answer our research survey. Feedback came from all over the world including Malaysia, UK, Czech Republic, China, USA, Serbia, Austria, Romania, Germany, France, Hungary, Greece, Italy, Slovakia, U.A.E., Kenya and Croatia. We would like to thank all our contributors; for those that agreed to have their name mentioned we would like to give our sincere appreciation – Csilla Mezösi, Sarra Temple, Heréb István, Ivona Hrdinová, Ioana Marian, Jane Wilson, Vladi Kovanic, Vladimir Mozetič, Chris Theyer, Adriana Svátková-Haluzová, Anita Bogó, Suzana Pretorian, Ádám Orgoványi, Nataša Ranitović, Szilvia Móricz, Sona Zabranska, Massimo Giovanetti, Gyula Bakonyi, Patricie Irlveková, Elena Bazzocchi, Alastair Graham, Marion Schneider, Kurt von Storch, Stavros Mavridis, Ilan Geva, Balázs Kovács, Klaus Pilz, Márta Vajda, Zseraldina Richvalszki, Tobias Bielenstein, Árpád Godra, László Puczkó, Andrew Gibson, Claire Way, Robert Landsman, Sheila McCann, Viktor Marsalla, Simon Saunders, Dr Anke Zeqiri, Lisa Starr, Tracey Welsh.

About the authors

Mike Wallace is a thermal spa and wellness expert, with over 25 years' experience working in the health, wellness and spa operations. He provides specialist consultancy advice on thermal/hot spring and medical spas and is a well known international speaker. He also lectures at several colleges and universities on health tourism/spa management and contributes articles for various spa and health publications and co-written two books on health and wellness and spa management.

Melanie Smith is an Associate Professor from Budapest Metropolitan University, Hungary and the University of Tartu, Pärnu College, Estonia. She has lectured extensively in Health, Wellness and Spa Tourism in Hungary, Estonia, Austria, Germany and Switzerland. She has undertaken research and consultancy in this field including for ETC/UNWTO, she has written numerous publications and has been an invited keynote speaker in many countries worldwide.

Foreword

The spa industry is growing dynamically – there are over 50 educational establishments worldwide offering a degree in spa management and over 700 other spa managment related courses.

Looking at the industry demands for spa management skills and comparing them to what educational establishments and educational materials currently provide, it is evident that there is a mismatch in terms of what is being taught and what is actually required. Industry leaders have stated that they are looking for spa supervisors and leaders with business and management skills, as well as practical professional skills, such as flexibility, problem solving, teamwork, attitude and ethics. According to the Global Spa & Wellness Summit over 95% of spa industry leaders stated that they found problems hiring managers with the right combination of skills/experience and 63% of them stated that they have to invest further in training and mentoring because the training the managers had received was insufficient.

One of the reasons for this is that existing spa management teaching materials and courses do not concentrate on the practical skills needed in the day to day operation. They also tend to be more focused on the 'pampering', 'wellness' and 'beauty' sectors leaving a gap in the learning materials for the many other different types of spas, such as resort/destination spas and the large thermal mineral spring spas common in central Europe.

Mike Wallace and Dr. Melanie Smith have teamed up to produce a book specifically targeted at today's spa managers and potential spa managers, including those who have not had any formal training and who wish to increase their knowledge in this field. The book is also designed for therapists or students interested in spa management, teachers lecturing on spa/health tourism management or indeed anybody interested in the field of spa and wellness from an international perspective, including those working in the mineral/thermal spring spa facilities.

Since working in a spa is a hands-on practical job, effort has been made to make the style 'easy to read' specifically pinpointing and examining the most important elements required to manage a spa successfully.

This book is divided into two sections: the first seven chapters cover the most important aspects of spa management (customer service, leadership, team management, sales, finance, quality and health and safety) whilst the second part of the book deals with essential product knowledge every spa manager should be aware of (health and wellness concepts, fitness and diet, sustainability etc). The book will appeal to an international readership, and spa managers working in Europe, particularly in mineral spring/thermal operations, will find all of the necessary advice and information to assist them in managing these types of facilities.

Culturally, particularly in Europe, spas have historically been places of rest, recuperation and healing – places to escape to, to slow down in and recharge. In today's increasingly manic, technology-obsessed world, spas have a crucial part to play in improving the quality of people's lives. They are also essential to a sustainable economy. They improve the lives and health of citizens, and compared to other industries, they have less of an adverse effect on the environment– spas, particularly those in rural destinations or resorts, help to contribute positively to the local economy. In view of the coronavirus pandemic all spas will have to change both operationally and conceptually if they are to survive, providing facilities that are hygienic and safe, as well as treatments that boost the immune system and promote holistic health. Spas do have a future in this new environment, particularly in attracting a local clientele who may be more reluctant to travel long distances – smaller, less crowded spa facilities having a distinct advantage.

The aim of this book is to help to improve the quality of spas, as well as to motivate and inspire the next generation of spa leaders and managers.

Mike Wallace & Melanie Smith
Budapest, 2020

1 The importance of customer care and service design in the spa environment

Good and bad customer service

Customer service must be at the heart of any successful spa operation. This is why, before discussing any other topics, this book begins by examining the ways that spa managers can both meet and exceed the expectations of not just today's spa goers, but also the spa goers of the future.

As people become more educated and travel more often, globally customer service levels are becoming more sophisticated. Spa goers are more discerning in both what they expect and what they will accept as an acceptable customer service. Spa customer service etiquette is therefore having to adapt and change – and it is evolving, constantly.

Meeting customers' expectations is the core essence of what a spa must deliver. Without good customer service a spa will run into problems. Beautifully designed spas have been known to fail because they were not able to consistently offer good customer service, and in contrast, excellent customer service can compensate for a spa operation that is past its sell-by-date.

People experience customer service on a daily basis and even the most undemanding of customers are now able to differentiate between good service and bad service. A bad experience will stick, it may also be shared between family and friends and, in today's digital world, to possibly hundreds of people via social media.

To understand what constitutes good customer service it is worth examining some of the common signs of what constitutes bad customer service – the list is not extensive, but its characteristics are unfortunately all too common:

- **Sloppy body language**: body language reveals the thoughts and attitude of the person serving – just through their posture the customer will be able to tell in seconds whether the member of staff is professional and has their best interests at heart, or not.

- **A low level of energy and/or poor attitude**: through body language and micro-movements the customer can immediately pick up on the energy of the member of staff. In the hospitality and spa industry a helpful, positive attitude and enthusiastic energy level are expected as the minimum starting point. If what is delivered is anything less, at best the customer will be disappointed, at worst it may be the beginning of the start of a conflict.

- **Disinterest**: when the customer gets the feeling that the person serving them is not 100% committed to serving them or putting in the necessary level of effort – again evident through the server's body language.

- **Speed**: going too fast for the guest (chivvying them along) or just being too slow.

- **Chatting**: with other staff members over or in front of the guest.

- **Keeping the customer waiting**: ignoring them whilst finishing off, or occupied in, another task.

- **Abruptness**: answering queries and questions to a minimum (i.e. just giving "yes" or "no" answers) and not being forthcoming in communicating the required information.

- **Giving negative closing responses**: "no", "it's not possible", "I can't do that" "sorry, it's not available", etc. and not giving suitable alternatives.

To say our health club was run down would be an understatement. The spa had not been renovated for 30 years and our fitness equipment was well out of date. We also had a serious damp problem. We even used to joke that we could grow mushrooms in our spa! However I made that spa work. I picked a team that were full of personality and who loved people. They were my most valued asset and I treated them with total respect. I had a rule that whenever a member walked in through the door we would run to them with a smile (not wait for them to come to us), hand them a towel and greet them by name. We made it our intention to make our guests feel special and loved. I ordered retail goods and displayed them all around the club (mainly to hide the mould), we made a little counter into a coffee and snack bar and encouraged people to stay after their workout and chat to other members. Our USP was our happy 'family-like' atmosphere. Our tiny little club was designed for 500 members, but at its peak we reached 890 members, even selling more retail products than the larger clubs. Eventually we had to close membership and make a waiting list, and of course once there was a waiting list, everyone wanted to be part of our little oasis in Watford!

Sarra Temple, previously manager of Watford Health Club, UK.

Poor customer service has a serious negative impact on any business operation, but more so in a spa environment where everything depends on human interaction. The moment the customer experiences a poor interaction, it will kick-start negative emotions and they will begin to lose trust. If this experience is at the start of their spa journey, then they will be more likely to look for other problems to complain about. If a spa is consistently not delivering acceptable service in an environment where guests chat and share their experiences with one another, problems will escalate.

Whilst in the past, customers might have been satisfied with basic politeness and a smile, because of globalisation, expectations have become much higher. Worldwide, as customer service and service design have evolved, these expectations are showing no sign of slowing down and this is something which today's spa managers should be acutely aware of. Here, we examine the minimum that guests expect when visiting a spa:

- **A kind, genuine smiling face**: is a must and a minimum expectation required by all staff, from the cleaner to the manager. In a spa, guests expect authenticity, sincerity and empathy. Most are coming to relieve their stress levels, so staff should be doing everything they can to help their guests achieve this. A supermarket checkout worker's smile and greeting are not enough for the spa environment!

- **Good energy**: as stated above, the staff's body language and micro movements mean that the customer will be able to read their attitude and feel their energy. The energy of staff in a spa should reflect positivity and an openness to please.

- **Speed**: going at a speed slower or faster than the guest, even if it is delivered in a positive style is likely to frustrate and annoy the receiver, staff should pay attention and adapt to the different tempo of the guest that they are serving.

- **Flexibility**: staff should be able to handle queries and problems and provide an acceptable solution to most requests and/or complaints.

- **A willingness to do everything to meet the guest's requirements**: the guest should feel that the member of staff will help them and will go the extra mile if necessary.

- **Correct, clear and fast billing**: guests should be able to see clearly what they have bought, what is charged for is correct and that it is presented quickly and seamlessly.

In a well-run spa the above points are now expected by spa goers as the norm. If professional customer service is offered consistently, it results in better staff-customer interactions and happier customers, which in turn helps to contribute to a healthier atmosphere and a healthier business (which could possibly result in more opportunities for the staff). When delivering customer service training the spa manager should emphasize this to the staff and make them realize how good customer service has the potential to benefit them personally, both through a pleasant working environment and possible bonus and/or promotional opportunities in the long term.

When customers are being served and paying for a service, they are judging the person who is serving them, more so than in other daily interactions. The more exclusive the service, the more critical the customer will be. In a spa environment, where the relationship between the customer and staff member is more intimate than other service environments, the customer will be extra sensitive to how they are being handled. In their customer service training the spa manager should emphasize to their team the areas in which they will be judged in their daily interactions:

- **Personality**: the spa goer will be making up their mind if they like the person serving them or not.
- **Appearance**: the customer will expect whoever is providing the service to be well-presented and have an appealing manner.
- **Hygiene**: cleanliness and smell are particularly important in the spa environment, especially so for therapists carrying out treatments – spa customers take hygiene extremely seriously.
- **Credibility and efficiency**: the customer needs to trust whoever is treating or serving them, they need to feel that the server has their best interests at heart, is reliable and able to carry out the service professionally and to a high standard.
- **Attention to detail**: reflected in the appearance, body language and personal hygiene.

We judge people in many ways and categorize them accordingly. In the spa environment staff should be perceived to be in the category of a 'friend' and therefore staff should communicate in a 'friendly' way even though this is not and never should be a 'friendship' in the strict sense of the word. This sounds obvious, however, in spas where often customers are repeat guests, the line between communicating like a 'friend' and actually being one can often become blurred, leading to potential problems and conflicts of interest.

The status of the customer

Another important aspect of customer service in the spa environment is to be clear on the status level of the client and to respect it. In the following diagram you can see how the staff member should consciously place themselves at a lower level than the client. It is saying to the guest, "I value you; I respect that you are paying money for my service and I will put your needs before mine". Whilst this may sound obvious, this subtle understanding of status is often overlooked and not given enough credence, particularly in the West, where hierarchy and boundaries between client and server are often less formal and structured.

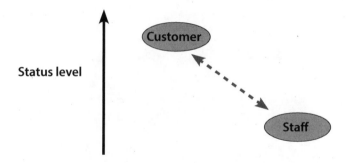

Figure 1.1: Correct status level for customer.

If the staff member starts to behave in a way or even feels that their status level is on the same (or in some cases higher!) than the guest, this will automatically cause an imbalance in the relationship. In a spa, where the relationship between client and staff can be extremely intimate, particularly in situations where customers frequent the same therapist over a long period of time, this status gap between the two can narrow. Providing excellence in customer service requires maintaining the boundary between client and guest, no matter how personal the connection and the for the staff member to always pitch their status level slightly lower than that of the guest regardless of how close their relationship has become. This should not be seen as degrading, but providing a professional service and giving the customer (regardless of who they are and how they have communicated) respect.

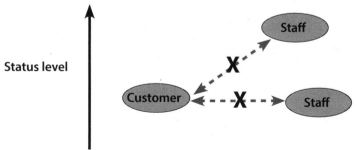

Figure 1.2: Incorrect status level for customer.

Customer service communication

In order for the spa manager to ensure that their spa is delivering excellent customer service it is necessary to understand the elements of how people communicate and judge each other. There are many theories on this, but perhaps the most popular, and one which is used in many customer service trainings, is Dr Albert Mehrabian's 7-38-55% rule.

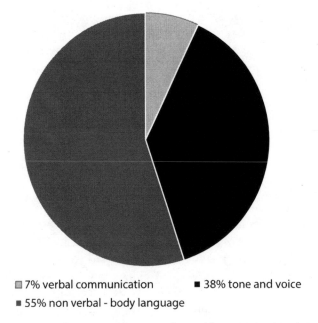

7% verbal communication   38% tone and voice
55% non verbal - body language

Figure 1.3: The components of communication. Adapted from Mehrabian's 7 – 38 – 55% rule.

What is important to note from this chart is how influential body language is. If 55% of communication is visual then how the staff dress and how they move has to be a priority in customer service training.

■ Appearance

Smiling is always emphasized as the starting point in customer service. For some staff members smiling will be easy, for others it will not come so naturally. Smiling is also related to cultural norms – in some cultures it is a natural expression, in other cultures people smile only when there is something to smile about. In a spa environment it is not enough to smile, the smile must also be perceived as natural and sincere, otherwise it will be considered fake. This is easy to say, but if a therapist has just finished a nine-hour shift of back-to-back massages, a smile becomes more of a challenge. Nevertheless, a natural pleasant smile and relaxed facial expression is the minimum of what clients expect to receive in a spa setting.

Each spa will have its own standards with regards to how they expect their staff to present themselves. Generally, however, spas are conservative work environments and will follow the expectations akin to a four- or five-star hotel. The general rules for this will be along the lines of:

- **Men**: Regular haircut, shaved or facial hair trimmed, nails cut short and trimmed, hands clean, no visible jewellery or tattoos, clean and smart uniform.
- **Women:** Orderly hair and tied back if long, nails clean and trim, minimum make-up, jewellery and perfume, clean and smart uniform.

Spa managers often underestimate or do not give enough credence to ensuring staff pay close attention to their appearance. Here are some of the main problems:

- **Name badges:** staff will often forget them. A manager should be prepared to say "can you put on your name badge, please" sometimes on a daily basis! Then there is the state of the name badge – is it clean? Has the logo worn off? Is the staff member's name blotched?

- **Men**: unshaved or unkempt trendy beards. The spa manager should be crystal clear regarding the company's policy towards beards and facial hair. They should keep a supply of razors handy to give to a therapist or member of staff should it be necessary to tell them to shave.

- **Nails**: it is obvious to state that nails should be trimmed and clean, this is particularly important in the case of the receptionists and therapists.

- **Odour**: the manager needs to tackle this discreetly but ensure that all staff are clean smelling for the clients. A treatment experience can be ruined by bad body odour, garlic breath or the smell of cigarette smoke. This can be a challenge in spas with a high volume of treatments, particularly for staff conducting physically demanding treatments, such as massage, mud packs, heat treatments etc. There should be facilities for staff to shower and the manager should also have reserve items of uniforms to give to a staff member if it is necessary to ask them to change. The manager should also make sure there is always soap, deodorant and mouthwash to give to a staff member if necessary.

- **Smoking**: Cigarette smoke stinks. It also lingers. It is not a habit that complements the job of people, particularly therapists, working in close proximity to a guest. For those therapists that do smoke, it should be spa policy that they should smoke wearing a coat or covering item of clothing (to prevent the smoke being absorbed into the uniform) and after smoking, to wash their hands thoroughly and take action to minimise the smell on their breath.

■ Body language

The biggest challenge which spa managers will face with regards to non-verbal communication in the spa environment is body language – getting the staff to understand that how they move and conduct themselves in the spa workplace is different to how they conduct themselves at home or in their private life. As to how challenging this will be, will depend on the local culture (whether it is hospitality orientated or not) in addition to the upbringing and training of the staff. In some cultures, body language and presentation will not be so much of an issue, in others it will require regular and ongoing monitoring and training. Any training in this area should be kept simple, targeted and cover the following areas:

- **Posture**: reinforcing confident upright posture, hands kept to sides wherever possible.

- **Gestures and movements**: that are slow and deliberate (fast excitable movements diminish the perception of professionalism).

■ **Eye contact:** it should be noted that in some cultures for example in the USA, prolonged eye contact is the norm, looking down or away can be seen as shifty. Alternatively, in other parts of the world, in certain countries in Africa or Asia for example, prolonged eye contact can be misconstrued as aggressive or intrusive. How much eye contact to give will be dependent on the culture of the guest being served.

The golden rule of hospitality!

It is a basic rule in the hospitality industry, particularly in hotels and spas, that the staff member should greet each guest (and other staff members and in fact anyone they meet) with eye contact and a smile. This is now the norm – globally. In spas with high volumes of guests, this can become a challenge. In one spa in Slovakia where 4,000 to 5,000 treatments are delivered each day, the spa manager, Sona Zabranska, used to say that just while walking from one end of the spa to the other she had to greet guests more than 50 times! Working on a cruise ship will mean greeting guests continually from morning till night. Whatever the circumstances and however demanding it may be, smiling and greeting is a must.

Customer service from behind a reception

Here are some basic expectations required of staff working behind a spa reception:

1 If the receptionist is seated, they should stand *before* the guest arrives to the reception desk whenever possible. This demonstrates both respect for the status of the guest and readiness to serve. Waiting until the guest arrives at the reception diminishes both the readiness of the receptionist and their respect for the client. Not standing up demonstrates little or no respect.

2 If the receptionist is busy but able to stop what they are doing they should do so, smile and turn to serve the guest quickly.

3 If the receptionist is busy and not able to stop what they are doing (for example being on the phone) they should turn, make eye contact with the guest and indicate that they will serve them as soon as they are able.

4 The receptionist always should try to use the name of the guest.

Speed and mirroring

Speed is often overlooked as being an important element of good customer service. Whilst some guests will be ponderous, wanting to take their time, asking detailed questions etc., at the other end of the spectrum there will be guests who are impatient and who want immediate attention and quick service. For a guest who likes to take their time, being rushed will unsettle them, for a guest who is impatient, having slow service will irritate and is likely to cause them to lose their patience. The person delivering the customer service must be able to mirror the tempo and energy of the guest that they are serving. In many cases, whilst the member of staff might be following all accepted customer service delivery expectations, this can all be completely undone by not mirroring speed. In certain scenarios, staff sometimes indirectly control the speed of the interaction and subtly force the customer adjust to their tempo. By doing so, they are putting their status level above that of the guest and thereby defeating the whole nature of service.

■ Verbal communication

According to Dr Albert Mehrabian's 7-38-55% rule, 38% of verbal communication comprises the tone and volume of what we say. If this is true, the tone and modulation of how the staff speak contributes strongly to the service result. In all communication with guests, the tone should come across as helpful and friendly. With regards to the words they use, these should be polite, efficient and well informed about the services.

On the telephone, (as there is obviously no non-verbal communication) the tone in which staff communicate with guests is critical. The general rule for telephone handling is as follows:

- To pick up the phone in under three or four rings.
- The staff member should make an effort to smile as this will impact their tone.
- They should greet the guest, announce the department, their name and ask if they can help. A standard response example is "Good morning/afternoon/evening, this is the spa department ……….. speaking, how can I help?"
- They should then answer any questions and queries with the aim of giving as much information as the customer needs.

■ Listening

The art of good customer service is being able to listen, not just to what the guests are saying, but also to what the guests are not saying and to what they are feeling. Quite often, what a guest is saying might be completely different to what they want. A question about a treatment might actually mean the guest would just like to chat and make contact; a complaint about the temperature of the pool water might indicate a more serious situation they are unhappy about.

In delivering customer service training the biggest challenge for spa managers is that most people consider themselves to be good listeners, when in fact very few of us are. Listening is an active process. Good listening requires focus, attention and energy. Good listening is hard work, which is why most people prefer to talk rather than listen. In guest interactions, the guest should do about 80% of the speaking, the staff member 20%. If the member of staff starts to take over the conversation, whilst the guest may not show it, their satisfaction with the interaction will diminish considerably. As mentioned previously, staff should be able to listen not just to what the guest is saying verbally, but through body language, decipher what the guest really wants. Through good body language, they should show the guest that they are listening. Here are some common key steps in listening etiquette for staff:

- Face the customer and maintain eye contact.
- Stand still, be attentive but relaxed, keeping hands by sides.
- Not pre-judge but keep an open mind.
- Listen to the words and try to picture them.
- Do not interrupt.
- Let the customer finish both what they are saying *and* what they are thinking.
- Ask questions for clarification.
- Remember to let the customer do 80% of the talking.
- Continue from what the customer is saying.

The last point is worth discussing. Quite often in conversations people will switch or link the topic to something they would prefer to talk about, or alternatively continue from what the person is saying but relate it to their own personal experience. In conversations with guests, the conversation should focus totally on and around the guest, not the member of staff. The guest, no matter how personable they may seem is rarely interested in who they are talking to – they are paying for a service and consciously or subconsciously they are expecting to be the sole focus.

Listening to the customer also means knowing when and when not to speak. Silence is as an important part of communication as speaking. Staff need to know when to talk and when to be quiet, what subjects to talk about and what are off limits (i.e. politics, religion, the operations of the spa and their personal life and life opinions).

■ Complaint handling

Staff are not always able to resolve a complaint, however what they can do is make the customer feel they have done everything they possibly could do to help and dealt with the complaint in a professional way. If the customer feels that that the staff member has put their heart into trying to resolve the problem, they are more likely to react favourably. Here are some common steps that staff should take in dealing with a customer with a complaint:

1 The staff member should *immediately* stop what they are doing and focus on the customer.

2 This is the time when it is not appropriate to smile – the staff member should look concerned and offer an apology for the customer's upset as soon as possible.

3 The staff member should then ask questions to ensure that they have a clear understanding of the situation.

4 They should repeat what they have understood to show the guest that they have listened.

5 They should offer a solution and check if it is acceptable to the guest.

6 They should follow up on what has been agreed.

7 They should get back to the guest with the result if appropriate.

It is in the spa manager's interest to ensure that staff are able to handle and resolve most complaints. Passing every little problem onto the manager will not only reflect badly on the staff member, but it shows disunity in the team and weak leadership.

Sometimes complaints cannot be rectified, in such circumstances honesty and directness are required.

Compensation: compensating guests with a complimentary treatment, drink or extra spa day visit is a common gesture to appease an upset client. There are two arguments for and against this, the first stating that giving compensation will encourage more guests to complain, the second realizing that offering compensation for a complaint, whilst in some cases might not be deserved, keeps the peace and saves time. The second argument in terms of maintaining a positive atmosphere, reducing drama and unnecessary time wasted on dealing with complaints tends to win the day. It is far better to have a complaint dealt with quickly, even at a small cost, than for it to drag on and spread bad energy throughout the spa.

Difficult guests: All spas have their difficult guests and chronic complainers. Some spas have guests from certain countries and cultures who are more demanding than others. Difficult guests should never become the enemy. Difficult guests should be seen as a challenge and opportunity to improve the customer service level. Staff will naturally want to moan about such clients, however if permitted to gossip or complain, tension will increase and singling out certain guests will become part of the spa culture, thereby negatively impacting the spa atmosphere. People do like to gossip and complain, however, the manager should keep an open eye and, through setting an example, ensure this does not get out of control.

■ ## Workplace etiquette

Again, this is dependent on local culture and training, but there should be a distinct understanding of what behaviour is expected in the spa as opposed to how the staff behave in their personal life. For the spa manager, making sure this line is properly understood and adhered to is likely to be one of the hardest challenges of the job. At off-peak quiet times, or periods when the manager is not present, staff will be more than likely to slip back into their natural ways of behaving. To continually remind staff to maintain their professionalism, many hospitality chains use the analogy of a theatre:

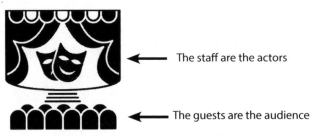

The staff are the actors

The guests are the audience

The spa manager should ensure that the staff stay in role!

Figure 1.4: Working in a spa is like being on stage.

Reminders like these can be put up on staff noticeboards and doors leading into front of house areas.

As they walk through the spa, staff should look like they are going somewhere and move confidently. The spa manager should be on continual alert to ensure that professional standards are maintained. As a part of the daily quality checks, a key priority should be to make sure that the staff have positive energy and body language, a professional appearance in the correct uniform, and smiling and greeting the customers.

Naturally the spa manager should set the example. Staff are more likely to follow what the manager does and how he or she behaves, rather than being told – in other words leading by example is more effective than telling.

Customer care training in a large spa chain in Central Europe

Because of fluctuating workforce of approximately 700 spa staff, large geographical distances between the spas and four different local languages, the recent customer care training had been mainly ineffective. As a simple solution, the spa director put together a short 20-minute film comprising the key points for good customer communication and professional behaviour in the guest areas. Most of the messages were conveyed visually, with humour, highlighting good and bad examples and 'dos' and 'don'ts'. It was implemented into the HR policy and each member of staff had to view the video at the start of their employment, and again once a year. This was effective on two fronts: first, it focused the staff on what was important in an entertaining way, and second, it made sure that all the staff were clear on the expectations and main points of good customer service.

Non-professional behaviour will often arise in the form of:

- Playing with mobile phones in view of the guest.
- Eating or chewing gum.
- Leaning on receptions or lounging in guest areas.
- Chatting with other staff in front of guests.
- Reading magazines or books.

Correct workplace etiquette and company do's and don'ts, should be clearly explained in the staff induction training, job descriptions and handbooks, but most of the work will fall onto the spa manager's shoulders to correct and rectify such tendencies on a daily basis. If reminded and corrected politely, staff will eventually get the message; if not sloppiness will escalate.

Service design

Service design in a spa is the organization of people (in a spa this means the staff and customers), the communication between them and the material aspects of the facility. Its aim is to improve quality of the guests' experience and the relationship between the spa and its customers.

As stated, customer service in the spa environment needs to be more than just delivering the basics but offering unique and fulfilling customer experiences. One of the main aims of the spa manager should be to ensure that the guest has a seamless customer journey. This means that from the first click on the website, through to the last moment of the spa visit, the experience for the customer is smooth and frictionless. In a spa visit setting, this will concern the following areas:

- Sales, promotions, website, booking.
- The service at the destination including the reception and therapies (sometimes referred to as software).
- The physical components of the experience, the facilities and design (sometimes referred to as the hardware).
- Infrastructure, operations and management.
- Billing and accounting.

Service design is challenging. To deliver a service well takes planning and imagination as it is necessary to visualize what the customers and providers cannot see. It is challenging also because it is built on the human factor, and unlike machines or computers, human nature can be both unpredictable and inconsistent.

Service design has what is called an 'outside-in' approach – looking at the customer's journey from the outside. It is guided by the belief that customer value creation, customer orientation and customer experiences are the keys to success (Lagerstedt, 2014)

There are a number of reasons for focusing on service design in a spa. The most common are to introduce a new service (normally a treatment) or to improve an existing one. There are others too:

- To meet the demands of the customer and business.
- To make use of new technology.
- To address environmental, economic and social challenges.

Ultimately, service design should always be about the customer, offering them a unique experience, which is user friendly, relevant, sustainable and competitive.

- **User friendly**: this means placing the customer at the forefront, before the business. In other words, the service experience comes first and the systems and business operations second. From the point of view of the spa customer, the service experience should be easy – or seamless. It should also be personal!

- **Relevant**: The service should be relevant. If it is a treatment experience, it should be a treatment that the customers want, not one that the spa manager or owner thinks the customer wants. It should be created for the user, not for the person designing the service, and clearly, there should be a demand for it, otherwise it will not be successful.

- **Sustainable**: When we talk about sustainability, we mean that from a social, environmental, personal and economic standpoint, the new service must put back more than it takes out.

Ultimately the service must be profitable, a win-win between the operational savings and value-added services. It should be charged for in palatable way (not with a surprise extra cost that could upset the customer) and if possible, the customer should be a part of the work process. (Frei, 2008). This means not getting them to do work, which may cause upset, but get them to take part in the service in a constructive way (e.g. reserve, pay and book their own treatment via the web rather than a receptionist doing it). Not only will this save time and cost, but can actually improve the customer experience as well.

According to Stickdorn and Schneider (2012), service design has five basic principles:

1 **User centred**: the service should be viewed through the eyes of the customer. In other words, when planning a new service, we should try to look at it imagining that we are the customer. It is therefore necessary for the spa manager to really understand who their customers are, what they want and what they are looking for. If appropriate, it would be recommended for the spa manager (and/or team involved) to try a similar experience to really see and feel what it would be like for the customer.

2 **Co-creative**: means actively involving all of the stakeholders in the experience. If it is a treatment this would mean everybody connected to and affected by the new service, from the receptionists to the therapists, to the cleaners and technical staff. If the new service is just driven by the spa manager or owner and the staff are not actively involved, it is less likely to be a success.

3 **Sequencing**: means breaking down the new service into steps or parts and analysing what needs to be done at each step to make the service work.

4 **Evidencing**: means visualizing the new service, even presenting it with visuals so that all the stakeholders and staff involved can understand it clearly, then testing the service in a live environment. This might mean doing trial runs and if the new service is a treatment, actually getting the staff to try out the treatment themselves, thereby enabling them to see it from the customer's perspective, and more importantly to get their professional feedback.

5 **Holistic**: in service design when we use the word 'holistic' we are not necessary meaning 'mind, body and soul'. 'Holistic' in this context refers to the entire environment of the service, the sustainability factors (social, environment, personal, economic), the physical and non-physical requirements, whether the new service will really be profitable and its overall effect on the spa operation.

■ The customer journey

When designing a spa customer journey, we want to make sure that it is memorable. If it is not memorable, it is not worth creating and it is unlikely whether the guest will return to repeat the experience. A spa customer journey is likely to be more memorable if it is authentic. This means creating a journey that links directly to the uniqueness of the location, culture and traditions. This is not to say that all journeys need to be authentic, Thai massage does not have to be just offered in Thailand (Thai massages are popular worldwide), but by tapping into the local environment and traditions and offering a service that is unique raises the chances of it being memorable and therefore successful.

A historical spa resort chain in the Czech Republic adds a surprise benefit

Having implemented standards and protocols for all of their treatments it was decided that in some way the 5-star hotels needed to offer something extra to differentiate themselves from the 4- and 3-star spa brands. The head therapist, in consultation with selected therapists put together an introductory ritual for all the main treatments inspired by their history of royal visitors and introduced it into their flagship 5-star spa. The ritual included an introductory foot bath in an attractive 19th century copper bowl decorated with petals followed by a short five-minute foot massage. This not only acted as a surprise added benefit for the customer, but the intimacy of washing and massaging feet added an extra layer of personalized service and luxury.

Based on the above there are certain key questions that the spa manager should ask before implementing a service:

■ What is my target market? Which guests do I wish to attract?

■ What are their needs?

■ What is the objective of the new service?

■ Is there a plan for every stage of the journey?

■ Is there a plan for testing and evaluating the service, both before its implementation and afterwards when it is up and running?

■ Are there enough resources?

■ Is there a clear goal of what is to be achieved?

■   Key words in service delivery

Imagine that a new treatment will be introduced into a spa: the customer sees the advert, clicks on the website, books the treatment, goes to the spa, gets undressed in the changing room, waits for the treatment has the treatment, gets undressed and checks out.

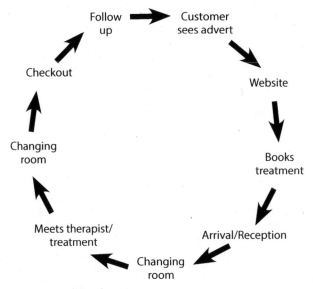

Figure 1.5: The spa customer service cycle.

Front and back stage

When designing the new service, we need to take into consideration the front and back stage areas. The front stage areas are everything that the customer sees and experiences on their journey; the back stage, everything that is affected in the back of house related to the journey. The front stage includes the initial impressions at the entrance to the spa, through to the reception, the changing rooms, the corridors, the treatment room etc. For example, does the entrance of the spa look inviting or are there weeds and cigarette ends? Is there clear information at reception for the customer, what about the body language and presentation of the receptionists? Are the changing rooms and showers spotless? What about the treatment rooms? Is the therapist in the correct uniform with name badge? What about the lighting, the music the temperature? etc. Backstage refers to the technical and administrative areas relevant to ensuring the smooth operation of the customer's journey.

Touchpoints

With each stage of the journey, we have what we call *touchpoints*. These are the important points of communication between the facility and the customer. These are important as if one of the touchpoints is not handled correctly then the whole spa journey can be negatively impacted. Looking at this example of a customer journey, we can see that the important touchpoints are: clicking on the website, booking the treatment, arrival to the spa and handling at reception, meeting the therapist and having the treatment, checking out and being contacted again for a repeat visit. There should be a clear protocol and plan for each of these touchpoints, not just so that they are smooth and seamless but delivered in a way to make the journey unique and authentic.

Channels

These refer to the advertising, the website and the booking system. The advert should have a catch (i.e. a voucher, discount, incentive – something to make the client go to the website); the website should be clear and navigable, directing the customer to easily make a booking for the treatment; and of course the booking should be simple and easy. If any of these touchpoints becomes complicated, unclear, slow or requires more than the necessary clicks, business can be lost.

Lifecycle and circular

The *lifecycle* means the length of time the particular service or experience will be valid for. For example, if the spa is going to offer a one-off special couples' treatment for Valentines, the lifecycle might just be for the month of February. However, if the spa is going to introduce a new salt cave to replace the sunbed, the lifecycle would be continuous and ongoing, at least anyway for the next five years. By *circular*, it means that the customer journey comes full circle. In most spa operations the aim is to make the customer want to return, so if possible, the journey should have a component in it that encourages the customer to come back and repeat the visit. This might be achieved by following up with an email, offering a special discount on the next treatment before a certain date or simply by getting the therapist to offer the same treatment again to the client. Whatever the approach, the aim is to ensure the guest returns.

Actors

When putting the journey together, it is necessary to really understand and involve everybody who will be connected to the service. There will be both front and back of house staff. In this case, the front staff will be your therapists and receptionists, the back staff, the management, administration, cleaning and technical staff. Input from all staff connected to the service journey will contribute to its success – both front and back of house team members. From a front of house point of view, the treatment might seem simple and easy to implement, but there could be complications regarding cleaning, turnaround time, or if it involves using a new piece of equipment there could be technical challenges – all matters need to be taken into consideration.

Naturally, it is not enough just to implement a new service; it has to be evaluated and checked for quality, guest satisfaction and that it is profitable. Feedback mechanisms, such as staff and guest feedback, website reports and mystery customers all have their part to play. These will be discussed in a future chapter.

■   Service design checklist

To put all these items together, before embarking on a new service in the spa, here is a quick checklist that the spa manager can run through:

- What is the purpose of the experience?
- Who will be the customer, what are their needs?
- What is the desired result or goal of the experience?
- What physical elements will be required both front and back stage?
- Who are the actors involved and what training do they need?
- What are the channels, what changes will be needed to the channels for the new service?
- What is the lifecycle of the new service – is it a one-off experience or will it be ongoing?
- How can we make the service circular, so that the customer will return?
- What systems will be required? (Standard operational procedures, treatment protocols, health and safety policies?)
- Is it user-friendly, relevant, sustainable and competitive?
- What resources will it require?
- How will the experience be measured?

Feedback from the interviews – what the experts say

Opinions vary quite considerably in terms of what are considered to be the most important touchpoints in a customer spa journey, however, there is also consensus:

- The website is mentioned several times emphasising that a clear menu and a straightforward booking system for treatments are critical.
- First impressions count, particularly the way in which the customer is welcomed and how the reception sets the tone for the whole experience.
- According to Sona Zabranska, previously Spa Operations Manager from Piestany, Slovakia, the final impression is also important, but often neglected (post-treatment, checkout, motivating customers to re-book etc).
- Managing customer feedback and reviews, and efficient complaint handling is also mentioned; a spa magazine editor stressed "All touchpoints are important, but the ones that are nearly always overlooked and the most lacking are the very start (i.e. website) and the end/aftercare. I can't help but think spas are missing out on a huge opportunity business-wise by ignoring these."
- The word 'quality' is mentioned by many respondents: quality of service, quality of treatments, high quality products, price versus quality, quality of facilities and equipment.

- More than one of the respondents refers to "smooth service" which implies that the whole process from pre-booking to after-care should be seamless. Zseraldina Richvalszki, Spa Consultant, states "the basic prerequisites for the effectiveness of the service are providing expertise, comfort, trust in the therapist – smooth service and constant courtesy".

- Atmosphere is considered to be instrumental in terms of creating a relaxing and calm space, as well as stimulating the senses. Ilan Geva, Wellness and Spa Consultant suggests that "Special attention should be dedicated to customer senses and their integration with what activates the senses". This also includes location, aesthetics, design and layout. Stavros Mavridis, Wellness and Spa Director, says that "Due to the fact that in spas we have tangible effects the whole atmosphere is important, such as colour, smell, temperature, music, elements".

- Staff behaviour is mentioned frequently, including the need to be kind, caring, courteous, professional, highly skilled, experienced and create trust. Chris Theyer, previously Training and Development Director of LivingWell Health Clubs comments "Professionalism is essential at every point of contact with team members, whatever the role, be that service or delivery of therapy". Natasha Ranitovic, CEO of Sunny Ltd Wellness Consulting emphasises the need for a "personal touch provided by an individual approach to guests".

- Several respondents emphasize the importance of natural, local and authentic treatments from the location in which the spa is situated.

Research and further reading

Spa managers need to know who their customers are in order to provide the best possible customer service, therefore some research can be useful in terms of finding out the profiles and motivations of guests. This can help to improve segmentation, marketing and experience creation. For example, in Central and Eastern Europe, Dimitrovski and Todorović (2015) examined the demographic profiles and motives of wellness tourists going to Serbian spas. Diana Dryglas and co-authors have undertaken a number of extensive studies examining the profiles, motives and segments of guests in Polish spa resorts (Dryglas and Różycki, 2017; Dryglas and Salamaga, 2017; Dryglas and Salamaga, 2018). Smith and Puczkó (2018) examined the profiles and motivations of spa-goers in Budapest, Hungary, including residents, domestic and international tourists. Several studies have emerged from Asia, which include an examination of the factors that influence spa visitors' intention to re-visit hot springs destinations in Taiwan (Lin, 2013); the cultivation of customer loyalty through quality and value in spas in Thailand, focusing in particular on wellness tourists (Han et al., 2017); lifestyle segmentation of spa users in Hong Kong, including day spas (Kucukusta and Guillet, 2016). Clark-Kennedy and Cohen (2017) looked at the characteristics, motivations and experiences of hot springs bathers in Victoria, Australia. Most of these researchers used quantitative questionnaires with representative sampling to collect their primary data. Some authors have also made the point that spa managers increasingly need to consider cross-cultural differences of their guests, which can mean nationality or religion (e.g. Tooman, Tomasberg and Smith, 2013; Hindley and Smith, 2017). There are also a few chapters on the spa consumer in *International Spa Management: Principles and Practice* by Rawlinson and Heap (2018).

References

Clark-Kennedy, J. and Cohen, M. (2017) 'Indulgence or therapy? Exploring the characteristics, motivations and experiences of hot springs bathers in Victoria, Australia', *Asia Pacific Journal of Tourism Research*, **22** (5), 501-511, Doi: 10.1080/10941665.2016.1276946

Dimitrovski, D. and Todorović, A. (2015) 'Clustering wellness tourists in spa environment', *Tourism Management Perspectives*, **16**, 259–265, Doi: 10.1016/j.tmp.2015.09.004

Dryglas, D. and Różycki, P. (2017) 'Profile of tourists visiting European spa resorts: a case study of Poland', *Journal of Policy Research in Tourism, Leisure and Events*, **9** (3), 298-317, Doi: 10.1080/19407963.2017.1297311

Dryglas, D. and Salamaga, M. (2017) 'Applying destination attribute segmentation to health tourists: A case study of Polish spa resorts', *Journal of Travel and Tourism Marketing*, **34** (4), 503-514, Doi: 10.1080/10548408.2016.1193102

Dryglas, D. and Salamaga, M. (2018) 'Segmentation by push motives in health tourism destinations: A case study of Polish spa resorts', *Journal of Destination Marketing and Management*, **9**, 234–246, Doi: 10.1016/j.jdmm.2018.01.008

Frei. F. X. (2008) 'Four things a business must get right', *Harvard Business Review*, April, 86 (4), 70-80.

Han, H., Kiattipoom K., Kim, W. and Lee, S. (2017) 'Investigating customer loyalty formation for wellness spa: Individualism vs. Collectivism', *International Journal of Hospitality Management*, **67**, 11–23, Doi: 10.1016/j.ijhm.2017.07.007

Hindley, C. and Smith, M. K. (2017) 'Cross-Cultural Issues of Consumer Behaviour in Hospitality and Tourism', in S. K. Dixit (ed.), *Routledge Handbook of Consumer Behaviour in Hospitality and Tourism*, London: Routledge, pp. 86-95.

Kucukusta, D. and Guillet, B. D. (2016) 'Lifestyle segmentation of spa users: a study of inbound travelers to Hong Kong', *Asia Pacific Journal of Tourism Research*, **21** (3), 239-258, Doi: 10.1080/10941665.2015.1025087

Lagerstedt. E. (2014) 'Business strategy: are you inside out or inside in', Insead - Business School for the world, https://knowledge.insead.edu/blog/insead-blog/business-strategy-are-you-inside-out-or-outside-in-3515 2014 (accessed 25/02/2019).

Lin, C. (2013) 'Determinants of revisit intention to a hot springs destination: evidence from Taiwan', *Asia Pacific Journal of Tourism Research*, **18** (3), 183-204, Doi: 10.1080/10941665.2011.640698

Rawlinson, S. and Heap, T. (2018) *International Spa Management: Principles and Practice*, Oxford: Goodfellow.

Smith, M. K. and Puczkó, L. (2018) 'Thermal spas, well-being and tourism in Budapest', in M. Uysal, M. J. Sirgy and S. Kruger (eds) *Managing Quality of Life in Tourism and Hospitality*, Wallingford: CAB International, pp.103-118.

Stickdorn, M. and Schneider J. (2012) *5 Basic Principles of Service Design*, New Jersey: Wiley.

Tooman, H., Tomasberg, K. and Smith, M.K. (2013) 'Cross-cultural issues in health and wellness services in Estonia', in J. Kampandully (ed.) *Health and Wellness Services*, Dubuque: Kendall Hunt Publishers, pp. 347-361.

2 Leadership skills in the spa environment

In order for spa managers to be effective, it is essential that they should have the necessary skills and self discipline to be able to personally manage themselves; if not, it is highly unlikely that they will be able to manage and control their team effectively. Strong and effective leadership skills are key to a well-functioning spa operation. This chapter covers the most important areas and behaviours that a spa manager needs to develop and focus on in order to lead their spa team well.

A point that is often overlooked is that spa staff will be more responsive to being led through example as opposed to being told. The more that spa managers can set an example through their own behaviour and communication skills, the more likely the staff are to follow suit. Watching a spa manager communicate with their guests with excellent people skills will be just as, if not more effective, than any customer service training. In short: the staff will do what the spa manager does!

Alternatively, bad habits such as coming in late, poor appearance etc, will also be picked up on by team members. Unprofessionalism puts the spa manager into a weak position – cutting corners, lax personal discipline and bad timekeeping will be mirrored in time by the staff. In order to build up his or her respect and maintain a strong position, the spa manager should always be aware of and be continually working on their professional and leadership skills.

Michael Solomon's PHD work at the Graduate School of Business of New York University (Polly, 2015) suggests that we make 11 assessments about somebody in the first seven seconds of contact. These are:

1 Economic status – where somebody is positioned in society, and their income level and wealth.

2 Educational status – how intelligent they are and what is their probable academic level.

3 How honest and/or credible they are.

4 How much they can be trusted.

5 Level of sophistication.

6 Gender, their sexual orientation, desirability and availability.

7 Level of success.

8 Political background.

9 Whether they share the same values and principles.

10 Ethnic origin.

11 Social desirability – how much you would like this person as a friend.

(Eggert, 2010)

For the spa manger, honesty, trust, a certain level of sophistication, values that complement a healthy lifestyle and having a likeability factor, stand out as being the most relevant. Guests need to feel that they can trust the manager, that the manager has a certain amount of elegance (spas after all sell experiences and treatments, not hamburgers!) and that the manager portrays similar values as today's spa goers, values such as humility, altruism and wellness. As mentioned in the previous chapter, most of all, the customer wants to see the manager 'like' a friend, a friendly host who is going to guide them through their experience.

In the previous chapter we looked at the percentages of communication, in particular non-verbal communication according to Albert Mehrabian's 7-38-55% rule. If personal presentation and body language is 55% of how customers will react to a spa team, the spa manager should be setting an exemplary example.

Presentation

Spa environments are normally conservative. Globally, spas tend to veer towards being a luxury experience, with many, though not of course all, situated in four- or five-star hotels. The expectations of how a spa manager should present themselves are high. Not only do spa managers need to demonstrate professionalism through how they dress and their attention to detail, but given that they are also selling health and harmony, they need to look the part. No one expects them to look like a supermodel or Olympic athlete, but they should be smart, impeccably groomed, relatively fit, and balanced.

■ What to wear

Often a uniform will be provided by the company. This is the preferred option as it will reflect the style of the spa operation; a uniform will also save the manager time and energy each day in selecting what to wear. Many companies, however, do not offer this option.

With respect to dress, the aim of the spa manager should be to present themselves in a discreet and professional way. Understatement is the key word. If the spa manager wants to make a statement and stand out, they should stand out through their personality and their excellent people and management skills, not through their dress or piercings.

The 3 'T's

The 3 'T's provide conservative guidelines for selecting clothing: traditional, tasteful and tailored. (Hankins, 2005):

- **Traditional**: in the spa environment the spa manager will normally be required to wear a suit. Whilst not particularly comfortable or practical, this is currently the common standard. The style should be formal – no extreme fashion, with white, blue or light coloured shirt or blouse.

- **Tasteful**: the suit should be in dark colours, black or dark blue, matt and of natural fibers.

- **Tailored**: clearly it should fit comfortably, not too light or not too loose, with a buttoned jacket.

Men

- **Grooming**: hair should be cut regularly, shaving should take place on a daily basis before the shift, if the manager has a beard, designer beard, moustache etc. this should also be trimmed regularly. Nails should be clipped, clean and cuticles taken care of. With age, as nose, eyebrow and ear hair become more prominent, these should be plucked or trimmed. Jewelry or visible tatoos would generally not be considered appropriate.

- **Attire**: depending on the formality of the spa environment, ties would normally be expected. Again, these should be conservative, tasteful and not gimicky. They should be tied properly and up to the neck, with a moderately sized knot, with its length to the belt. Shoes should match the suit, and be clean and shiny on all sides. Socks should be of a dark coordinating colour.

Women

- **Grooming**: if hair is long, normally it would be expected to be tied back, particularly if the spa manager is also multi-skilling as a therapist. Nails should be of a reasonable, practical length, clean, with nail polish of a discreet colour. Miminium is the key word when it comes to make up, perfume and jewelry. Any accessories should be understated.

- **Attire**: in addition to a suit, either with skirt or trousers, a contrasting blouse with collar should be worn. The blouse should avoid being low cut. The more revealing the outfit, the less authoratitive the impact. Shoes should be business-like but practical – spa managers will spend most of their day on the their feet – and naturally the shoes should match the outfit

■ Body language

The previous chapter focused on customer service and the importance for staff to be aware of their body language. Given that the spa manager will be setting the example, good body language in this case is even more relevant – if the staff are expected to have a good posture, slow, confident movements and eye contact, the spa manager should set the example.

Developing good body language comes from both looking at how other people communicate and developing self-awareness. Yoga, meditation, Tai Chi and continual personal development (services conveniently promoted and practiced in spas) are excellent ways to help spa mangers become more self-aware and improve posture and bodily control.

■ **Facial expression**: Guests want to see a manager who looks in control, content in their job, particularly in today's yoga centric and 'living in the now' world. Guests in a spa are on their leisure time. They want to experience an atmosphere that is calm, peaceful and conducive to it. A manager who is running around stressed with a pained expression is not what they are paying for and not what they want to see. The manager's facial expression matters. It should appear open and friendly, with a warm smile and alert glint in the eye.

> In an aerobics class, if the teacher lifts their arms to the ceiling, the class will normally lift their arms to just above their shoulders or moderately less than what has been demonstrated. The aerobic teacher therefore demonstrates the movements larger and bigger than what the class will do. It is the same with the spa manager. If they want the staff to smile then they need to lead the way. If they want the staff to smile with sincerity, then they need to be smiling exuding super sincerity.

■ **Standing and walking around the spa**: Standing tall with a good posture gives a good initial impression. Keeping still, when either standing or sitting, with hands by the side will convey confidence (Eggert, 2010). If the spa manager is seen by the guests to be walking tall at a strong even pace, it inspires a certain level of trust. Rushing around looks panicky, hurrying or talking in an irritated manner on the mobile phone looks even worse – a stressed manager will unnerve both guests and staff. At the other extreme, wandering aimlessly or drifting about gives the impression that the spa manager is either not busy enough or does not know what to do. Spa managers should look like they are focused, doing something and going somewhere.

■ **Handshakes**: In many body language and communication books, the handshake is always discussed as a matter of importance. There are three points to consider, the manager should always initiate the handshake, it is their spa and they are the host. The hand being offered should be dry and not sweaty or wet. The thumb groove should fit into the other person's thumb groove. Then the general advice is to give a firm grip and three shakes, however what is considered firm to one person may not be to another. As spas are about communicating and listening to people, so this should be reflected in all areas of communication as well as handshaking. If the person gives a weak handshake, the spa manager should have the sensitivity to mirror it. If they receive a strong handshake, they should mirror that too. Likewise, return the number of shakes received.

- **Role models**: For good examples of body language, communication and to some extent appearance – newsreaders, TV presenters and TV anchors can act as appropriate role models. In one short clip, a good TV anchor, through their body language and dress can convey intelligence, education, sophistication, trust and even social desirability – all the qualities that a spa manager should look to emulate.

What not to do

There are certain behaviours that will immediately lower the perception of the spa manager's professionalism. Looking stressed and 'busy' have been mentioned, but there are other distracting mannerisms which can have a negative impact on how the spa manager is perceived whilst communicating with staff, guests or work colleagues – these include:

- Touching one's face.
- Fiddling with phone or pens.
- Adjusting ties, glasses.
- Playing with hair, moving hair away from the face.
- Scribbling on bits of paper.
- Jigging one's leg.

Any behaviour that reveals impatience, an inability to listen, or a short attention span should be nipped in the bud as it conveys unprofessionalism a level of immaturity. Keeping hands still and to the side is a good starting point.

Qualities needed in a spa manager

In the previous section intelligence, honesty and trustworthiness were mentioned in connection with communication skills. There are also some notable qualities and attributes that a spa manager should develop if they are to build a professional spa team:

- **Consistency**: no staff member wants a manager that is super nice and motivated one day and crabby the next. They want to know when they come into work what they are going to get. Volatility and unpredictability erode trust and unsettle the team. Challenging as it may be, the spa manager should endeavour to be as consistent as possible.
- **Fairness**: every team member should be treated equally by the spa manager. Having favourites, or 'friends' within the team can cause resentment and division.
- **Confidence**: as mentioned earlier, the staff and guests have to believe that the manager is in control and able to deal with any problems and emergencies in a smooth and calm manner. Good body language, listening and communication skills will help inspire confidence.

- **Calmness**: spas are places of tranquillity. Guests go to spas to relax and wind down. The manager, through exuding serenity and a peaceful energy should help to create this atmosphere in the spa.
- **Listening skills:** listening skills are perhaps more important in the spa environment than in other hospitality environments. The staff, and in particular the spa manager, need to be expert listeners. They have to know what the guests and staff are thinking and feeling and be able to react accordingly.

■ Listening skills

Whilst listening skills were covered on a basic level for staff in the previous chapter, the demand for spa managers to have advanced listening and empathic abilities is much higher. To assess one's level of listening skills try this exercise:

Answer 'True' or 'False' to the following statements, honestly:

1 I like to listen to other people talk.

2 I listen equally well to a friend, stranger, manager and my parents.

3 I don't tend to interrupt.

4 I look at the speaker when I am listening.

5 I am able to block out distractions when I am listening.

6 I am able to listen even if I do not like the person who is talking and what they are talking about.

7 I try not to let my mind wander when the other person is talking.

8 I try not to think about what I want to say when the other person is talking.

9 I let the other person finish what they want to say.

10 I remember what I hear.

11 I don't get distracted by sounds around me, other people talking or things I am thinking about when I am listening.

12 I follow on from what the other person is saying and don't change the subject to me or what I would like to talk about.

13 I try to let the other person talk for 80% of the conversation.

14 I am good at following directions and instructions.

15 People say I am a good listener.

Total up the 'Trues' – each 'True' equals 1 point, so there is a maximum of 15 points. A spa manager should aim to have at least 11 or 12 of these. The exercise is also useful as it will highlight those areas of listening which need working on.

Spa management is primarily a listening and a demonstrating job. Much of the work will involve talking to guests and staff – both generally like to talk. Guests in spas in particular like to talk to the host – the spa manager. Part of the spa manager's daily routine should include time walking around the spa facility, making a point of interacting with the guests – for example having a coffee or a sit-down chat with long-term members or regular guests. Likewise, they should also allocate time to be out in reception or therapy areas mixing with the staff. The more open the spa manager is perceived to be, the more information they will be able to pick up regarding the strengths and weaknesses of their operation, however, they will only be able to do this if they have good listening skills. Here is a recap of some basic good listening habits:

- Always be sure that full focus is given to the person talking.
- Check body language and that there is no fidgeting – hands should be by the side or still.
- Never interrupt.
- Let the person finish both what they are saying and what they are thinking.
- Leave a pause between what the customer has said before replying.
- Try to find out what the person really is saying – is it what they are talking about or is it something completely different?
- Try to find out what the person is feeling.
- Continually ask the question 'how can I make this interaction as satisfying as possible for the other person?'
- Make sure that they are doing 80% of the talking.

People often presume that listening is a passive behaviour. Far from it, being a good listener is an active process, a skill which few people do well, a skill that requires concentration. Active listening requires certain steps. Here are six important *Active Listening Components* described by Peter W. Cardon (Cardon, 2016):

1 Paying attention – really focusing and preparing to listen to the guest.
2 Holding judgement – not jumping to conclusions or pre-judging the person speaking.
3 Reflecting – taking in the information given and thinking about it.
4 Clarifying – asking questions to make sure that what has been said is understood.
5 Sharing – expressing one's own ideas if appropriate.
6 Summarizing – showing understanding and agreeing the next steps.

Paying attention

In the spa environment this means turning to the guest, zooming in on them and giving them full attention. If sitting, the manager should stand immediately and smile. In the rare exception when it is not necessary to stand, the manager should adjust their posture, sit up straight, lean forward with eye contact and smile.

Holding judgement

Regardless of who is the guest and what is their track record, each interaction should be dealt with as if it were new. This is to say not prejudging the person and anticipating what they are about to say. Each spa has their chronic complainer and it is easy for the spa manager to assume what they are going to say, but even in such cases, the interaction should be approached in a completely new and non-anticipatory manner. After all, this time the guest might have something urgent and important to say.

Reflecting

This means really listening and taking in the information that the guest is imparting. It is not only important to try to understand the information that is being communicated, it is even more important to try to understand the emotions and thoughts behind what is being said. Questions can be asked to check that the manager has understood correctly, for example:

- It sounds to me that you are saying you weren't 100% happy with the treatment, am I right?
- If I understand rightly, it would be fair to say that you feel we should offer another level of yoga class more appropriate for younger clients?
- Let me make sure I am understanding the situation correctly...

Clarification

This is where questions are asked by the manager to double check that what has been communicated has been totally understood. These questions also show that they have listened and understood what the other person has communicated:

- Could you explain the most important points that caused you to be unhappy with the treatment?
- Could you go into more detail for me the reasons why you feel we need another yoga class for younger clients?
- What are your thoughts on.....?

Summarizing

This is where the manager summarizes the essence of what has been said. Summarizing questions would sound like:

- So, your main concern is that you feel that by complaining about the treatment it will upset your relationship with the therapist, am I right?
- You would strongly advise that we put another yoga class in our timetable, is that correct?
- Let me summarize my understanding of the situation...

Sharing

Now is the time for the manager to share their opinion and views on what has been said. This should only happen once paying attention, holding judgement, reflecting, clarifying and summarizing has taken place. Interrupting and sharing one's opinion too quickly is a sign of impulsiveness and immaturity. If a response is given too quickly this will irritate the guest and may cause a loss of trust. The manager should share their opinion and views as quickly and concisely as possible. Rambling answers and too much talking and explaining will have a detrimental effect

In most interactions with clients, the client rarely gives an opportunity for the manager to share too much information, in many cases they are not interested in the manager's opinion anyway, definitely not long rambling explanations. Most of the time they just want to speak and get their point across.

In addition, it is worth emphasizing that what is not said by the manager is as, if not more important, than what is said.

In my opinion the most important qualities for a spa manager are perception/empathy (understanding customers' expectations needs and desires) and ability to communicate clearly with both customers and team members and the ability to motivate staff, in addition to financial focus to ensure business success.

Chris Theyer, previously Training and Development Director, LivingWell Health Clubs.

■ Organisation

A spa manager has to have good organisational skills, and the larger the spa operation the more experienced their organisational skills need to be. A manager who is organised will be more in control of what is about to happen in their day, whereas a disorganised manager will be at the mercy of the day's events. An effective spa manager starts the day with a plan and ideas of what they intend to accomplish; an ineffective spa manager starts the day with no plan and lets the day take its course. Good organisational skills will mean that the manager will be in control of the spa and their day, not the spa being in control of them.

The body language and behaviour of a spa manager who is not in control of their day will be rushed, disjointed and out of control. Other signs of being disorganised include forgetting things, having to be reminded several times and not being able to complete tasks on time. The biggest and most serious sign of a spa manager who is not organised or disciplined will be no new developments in the spa operation. Such a manager is sometimes referred to as a 'status quo' manager, in that they keep the spa ticking along as it is, but with no development or noticeable improvements. In such cases, the day to day operations tend to dictate their focus, and ideas for projects and improvements in the spa, remain just that – ideas. The goal of being organised is not just to appear efficient, by being organised the spa manager will be able to focus on the main part of the job, which is not only daily operations, but more importantly developing and improving the business.

For a spa manager to be organised is not a complex job if certain basics are put into place – these should include the following three simple tools:

1 A diary / calendar
2 Yearly goals
3 A daily job-list.

Diary / calendar

In today's digital world, a calendar can now be viewed anywhere and synchronised in all devices. The spa manager should get in the habit of writing in all their commitments – the time, the location, who the appointment is with and the contact number in case of a last-minute emergency or change of plan. It is also advisable for the spa manager to have their calendar synchronised to their team member's calendars, or if it is a large operation, synchronised with their head of departments'. Here, they should be able to see the working shifts, holidays, meetings and main work-related events. In such a case, if the spa manager wants to hold a meeting or check where a member of staff should be, they can see it at a glance.

Strategy and yearly goals

These are the most important tools for the spa manager. Having a strategy will mean having a direction, but without goals being planned into a strategy, developments are unlikely to materialize. Every year or two years, the spa manager should put together their goals and vision for the next few years with dates and deadlines. How the plan is formatted will depend on the company guidelines and the spa manager's approach. Just having the plan, however, is not enough, as the aims will remain on paper unless the spa manager is focussed on them and being proactive on a daily basis to push the items along. This means looking at the goals and planning every day, and deciding what jobs or activity can be done there and then that can move the projects along:

Daily job list

The daily job list should be created from three sources:

1 By looking at the yearly goals and deciding what immediate actions are needed to help the projects progress.
2 By looking at the calendar, seeing what events are scheduled and deciding what preparation if any is needed.
3 By going through the email inbox and deferred items.

Many spa managers either tend to start their day by checking in at the reception or by opening their email inbox, meaning that they will get sucked immediately into whatever hits them first and before long their day will have disappeared. Putting together the daily job list should therefore be carried out at the beginning of the shift before any other duties, so that the spa manager can prevent him/herself being pulled into the minutiae of the operations and having their day derailed.

Organising the desktop

Being flooded with information comes with the territory of the job – phone calls, emails, guests wanting immediate attention, etc. To deal with the volume of multiple interruptions and tasks, it is best to have a clean, organised desktop and an effective system of working. Once a week, the manager should attempt to clear out all unwanted documents and emails.

■   Time management

There are many time management and organisational techniques and systems. One recommended system which works well in the spa environment is by David Allen (2009) described in his book *Getting Things Done*. His recommendation is to separate all information into tasks requiring action and tasks that do not require action. In both the emails and in computer files, all emails and documents should be filed as:

- **Actionable**: requiring tasks with a time and action
- **Non-actionable**: information that may or not be useful. In such a case there are three possibilities:

    1   It is trash and no longer needed.

    2   Action is not required immediately now but something might need to be completed later on.

    3   Action is not required at all but the item is potentially useful information. (Allen, 2009)

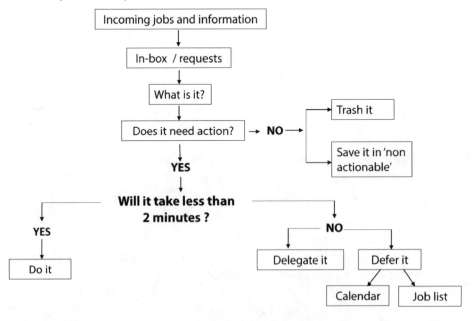

Figure 2.1: Assessing incoming jobs and information. Adapted from Allen D. (2009).

With items that require action the critical question is "will this take less than 2 minutes?" If the answer is yes, then the spa manager should do it and get it out of the way. If the answer is no, then they can either delegate it or defer it by putting it in either the calendar and/or the job list.

If the item is not actionable then it should either be deleted or trashed or saved in a non-actionable reference file.

The reason that this system is so effective is that the small, short jobs (which will comprise of most of the spa manager's daily tasks), get rectified quickly and immediately. Not only does this reduce the danger of a build-up of tasks, but it also increases efficiency dramatically. This system is highly recommended for the spa management organisation.

Another organisational system often used is the "urgent and important" system, following Eisenhower's *Important/Non-important Principle*.

	Urgent	Not Urgent
Important	Do	Plan
Not Important	Delegate	Eliminate

Figure 2.2: Jobs can be sorted into four boxes using the urgency and importance criteria.

There are many other time management and organisation systems which the spa manager can choose from. The aim however is to have a system that is effective and prioritizes tasks that do not just maintain operations but develop the spa business as well.

Other tips

- **Creating a 'junk' email address.** Many shops/airport WIFI requests etc, ask for email addresses and then take the liberty of sending out unwanted advertising. A 'junk' email address will keep these out of the daily work flow.
- **Diverting to spam.** Non-essential emails should be diverted to spam or trash.
- **Setting up direct diversions for non-essential emails to an allocated folder.** For example, a spa magazine might be sending their regular weekly bulletin which could have some useful information. The spa manager might not want to see this every week, but having it automatically diverted to its own folder

titled something like 'interesting articles', means the manager can dip into it whenever they feel like it or have some free time, rather than having it clutter up the inbox

- **Avoiding the out of sight out of mind habit.** In other words, not putting to one side or ignoring unpleasant jobs and tasks in the hope that by not seeing about them they will go away, but confronting them and getting them done.
- **Prioritizing.** Building up the habit of doing the jobs which are urgent and important (and possibly unpleasant) first and not the jobs that are the most enjoyable.

In today's world, a spa manager must have excellent communication and problem-solving skills combined with values that are in harmony with the corporate culture of their company. They need to be trustworthy, determined, and confident, with a certain amount of sophistication in their style. Strong organisation skills, time management and an entrepreneurial spirit are absolutely key. Understanding their business processes and finding ways to increase profits and develop the business, sales experience and professional skills are essential.

Zseraldina Richvalszki, Spa Consultant.

■ Reliability

It would be stating the obvious to say that a spa manager needs to be reliable, but there are certain points that should be highlighted.

Timekeeping

The staff will do what the boss does. If the boss expects the receptionists to be on time to open up the spa on a Sunday morning, then they need to set an example. Good timekeeping obviously does not just include arriving at work on time, it also means keeping appointments and not letting people hang outside the office waiting because of poor time management.

Always returning telephone calls

The hospitality rule used to be to return calls within 24 hours, but times have changed and now the unwritten rule in spas means it is more like 12 hours – or as soon as possible! If someone has called and left a message, it should be answered with a return call. If the person does not pick up, then a message should be left. Whom the call is from is not important, it could be a director, a beauty product sales person or the toilet roll supplier. Every call should be returned. This also includes missed calls, even if the number is not recognised.

Emails and texts

The same rules apply for emails and texts. Emails should be returned within 12 – 24 hours at least. If somebody requests something, every effort should be made to fulfil that request. The text and email should be written with good grammar and no spelling mistakes (spellcheck is available in all languages). The style of the language should be polite, with a greeting and a thank you at the end if appropriate. Politeness should be expressed in all correspondence, whether it is a guest, a colleague, the boss or the cleaner.

Being clear

The spa manager should never leave people or jobs 'hanging' or drifting. When asked to do something, regardless of who it is, whether it is by phone, text, email or in person there are three possible responses:

1 Yes, I can!

2 No, I am so sorry I won't be able to do that.

3 Could I have a think about it and get back to you by……

Clarity, with respect to what can be done, what cannot be done, and by when, should be communicated clearly.

■ Decision making

It has been said that the most successful people have a characteristic of making many decisions and making their decisions quickly. It is the quantity of decisions that are made as opposed to the quality. This might seem contradictory, but it is based on the premise that by making lots of decisions we broaden our experience and learn from our mistakes. The more decisions a manager makes will reflect the fact that they are more active – active people normally are people that make things happen. On saying this, there are certain steps that can make decision making more effective:

1 Before reacting to a situation, question or request, stop and follow the six listening steps.

2 Think through the options and make a decision.

3 If necessary, consult with a colleague, boss or friend who is *successful in the area that the decision concerns*. This is important. It clearly can be detrimental seeking advice from someone who either knows nothing about the subject or has not been particularly successful in that particular area themselves.

4 If necessary, think through it again.

5 Act.

■ Attitude and enthusiasm

A positive 'can do' attitude and an enthusiastic approach are essential if the spa manager is going to lead and motivate their team. This is not just necessary for the staff, but also for the guests who are expecting to have their spa experience in a positive atmosphere. Spas are as much about energy and atmosphere as they are about facilities and treatments. Energy and positivity start with the boss and trickle down to the team. That means every day, and all day, the spa manager should appear, positive and enthusiastic. Again, this is easy to say, but after a week of being understaffed and firefighting technical breakdowns, it is not always easy to maintain such a level of positivity, but this is what is required.

■ Behaviour to avoid

Anger and irritation

These are not admirable qualities and a spa manager who displays them will lose respect. At work, a spa manager should "retain their cool at all times and never lose their dignity" (Templar, 2013).

Gossiping

A manager who gossips will lose trust. The person who hears the manager gossiping will be thinking "if this manager is gossiping about so and so then they are likely to gossip about me". The spa manager should avoid discussing people altogether. If it is necessary to discuss another member of staff's professional behaviour, this should be done with discretion and careful thought about what is being said and to whom. Generally, if a spa manager is not able to say something constructive about someone, a guest or member of staff, they should refrain from saying anything at all.

Conflict

When managing staff, working in a large company and dealing with customers conflict is unavoidable. Conflict situations, however, should be avoided at all costs. A spa manager who is constantly in battles and attracting drama is unlikely to gain long term respect and most certainly is unlikely to progress into higher management. Sometimes, of course, conflict is unavoidable, but it should be dealt with in a planned, strategic way with the goal of resolution and moving on. There are no winners in a long term war. Not everybody clicks with everyone and the best way for the spa manager to deal with such customers, staff or colleagues, is to keep the contact with such people to a minimum. If contact is unavoidable, it should be as polite, friendly and professional as possible. In short, the manager should aim to be like a Teflon pan – smooth, effective, easy to deal with, where nothing sticks!

Being friends with staff

A good boss is friendly but not a friend. Employees do not want a boss who is overfamiliar, they want a boss. Employees want to spend their leisure time with their friends not their employer. Friendship with individual members of the team can lead to favoritism which diminishes respect for the boss and fuels contempt for the favorite.

■ Being motivated in the job

Every job has a shelf life. That is to say, a person will feel motivated in a position for a period of time, but then there comes a point where the job becomes less interesting. This is not a failure; it is human nature. It is the same with managing a spa. Generally, a spa manager should be able to keep themselves motivated for a period of at least 3 to 4 years (changing jobs every year does not look good on a C.V.) after that time it is likely the job will become less challenging. This is not a blanket rule, for some people are able to continue in the same job for years on end, while others lose motivation faster. It is not possible to manage a successful spa on less than a full tank; the staff will sense it and therefore ultimately the guests will too. If the spa manager is feeling unmotivated over a period of time, they should think about moving on.

A good exercise is for the spa manager to ask themselves this question every so often: "on a scale between 1 and 10 (1 being no motivation and 10 being super motivated) where do they feel in the job?" If the score is under a seven for longer than six months it could time for them to consider looking for the next move. Staying in a job feeling demotivated and unfulfilled is unfair on everyone, including the spa manager. If it is time to move on, the manager should keep working as best as they can, maintain their professionalism and look for another position. When it is time to give their notice, they should do so well in advance, giving support to whoever will take their place and leave the position and spa in the best possible way for their successor to take over.

Feedback from the interviews – what the experts say

Spa managers were asked which professional skills they think are most important for a spa manager. Here is a summary of their responses:

- The most important characteristic of a spa manager according to many respondents was 'empathy', and the most important skills identified by the respondents were people management skills relating to both customers and employees. Hospitality, interpersonal skills and customer friendliness were all emphasised, as well as taking care of staff through motivation, development, training and team building.

- The second most listed skills were those relating to knowledge, including knowledge of products, treatment, equipment, resources, and in some cases, medical knowledge. This was followed by a need for business acumen, especially good financial sense, but also resource management, marketing, media, sales and IT systems. Andrew Gibson from SVP, Los Angeles, suggested that "for a hotel spa manager, it's all about staff management and guest experience….. for a day spa manager, the basic small business skills are also important - accounting, marketing, legal, etc. A spa manager needs to juggle six variables in yield management (compared to three in a hotel)".

- The third most important skills cited related to being professional, well organised, and a good communicator, as well as being flexible and adaptable. Problem solving skills were also cited several times.

- A long list of ideal characteristics were given for spa managers. These are the most mentioned: attention to detail; conflict resolution and crisis management skills; open mindedness; creativity and innovativeness.

- Ilan Geva, Spa Consultant, also emphasised that spa managers need to "be aware of wellness trends worldwide and have a global view of social, economic and political situations".

- Overall, it was agreed that a spa manager should be multi-skilled. As described by Vladi Kovanic, Managing Director VK organisation from Paris, "The spa manager should be a perfect leader and 'spa orchestra conductor'".

Research and further reading

There has been relatively little research on spa leadership compared to spa management more generally. It is also more common for research to focus on employees within spas, but this can also include spa managers. As this chapter explains, the spa manager plays an important role in leading and motivating their team, but their own wellbeing should also be considered. A few years ago, SRI (2012) analysed the spa workforce and education, highlighting some of the problems with working conditions, job satisfaction and retention. ISPA (International Spa Association) undertakes an annual workforce study in the United States. The 2018 study emphasised in particular the employee experience as an area that requires attention, including training and career development opportunities. It also demonstrated that there is an employment deficit, including for spa managers, due to the lack of qualified talent, especially in smaller, seasonal and rural spas. Hodari, Waldthausen and Sturman (2014) undertook a study of 166 hotel spa managers. Their study emphasised the difficulty in attracting and retaining qualified spa managers, especially hotel spa managers, because they have to span both businesses and this can lead to role stress and dissatisfaction. A recent study by Wisnom and Gallagher (2018) focused on the quality of working life in spa resorts; 63% of their 107 respondents were spa managers. In addition to good wages, working conditions, feeling appreciated and interesting work, suggestions from the respondents also included allowing employees to have involvement in the decision-making process or choosing their own incentives as effective ways to influence a worker's motivation, improve performance and prevent disengaged employees. An even more recent study by Lagrosen and Lagrosen (2019) examined workplace health and wellness in spa hotels in Sweden and proposed a health leadership framework for the wellness industry. They suggested that respect and control are related to quality leadership, as well as empathy, presence, communication, integrity, empathy and continuity.

References

Allen, D. (2009) *Getting Things Done: The art of stress-free productivity*, Loughton: Piatkus.

Cardon, P. (2016) *Business Communication*, 2nd edn, New York: McGraw Hill.

Egert, M. (2010) *Brilliant Body Language*, New York: Pearson.

Hankins, G. (2005) *The Power of Pitch*, Chicago: Dearborn.

Hodari, D., Waldthausen, V. & Sturman, M. (2014) 'Outsourcing and role stress: An empirical study of hotel spa managers', *International Journal of Hospitality Management*, **37**, 190–199, Doi: 10.1016/j.ijhm.2013.11.006

ISPA (2018) *Spa Workforce Survey*, Lexington, KY.

Lagrosen, Y. and Lagrosen, S. O. (2019) 'Workplace health in wellness – a study of Swedish spa-hotels', *International Journal of Quality and Service Sciences*, **11** (3), 395-408, Doi: 10.1108/IJQSS-03-2018-0025

Polly, S. (2015) 'First impressions the 7 – 11 rule', *Positive Business*, http:// positivebusinessdc.com/711-rule/ (accessed 25/06/2019).

SRI International (2012) 'Spa Management Workforce and Education: Addressing Market Gaps', Global Spa Summit, Arlington, VA.

Templar, R. (2013) *The Rules of Work*, 10th edn, New York: Pearson.

Wisnom, M. and Gallagher, K. (2018) 'Quality of work life in the resort spa industry', *International Journal of Spa and Wellness*, **1** (3), 159-177, Doi: 10.1080/24721735.2019.1596658

 Effective team management in the spa environment

A great atmosphere and a successful spa normally go hand in hand – it is not usual to find one without the other. Similarly, behind every great spa atmosphere will be a competent and effective spa manager. Atmosphere comes from the top and trickles down from the spa manager and their boss, and the boss above them, into the spa.

It is not just the guests who demand a good atmosphere, the staff do too. According to an inaugural ISPA workforce study which surveyed 1200 participants, a positive culture and working environment was the number one priority for staff (Kitchen, 2018).

> The key to create a great atmosphere is 'the team'. And remember there is no 'I' in 'team'. Keep them happy and motivated, training is key, communication is key, and to be their boss, mummy, agony aunt. In our club our members could see how well we all got on, and it was infectious. Our staff retention was excellent and we all became like a little family. Even though our club was old and rancid, we loved it, we were proud of it, and this shone through!
>
> Sarra Temple, previously manager of Watford Health Club, UK.

In most spas, the staff will be working out of love for the job as opposed to financial gains. Like most industries in the hospitality sector, the spa industry does not normally pay particularly well and staff are aware of this. Many will be prepared to put up with the shift work, the long hours and back to back treatment schedule if the spa is a pleasant atmosphere to work in. The ISPA study shows that spa staff are loyal and do not like to job hop – 76% said that they had worked for less than 5 employers (Kitchen, 2018). That is not to say spa managers should become complacent about how they treat their staff, for if the work environment turns negative and nasty (and if there are other opportunities available), staff will more than likely leave. The spa manager therefore has a vested interest in closely monitoring and managing the energy and atmosphere in their spa.

> "Clients do not come first. Employees come first. If you take care of your employees, they will take care of the clients."
>
> Richard Branson

3

Weak leadership, an imbalance of personalities and abilities, unclear roles, lack of motivation, a culture of bad behaviour, unpleasant communication – are all factors that are characteristics of bad teams. Good teams on the other hand focus on performance and have a work culture built around values, norms and goals. They meet regularly and embrace differing viewpoints, evaluate their performance, give positive feedback and have common sense of purpose (Cardon, 2016).

The main role of the spa manager is to motivate and manage their team effectively. If the manager gets this right, then their job will be relatively easy and a joy to do. It they get it wrong, a dissatisfied team or two bad apples can turn the job into a nightmare. A nightmare in a spa means: telephone calls on a Sunday morning at six am because the receptionist has not shown up for work or a fire in the sauna because a member of staff did not bother to turn it off.

Investing time and energy in people are the building blocks to creating a good team, knowing how much time to spend with them and also when to leave them alone. This takes experience – "great relationships with customers, colleagues or loved ones don't just happen magically. They take time…" (McGee, 2013).

So how does a manager create a good working team? There are some key actions for this:

- Leading by example, as discussed in the previous chapters.
- Having a positive attitude.
- Good listening skills.
- Being able to adapt communication styles to different personalities.
- Being effective – having good organisation and business communication skills.
- Using tried and trusted management tools such as meetings and performance appraisals.
- And of course, making sure the team is right in the first place – recruitment.

Human resource in the spa environment

One of the mistakes spa managers make is in assuming that human resource in spas is an administrative role – sorting out contracts and personnel policies etc. However, this is only part of it. The main function of human resource and team management in a spa environment should be actively driving the development and motivation of the staff. This includes:

- Being able to hold good interviews and recruit the right people.
- Giving good orientation and induction training for new staff.
- Supporting career development and job training.
- Introducing benefits and motivational programs for employees.

■ Recruitment

To have the right team the spa manager needs to have employed the right people in the first place. One bad decision and the whole balance of a team can be thrown out of sync.

Recruitment can often be challenging and finding staff in some locations is sometimes almost impossible. However, there are certain actions a spa manager can take to help:

1 **Building relationships with higher educational facilities**: encouraging local college and university leavers to apply for positions. Building personal relationships with key decision makers in the facility (i.e. career advisors), inviting students for show-arounds, conducting presentations and lectures in local colleges and educational establishments etc.

2 **Offering students work experience in the spa**: many spas offer this opportunity. The advantage is, that if a student has had work experience, they will also have had on the job training and acquired some of the necessary skills, in addition they will know and have worked with the team.

3 **Interviewing potential staff even when there are no positions available**: this might seem illogical, but continuous interviewing not only keeps the spa manager in good practice at carrying out interviews, it also enables them to build up a CV bank. Therefore, if a receptionist walks out on a Monday morning, the spa manager will have a list of potential job candidates to call. If none of those candidates are available, maybe they can suggest someone who is.

4 **Recruiting through existing staff members**: approaching the best performing staff and asking them if they know anyone who would be interested in working in the spa. Some spas even offer financial incentives (for example, if the new recruit stays more than 1 year then the referrer employee gets an extra month's salary).

5 **Promoting up**: promoting from within is normally smoother than recruiting new blood from outside. An existing employee will know the systems and the team. When someone is recruited externally, it often takes several months before they find their place – if it works out at all.

6 **Being able to conduct good interviews and check references**. This will be analysed in the next section.

Preparing for the interview

It is important to remember that the person being interviewed is interviewing the interviewer as much as the interviewer is interviewing them!

There are key areas to take into consideration when preparing for an interview;

1 Properly examining the CV.

2 Being able to conduct a professional, effective interview.

3 Checking the references.

Examining the CV

There are certain items to check when looking at a CV.

First, it should be in a logical order, essential information (name, address, contact details etc), education history and employment history. For a normal spa position, it should fit onto one page. There should be no spelling mistakes and the graphic layout should look professional. A sloppy CV will most likely indicate a sloppy member of staff.

Second, there are key points which the spa manager should check:

■ **Age:** (Be aware, in some countries it is not permitted to include age on the CV as this is deemed as 'age discrimination'). The age of a candidate may have implications however. For example, if Peter is 58 years old and he has applied to work on the spa reception desk with staff who are all in their early 20s, there may be questions about whether or not he will fit in with the team.

■ **Photo**: again, in some cultures face photos are not permitted (as it could lead to race or disability discrimination), whereas in other cultures attaching a photo to the job application is the norm. If there is a photo attached, whilst they do not need to look like a supermodel, the applicant should clearly be well groomed and look appropriate for the part.

■ **Where the person lives**: this is extremely important, especially if they are going to be working in key positions such as the spa reception desk. The spa manager needs to know that realistically this person will be able to get to work on time, taking into consideration the local transport constraints. They might be brilliant for the job, but if they live 50 kilometres away and will have to rely on an intermittent bus timetable, are they realistically going to be able to arrive on time for work and keep up with the commuting on a long-term basis?

■ **Career breaks**: could be a cause for concern as it often is preceded by an abrupt employment termination. If there are breaks, the spa manager should make a note and prepare questions about this for the interview.

■ **Frequency of job changing**: this is perhaps the most important area to examine. An analogy can be given that if someone has been changing their girlfriend or boyfriend every six months for the past ten years and then they suddenly meet 'the one' it is highly unlikely the relationship with 'the one' will last forever after. It is the same with work positions – if a potential recruit has moved jobs repetitively, then it is highly likely they will repeat the pattern. For a spa therapy position, moving once every 2 to 3 years would seem reasonable, but any more than that and it could be a cause for concern.

- **Changing careers**: is related to the point above, if the CV has dramatic changes in it (for example, hotel receptionist, to flower arranger, to trapeze artist) this would be worth making a note of and going into more depth with the applicant during the interview.

- **Moving down positions**: for example, if the person being interviewed has had the career path of therapist, then assistant spa manager, then spa director but then decided to apply for the job of therapist, there would definitely be a reason to ask why.

- **Salary expectations**: by looking at the CV it is possible to make an approximate estimate as to what salary range the person would have been used to. If it is blatantly clear that an applicant has been in a position where the salary was of a much higher bracket than what the spa manager can offer, it would be worth checking that the applicant is prepared to accept the offered salary before the interview, so that time on either side is not wasted.

Conducting an interview

The fact that the spa manager has called the applicant in for an interview means on paper that they look as if they can do the job. The reason for the interview is not for the spa manager to find out if the applicant has the skills to do the job – that should be evident through the CV – but to find out through preparation and clever questioning if the candidate is able to do the job consistently and to a high level over a reasonable period of time; and in addition, if they will bring good energy to the spa and fit in with the rest of the team.

Most people can hold a job down well for the first month, but the question should be what will they be like in a year or two years? Are they going to be easy to manage or high maintenance? Therefore, preparing for the interview is a must. The spa manager should not forget that the applicant will be assessing the workplace/ spa manager as much as the spa manager is assessing the applicant. In short, the spa manager is representing the company, and therefore, they should do everything possible to make a good impression. They should carefully read the CV beforehand, make notes and prepare their questions. There are cases where managers do not bother looking at the CV before the interview, or even remember the name of the person they are interviewing, which gives an extremely poor impression of the company.

When the applicant arrives, they should be asked if they would like a tea, coffee or water and be given the job description (which should include all the job expectations). This should be done before the interview – if it has not been sent to them already. This means that the spa manager can spend the interview on getting to know the applicant and not waste time explaining the job.

Interview steps

1   It should start with an icebreaker – short chitchat about the weather or travel to the spa to help the applicant relax.

2   These informal questions should then lead smoothly into the applicant's career history, coaxing the applicant to talk about each job and their experiences. The questions should be open ended – 'how', 'what' 'why' targeting any unclear areas or concerns that have stood out during the CV analysis. If the applicant appears evasive, then polite probing questions should continue until a satisfactory explanation is offered.

3   If there are concerns, the spa manager should take the opportunity to express them, should they feel it appropriate.

4   A brief summary of what is expected in the job can be given, even though this should have been explained in the job description sent before the interview.

5   The spa manager also has the choice to reveal the salary and conditions (if appropriate and if it has not been done already) or alternatively they can let the applicant know, that if they are successful, that the salary will be communicated at a later stage.

6   The spa manager should ask the applicant if they have any questions and answer them accordingly.

7   They should escort the applicant out to lift or entrance making polite, friendly chat.

Checking the references

Checking references is of critical importance. There are people who can give an excellent interview which may or may not be reflected in their day to day job performance. At least two references should be checked. Preferably the reference check should be done by telephone call covering the following areas:

1   That the position and time and date of employment on the CV matches the reality.

2   Questions about timekeeping, professionalism and honesty.

3   Customer service skills.

4   Strengths and weaknesses of the applicant.

5   Asking why did the applicant leave their position.

6   The question: *'Is there anything that I need to know about, or be concerned about, regarding this person's character or performance?'*

The last question is crucial, as sometimes, for whatever reason, a previous employer may not divulge or be forthcoming about deficiencies without some form of probing.

All of the answers should then be compared with the candidate's answers given in the interview.

Deciding on the candidate

The spa manager then needs to ask themselves the following questions:

■   Does the applicant have the right attitude and energy for this spa?

- Will they complement and work well with the other team members?
- Do they have the right level of communication skills and style for this environment?
- Are they customer focused?
- Will they be reliable, professional and committed on a long-term basis?
- Do they have the professional skills for the position?

With regards to the last point, a person can be trained in skills, however attitude and behaviour are far more challenging. Some spas offer the opportunity for new recruits to come in for the day to see if they feel comfortable in the environment and if the team feel comfortable with them.

> In the spas that I have managed, what we do is ask the applicant to come and work for a few hours alongside a member of staff. This gives the person a taste of what it is like to work in our spa environment. The member of staff also can observe the strengths, weaknesses and what possible training requirements the applicant for the job might have. It also is an opportunity for the team to see if there are any major concerns. I find this a very useful tool to ensure that we recruit only the right people for this work environment.
>
> Zseraldina Richvalszki, spa consultant and owner.

With respect to therapists it is also appropriate for the spa manager to ask the applicant to give them a trial treatment (i.e. a massage or a facial). In this way the spa manager can get to judge both the communication style of the therapist as well as their touch.

For those applicants that have not been successful, the spa manager should write a polite letter informing them.

■ Induction and orientation training

The induction training is perhaps the most important training that a member of staff will have. This is where, in addition to essential knowledge about the facility, the expectations of the job and the "do's and don'ts" will be communicated. In many spas or hotels, induction training will be held once a month on a particular calendar day (normally to the convenience of the HR team). This can mean that the person can start employment without having the essentials explained to them before starting work. This is both unfair on the new employee and unprofessional of the organisation. Induction training should take place before the new employee starts employment and is let loose in the spa with the guests!

Induction training should cover the following areas:

- Job and expectations of employees as well as what the employee can expect from the employer.

- The company rules, the "do's and don'ts".
- A show around of the entire facility and if the spa is connected to a hotel, then also the hotel departments as well.
- A personal introduction to all key members of staff and heads of departments if possible.
- Emergency procedures.
- Basic customer care training.

The following materials can be used to support an induction training program:

- **PowerPoint presentations and/or film**: covering all of the above topics
- **A staff handbook**: this should contain the spa's mission and vision, the company structure with photos of the owners, VIPs and key people in management, a description of the different departments and a summary of what was delivered in the induction training – customer care and quality standard expectations and emergency procedures.
- **The job description**: quite often job descriptions can be overcomplicated and full of HR buzz words and jargon. It is worth putting in the effort to make sure that the job descriptions are up-to-date, clear and easy to understand and most of all describe accurately the tasks that the new staff member will carry out. Not only will this be constructive for the member of staff, but if in the future, should conflicts and performance issues arise, it can be referred to.

Figure 3.1 is an example of a simple, clear job description for a group beauty and wellness treatment trainer for a large spa chain.

What stands out about this particular job description is how simple it is. The key word when creating job descriptions is 'minimal'. The job description should be absolutely clear and describe exactly what the role requires and what the expected duties are.

E-learning: there are some very good e-learning programs on the market that are very effective for staff inductions. Power point, films, presentations and short tests can also be easily integrated into an e-learning training program. These tests can check whether the new employee has fully understood the information. The other advantage of e-learning, particularly for spas with a high volume of staff and turnover, is that it can be delivered at any time – the person can even do an e-learning training at home if necessary. E-learning also has the advantage of being able to be connected to the HR administration of the staff member, saving administration time and energy for the spa manger.

GROUP WELLNESS MANAGER AND TREATMENT TRAINER

Main responsibility:

- To oversee, develop and lead the wellness treatment departments for the spa chain

Tasks:

- Ensure that all action is taken to ensure that the beauty and wellness treatment departments meet their financial targets.
- Monitor, motivate and support the therapy teams in cooperation with the spa managers.
- Conduct a detailed quality audit all wellness treatment departments at least once per year.
- Maintain the quality of the wellness departments through spot checking, monitoring the guest feedback systems and following up on the mystery customer audits.
- Carry out regular training in the following areas: customer care, treatment protocols, up-selling, complaint handling, privacy (2 per month minimum).
- Monitor, control and give active support to the internal spa trainings carried out by the spa managers.
- Maintain the training administration system so that it is up to date.
- Support the Group Spa Director with spa quality control audits when required.

Requirements:

- Good English
- 4 years therapy experience
- Training experience and qualification
- Excellent communication, motivation and people skills
- A Master Cosmetician Certificate
- Experience in using the cosmetic brands currently used by the spas
- Self-motivated and disciplined
- Excellent problem-solving and innovative skills
- Energy, enthusiasm and politeness
- Adaptability to fit in and work with other cultures
- Flexible and able to travel.

Figure 3.1: Example job description for a group beauty and wellness treatment trainer.

■   ## Regular training

Effective training in a spa will involve a combination of both outside trainers and internal training sessions. More likely than not, most of the training will be delivered internally as outside training comes at a cost (except for treatment training connected to a spa product brand, when the training should be free and a part of the product brand contract). The ability to hold a good and effective training workshops is an essential skill for the spa manager. A 'train the trainer' qualification should be in every spa manager's resume. The trainings that a spa manager should be able to give should include:

- Customer care training – listening and communication skills.
- Complaint handling.
- Selling and upselling.
- Treatment protocol training (greeting the guest, do's and don'ts during the treatment, respecting privacy, etc).
- Emergency procedures (fire, accident, pool chemical gas leak, etc).

Such trainings should be delivered regularly throughout the year. Training in spas with spa staff tends to be more effective if the trainings are short (1 or 2 hours maximum) but regular. Pulling spa staff off their shift is both disrupting for the staff member and the operation and comes at a cost. It is recommended to put into the employee's contract that 3 or 4 times a year they will be expected outside of their shift to attend a training.

■   ## Training administration

As important as the trainings is the training administration – keeping track of which staff member has attended which trainings, when and how often. Because spa work is shift work, it can be a challenge to get all the necessary staff together at the same time. This means that there should be an airtight training administration system in place to ensure that the spa staff have attended the training necessary for their position. Unless it is a small spa with 4 or 5 employees, Excel spreadsheets or manual systems are not advised for controlling the training administration, instead a training software is strongly advised. This should include:

1 A training calendar with all the training planned in the future (subject, attendees, trainer) and all training that has taken place in the past (subject, who attended, trainer).

2 A staff member profile with the following information:
   - Their name, personal details and qualifications.
   - A list of what skills and treatments they are able to perform
   - A list of all the dates of the training they have attended.
   - A list of all the training that they need to do and by when.

3 Easily downloadable reports (upcoming planned training, training attended according to staff member/department, who missed training, who requires

training, which training should be scheduled before certain deadlines, training feedback scores etc.)

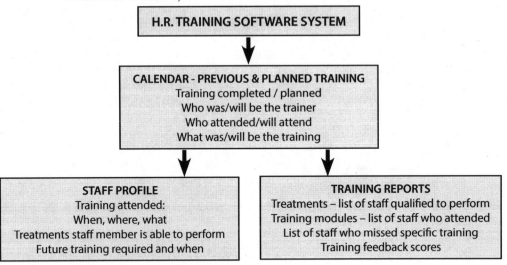

Figure 3.2: The essential features of an HR training software system.

```
                           Training Record

  Training Subject:

  Date: ................................................
  Time: ...............................................
  Location: ..........................................
  Name of Trainer: ..................................................


  Attendees:
  Name:                                Signature
  1. ..........................................     ............................................
  2. ..........................................     ............................................
  3. ..........................................     ............................................
  4. ..........................................     ............................................
  5. ..........................................     ............................................
  6. ..........................................     ............................................
  7. ..........................................     ............................................
  8. ..........................................     ............................................
  9. ..........................................     ............................................
  10. ........................................     ............................................


  Notes:
  ...........................................................................................
  ...........................................................................................
  ...........................................................................................


  Signature of Trainer: ...............................................................
```

Figure 3.3: Example of a training record sheet.

If the training administration is controlled on Excel or manually, it will be extremely time consuming, particularly in spas with a high number of staff. Keeping track, and ensuring that everybody has had the necessary training, without a good software system can be incredibly difficult to monitor. One of the main reasons why training in spas often falls short, is not because of the quality of the actual training itself but because not enough energy is being put into the planning, monitoring, control and administration.

As a basic rule, all staff should sign that they have attended the training (Figure 3.3), and this information is then inputted into the system.

3

Top training tips

Providing effective and regular training on different topics will make your team more motivated, confident and engaged to their workplace. It will also make them feel more valued. Here are my tips:

1 Set your educational goals for a year ahead. What do you want to achieve by the end of the year?

2 At the same time create a list of the strengths and weaknesses of your spa and think how often your employees actually need training sessions. Decide on the priorities.

3 Make a list of the customer care related training topics (upselling, proper behavioural etc., complaint handling etc.), also create a list of the trainings that your employees need to improve their professional skills.

4 For the inhouse training topics prepare the educational materials (the purpose, message and execution of the training). Be creative – *if your staff enjoy the training, they will take on board the message faster. Regular short humorous trainings are the most effective, max 30 – 60 minutes.*

5 Make sure you plan to involve them as much as possible, trainings are not lectures.

6 Check if all your employees can join the training at the same time, or you need to schedule the same topics for multiple times. Make sure that *all of your employees* are scheduled for all of the trainings that you have planned.

7 Decide who is going to be the trainer? Do you have one person who will execute all of the different trainings, are you going to be a trainer, or you will you ask different experts for the different topics? *Make sure that whoever the trainer is that they are the best in the topic that they are covering.*

8 Create a yearly training calendar draft (schedule all the external trainings that you already have a date for and draft your internal trainings as well).

9 2-3 months before the training make sure that your dates are finalized. *Keep them!*

10 After each of the training sessions you have to show that something has changed due to the training. Ask staff for their feedback! Monitor the progress.

Anita Bogó (Group spa trainer and beauty therapist)

■ Holding meetings

Holding meetings and getting the staff together are key tasks for a spa manager. A meeting that is not managed well will result in resentment for time being wasted and a loss of respect for the manager. A spa manager who holds meetings rarely or not at all, will miss out on what is going on in the team, putting themselves into a weak position. In a spa setting, meetings should have certain aims:

- **Motivation**: the main reason for holding the meeting should be for the spa manager to gauge what is the mood and direction of the team and use the opportunity of the get-together to refocus and motivate the team.

- **Gathering, information and goal setting**: meetings are an ideal tool for the manager (and other staff) to find out what is happening in the various departments, it also is an opportunity to set goals and objectives.

- **Sharing and listening to ideas**: meetings are an ideal setting to brainstorm, get new ideas and inspiration.

- **Problem solving**: discussing problems rather than solving them can sometimes take over a meeting. It is important for the manager to find out what the problems are, but obviously the goal should be to focus on quick and effective solutions as opposed to wallowing in them.

Perhaps the most useful result of holding meetings is that the spa manager will be able to very quickly assess the focus and motivation level of each individual attending and, if necessary, take action to rectify it.

Cardon lists three types of meeting (Cardon, 2016):

1 Coordination meetings: discussing roles, goals, accountabilities and tasks.

2 Brainstorming problems and solution discussions.

3 A combination of both.

In the spa workplace where time is short, most meetings should be fairly brief and will be a combination of points one and two.

In a normal business setting, the person holding the meeting would be expected to provide and send out an agenda, but in day-to-day spa operations this is not normally necessary – a quick email will suffice. Before the meeting, the manager should have prepared the following:

- Date, time, location.

- The purpose (even if it is a weekly regular meeting the spa manager should have some idea of what they would like to achieve).

- What items will be discussed.

- Who the participants are.

Minutes

Minutes are a written record of the meeting. During the meeting, notes should be taken, in bullet form, of the key points and actions agreed. For each action there should be: a clear understanding of what needs to be done, by whom and a deadline of by when. Failure to do this can make the whole meeting ineffective. Minutes of the meeting should contain:

- Date, time and location of the meeting.
- Who attended.
- Main items that were discussed, in short bullet form (spa staff do not have the time or interest to read long documents describing everything little thing that was said).
- What was agreed, what actions are expected, by whom and by when.

For short meetings (weekly update meetings for example) the minutes can be sent around just in an email. For larger meetings (full spa staff team meetings) proper minutes should be typed up and staff should sign an attendance sheet (similar to the training record sheet).

In a medium sized spa setting of a spa with about 40 staff, it would be recommended for the spa manager to have a meeting once a week with the heads of department (i.e. reception, beauty, fitness etc) and 2 or 3 times a year a full staff meeting. Getting all the staff together for a meeting at one time can be challenging to coordinate and for this reason many spa managers avoid organising them, but full team meetings are vital for the smooth running of the operation. Failure to do so can result in division and a lack of communication between management and staff, and a decrease in productivity.

■ Appraisals

Perhaps one of the most effective staff management tools is the performance appraisal. This can either be done informally in short one-to-one meetings throughout the year, or formally once a year. Interestingly, according to a recent survey (SHRM, 2018), it was shown that spa staff prefer the option of continuous performance management appraisals as opposed to a formal appraisal annually.

The goals of an appraisal are straightforward:

- To give feedback on the staff member's performance.
- Set goals.
- Find out how they feel in the job.
- Motivation.

The last two points are the most critical.

Finding out how they feel in the job: by having an honest conversation, the spa manager should able to discover if the staff member is happy or not, and if not, what the main reasons behind their dissatisfaction are and how this can be rectified. It may just be that the person is coming to the end of their time in the spa and feels it is time to move on. By being open and frank, the departure of the spa member can be worked through together with the knowledge and sometimes help of the spa manager. This will give time for the manager to prepare themselves and to find their replacement. In some cases, the manager might be able to support the spa staff member in their transition to a new position either within or outside the company.

Motivation: if handled right, an appraisal can be extremely motivating and constructive. It can even improve the relationship considerably between the spa manager and the staff member. Honest criticism, if delivered well, with the best interests of the employee, is normally welcomed. Likewise, complimenting the staff member on their attributes, if communicated sincerely and from the heart, will definitely motivate them. Throughout the entire appraisal motivation should be the main goal of the spa manager.

What not to do: the appraisal is not a forum to give deep criticism or a disciplinary. If there are serious problems with the employee's performance, it should be dealt with separately. The purpose of the appraisal is to motivate, improve communication and set goals, not to combine it with a disciplinary warning or very serious conversation about poor performance.

The structure of an appraisal from should be simple and although some zealous HR departments may want overcomplicate the format (by making the appraisal forms long and bureaucratic) it should not be forgotten that the main focus of the appraisal should be on the communication between the manager and staff member, not filling out complicated forms. The general structure of the form should be along the lines of:

- Professional skills and knowledge: knowledge of their given field, ambition, language skills.
- Quality of their work: consistency, inter-team communication skills, customer care skills, team work.
- Personal qualities: reliability, punctuality, personal presentation, attendance, initiative.
- Achieved goals that were set in the previous review.
- Goals for next review.
- Any other comments.

For each area there can be a scoring system, for example: 'unsatisfactory', 'satisfactory', 'good', or 'excellent'. It is recommended to keep the scoring system as simple as possible to avoid the appraisal turning into a big debate about scores or marks.

Ideally the form should be given to the employee a few days before the review and they should be asked to fill it out. Likewise, the spa manager should fill out the same appraisal form, prior to the review, with their opinions and scores of the staff member's performance. During the appraisal these scores can be compared. Depending on the culture, it might not even be necessary to have any forms at all, informal appraisals, if carried out professionally can work just as well.

Whether it is a formal or informal appraisal the spa manager must prepare for the appraisal in advance. It is important to judge the behaviour and not the person – criticism needs to be specific (Robbins, 2003). If the spa manager gives criticism and the employee then asks for a specific example, the manager must be able to answer and provide one.

It is also necessary to bear in mind the limits of the person that is being appraised. Pushing somebody above and beyond what they are capable of delivering, will cause frustration and tension for everybody concerned – both staff member and the manager. The spa manager's job is to make sure their staff are working to their best and putting their heart into their work. Trying to change somebody or remind somebody of something of which they have no control has little constructive value (Robbins, 2003). Similarly putting the wrong person in the wrong job, or a job which they have little interest in and forcing them to do it is a sure recipe for underperformance.

■ Conflict and poor performance

Team performance in a spa is never consistent – unfortunately. There are good days and bad days, ups and downs. The job of the spa manager is to keep these ups and downs as minimal as possible. The worst habit a manager can get into, is to ignore small conflicts and tensions in the hope that they will somehow disappear on their own. In the spa environment, which is all about relationships, they will not – more likely than not, small problems will morph into something bigger.

Poor performing team members must be dealt with. Like a bad apple in a box, their behaviour and energy will spread in the team. Normally poor performance will arise from having hired a person with a wrong attitude (hence the importance of being able to hold a good interview), or simply having the wrong person in the wrong job. When dealing with a staff member who is underperforming the following should be taken into consideration:

1 The person and problem must be addressed, pushing the matter under the carpet may have serious implications later on.

2 The spa manager should be clear on what they are prepared to accept and tolerate and what they are not.

3 The spa manager should be clear in their own mind about the result of what they would like to happen.

4 They should recognise the difference between bad behaviour and mistakes. For example, inaccurately calculating the cash register is a mistake, which is

forgivable within limits (of course if it happens on a regular basis then maybe the person is in the wrong job); bad behaviour, however (for example, lateness, rudeness, gossiping, negativity and causing friction in the team) should be cracked down on immediately. Bad behaviour is more challenging to deal with, particularly in cases where a staff member is stirring up negative energy and conflicts – as pinpointing actual specific examples can be difficult, but such behaviour must be addressed and dealt with quickly.

■ Difficult conversations

One way for the spa manager to deal with difficult situations is to not view them as a negative event, but rather as an opportunity to address a problem and a challenge to overcome. Here are some possible steps:

■ The manager should have all the information and specifics regarding the problem.

■ The manager should prepare their desired outcome before the meeting.

■ They should invite the person to speak first, and much like an interview, let the person do most of the talking following the six active listening steps described in the last chapter – this will give the manager time to gather as much information as possible.

■ The manager should stay calm, respectful and polite at all times – showing irritation or revealing anger will diminish their control of the situation.

■ Generalisations and exaggerations should be avoided. What the manager says should be specific and to the point.

> I employed a spa administrator. The administrator was excellent, worked hard and stayed late. There was one problem that the administrator always arrived late to work, sometimes up to 30 minutes. When I addressed this her reply was "but I work hard and I always stay later than I am supposed to". I dealt with the problem by explaining, that if I allowed her to come in late this would set a precedent for the team and that I expected her to follow the rules like everyone else. I also made it clear that she had every right to leave on time according to the conditions in her work contract if she so felt.
>
> Viktor Marsalla, Spa Manager.

■ Disciplinaries and firing

Sometimes mistakes are made and the wrong person is put in the wrong job or team. Ignoring the problem or letting it drift on for months or even years is unfair to the person, unfair to the team and also unfair to the manager. Depending on the local regulations, there are various legalities concerning letting staff go. The spa manager needs to ensure that they follow the local procedures exactly and use, as much as possible, the support of the HR department and/or company lawyer (if there is one). If this support is not available, outside professional advice is advised even if it comes at a cost. A mishandling could result in a court case and far higher expenditures! The spa manager should do everything to make sure that they have followed all the procedures in order to avoid an ongoing legal complication.

It is normally possible to dismiss a member of staff if they are not capable of doing the job to the required standard, if they are unwilling to do the job in their job description or they have committed a gross misconduct. In brief, these are normally the steps:

1 The spa manager should in a meeting with the employee, tell them the reason for it. At the meeting, the staff member should be given a chance to explain and issued a first written warning if the manager is not satisfied with their reasons. In the warning, the manager should tell them how they expect them to improve and over what period – warning them that if they do not improve enough, that they will be given a final written warning.

2 The manager can then hold a second meeting if the performance or behaviour has not improved enough by the deadline – the staff member should be given a chance to explain and be issued a final written warning if the manager is not satisfied with their reasons. The manager should revise the action plan with timescales for improvement and warn them that dismissal will be considered if there is no improvement.

3 The manager should then hold a third meeting if the performance or behaviour is still not up to standard by the new deadline. They should warn the member of staff that the dismissal is now possible. After the meeting – or appeal if there is one – the manager can decide whether to give the employee a further chance to improve, or dismiss them. The employee must be informed of the decision, whatever it is (UKGOV, 2019, adapted).

When evaluating the staff member's performance, the manager should keep a written record of all misconduct with the times, dates, of what they did wrong and if possible, with witness statements recorded. The more watertight the case, the less chance there will be for unpleasant repercussions later.

■ **Serious misconduct**: In most countries the spa manager can issue a single 'first and final' written warning if the misconduct or underperformance is serious enough. He or she should explain that not improving could lead to dismissal. 'Serious enough' includes if it is likely to or has caused serious harm to the organisation itself (UKGOV, 2019, adapted).

■ **Gross misconduct**: Gross misconduct can include things like theft, physical violence, gross negligence or serious insubordination. With gross misconduct, the spa manager should be able to dismiss the employee immediately as long as he or she follows a fair procedure. The spa manager should investigate the incident and give the employee a chance to respond before deciding to dismiss them (UKGOV, 2019, adapted).

■ Motivating a team on low salaries

Motivating a team in the best circumstances can be a challenge, however motivating a team on low salaries can sometimes feel like a never ending battle. However, it is important not to forget that what cannot be made up for in wages can be compensated for in a positive work environment. Through professionalism, energy, style, good management and people skills the spa manager should be able to create a pleasant positive work environment that people enjoy coming to work in. Offering flexible hours, reacting to feedback in the employee surveys, holding regular meetings and being able to give excellent staff appraisals are tools that really can make a difference.

■ Staff turnover

Staff turnover is a problem that is regularly highlighted as a spa industry challenge. Staff turnover however is also not always related to salary levels as this example shows:

> I had an excellent head therapist, who began to act less motivated than before. He asked to meet me and said he was unhappy with his wages. We agreed a 10% rise. At first, the head therapist seemed happy, but then a few months later reverted back to his previous level of motivation. Another time I encountered general disatisfaction from the team regarding salary conditions. This was also reflected in the employee feedback surveys so we decided to introduce a new bonus system which was linked to the number of treatments delivered and guest satisfaction levels. At first, the team seemed satisfied with the system, but after a period of time, their motivation and efficiency levels returned to almost what they had been before. In my opinion whilst bonus systems and salary raises can help increase motivation for a period of time, it should not be seen as a one-stop solution.
>
> Sona Zabranska, previously Spa Operations Manager.

As the examples above show, wage rises, unless they are raised considerably may have little effect. Increasing wages by 10 or 20%, which is the most a spa would be able to consider, will not resolve staff motivational issues in the long term. Spa therapist and spa reception positions are never going to be highly paid professions – this is something that a spa manager needs to be aware of, and diplomatically the staff can be reminded of this too.

Staff turnover can be reflective of poor management but it can also be related to location and the local business environment as well. A spa in Central London is likely to have a high turnover in a city where people tend to job hop at fairly rapid pace. A spa out in the Romanian countryside may not have any staff turnover at all (in such locations it is common for staff to remain in the same position for their entire career!).

What is important for the spa manager to recognise, is that every job has a shelf life. After a period of time the spa therapist or receptionist will lose motivation and want to move on and try something new in a different environment. Rather than resisting this, the spa manager, through open communication (and using the tools such as performance feedback) should work with the employee, so that when they decide to move on, it comes as no surprise and a replacement has be recruited and trained to take their place.

In locations where staff turnover is naturally high, the spa manager should be interviewing on a continual basis, building up a good potential CV recruitment bank and have simple, quick and easy to implement training systems and inductions that fit into the day to day operations, without taking too much time.

The main issue for spa managers regarding staff turnover is their own resistance and inability to recognise that in some jobs the timespan of the average employment period is 2 or 3 years. By recognising this and building systems around it, rather than fighting against it, the spa manager can save themselves a lot of energy and time.

Feedback from the interviews – what the experts say

Spa managers were asked which were the best ways to motivate their employees. The responses were varied but there was a consensus too.

- One of the most important aspects, according to respondents, is ensuring that staff are offered ongoing educational and training opportunities, partly to help with career development. This is followed by fair salaries, financial rewards, bonuses and incentives.

- Another really important aspect is leading by example and being a good role model. According to the respondents, typical characteristics of a spa manager should include being fair, honest, consistent, friendly, enthusiastic and a good communicator. This can contribute to creating a happy and productive working environment, which is also deemed important. Andrew Gibson from SVP, Los Angeles, summarises this rather well "Recognition, positive reinforcement, comprehension of the skills required and energy flow, sufficient time between treatments to reenergize, fairness to all and clear targets and objectives on a daily basis."

- A few respondents mention the need for fair and flexible working hours which facilitate a good work-life balance.

- The need to understand team members and encourage team spirit is seen as a relatively important part of a spa manager's job too. This includes identifying individual team members' needs as well as working towards common goals. Listening to feedback from staff and knowing how they feel about their job is part of this process. As stated by Chris Theyer, Training and Development Director of LivingWell Health Clubs, "Consideration of what each person is looking for in their work and their abilities and skills allows a manager to develop both individuals in the team and the team as a whole".

■ Following on from this, several respondents emphasise the importance of what Ioana Marian, Secretary General of the Organization of Balneo and Spa Tourism in Romania calls "Custom-made motivation". This means understanding what motivates individual team members, which can vary from person to person (e.g. more money, a better title, learning and gaining experience or simply going home on time each day).

Research and further reading

There have been numerous studies of employee motivation in different contexts, but the spa and wellness context is rather different because the levels of intrinsic motivation may be higher (i.e. employees go into this profession for love of the job rather than financial rewards, which can be quite low). However, Perić, Gasic and Ivanović (2015) analysed the motivation of employees in spas in Serbia and concluded that the financial factor is the key motivating element for employees, because of the low standard of living there. Khadka (2015) undertook interviews with spa and wellness therapists in Nepal, where salary and financial bonuses are also the most important factors for employee well-being, followed by quality working life and high job status. Craig (2018) points out that high-volume massage can impact negatively on the mental and physical wellness of spa therapists, potentially leading to turnover.

Several articles have expressed concern about the difficulties in attracting staff to the spa profession and retaining them. Jager (2016) lists four reasons why good spa employees leave their jobs which are not related to financial compensation. These include: not liking the manager; lack of support from managers in difficult situations; being over-worked; no growth or advancement opportunities. Bromstein (2018) cites ISPA and Global Wellness Institute data which emphasise the growth of the spa and wellness industries, but laments the challenges of finding qualified managers and staff, as well as the huge turnover. Experts interviewed in this article attribute this to perceptions of the industry and lack of career development opportunities; being overworked and underpaid; cost of education and training versus earning potential; lack of training in business management as well as treatment and service providing (especially important for spa managers); lack of rewards for top performance and loyalty.

On the other hand, an ISPA research report including 1,200 spa professionals in 2017 showed that the spa industry has a loyal workforce full of positive professionals. It suggested that turnover was not so high; they generally felt loyal to their employers and positive about working culture and environment; and 87% of management respondents hoped to have a long-term career in the spa industry. However, it was noted that training and education are needed for high quality service providers and flexible scheduling for the ability to balance work and home life are of high importance (Reed, 2018). It should be noted that there is a growing number of studies on the need for work-place wellness and stress management (e.g. Richardson, 2017), but most of these do not focus on employees within spas or the wellness industry. On the other hand, one consideration for spa managers in the future may be how their spa or wellness activities could contibute to work-based wellbeing.

References

Bromstein, E. (2018) 'Special Report: can the spa industry solve its staffing problems before it's too late?', *Spa Executive*, 23 January, https://spaexecutive.com/2018/01/23/special-report-can-the-spa-industry-solve-its-staffing-problems-before-its-too-late/ (accessed 20/11/2019).

Cardon P. (2016) *Business Communication*, 2nd edn, New York: McGraw Hill.

Craig, V. (2018) 'The impacts of high-volume massage on spa therapists' physical and mental wellness', *International Journal of Spa and Wellness*, **1** (3), 218-227, Doi: 10.1080/24721735.2019.1596659

Jager, L. (2018) 'Four reasons good spa employees quit their jobs', *Spa Executive*, 16 June, https://spaexecutive.com/2018/06/16/four-reasons-good-spa-employees-quit-their-jobs/ (accessed 20/11/2019).

Khadka, L. (2015) 'The significance of employee well-being while delivering wellness and spa services', Master's Thesis, University of Tartu Pärnu College, Estonia, http://dspace.ut.ee/bitstream/handle/10062/49491/khadka_laxmi.pdf (accessed 20/11/2019).

Kitchen J. (2018) 'Inaugural ISPA workforce study', *Spa Opportunities*, 20 April, pabusiness.com/index.cfm?pagetype=news&codeID=337201 (accessed 20/11/2019).

McGee, P. (2013) How to succeed with people, Chicago: Capstone.

Perić, G., Gasic, M. and Ivanović, V. (2015) 'Research of Employee Motivation in the Spa Tourist Centers in Serbia', *Proceedings of the Faculty of Economics in East Sarajevo*, **10**, 65-76, 10.7251/ZREFIS1510065P

Reed, S. (2018) 'Study shows spa industry filled with loyal employees and meaningful careers', *American Spa*, 20 April, https://www.americanspa.com/news/study-shows-spa-industry-filled-loyal-employees-and-meaningful-careers (accessed 20/11/2019).

Richardson, K. M. (2017) 'Managing employee stress and wellness in the new millennium', *Journal of Occupational Health Psychology*, **22** (3), 423–428, Doi: 10.1037/ocp0000066

Robbins, S. P. (2003) *The Truth about Managing People*, New Jersey: Prentice Hall.

SHRM (2018) 'Look ahead at HR trends for 2018', www.shrm.org/shrm-india/pages/look-ahead-at-hr-trends-for-2018 (accessed 20/11/2019).

UKGOV (2019) 'Dismissals', www.gov.uk/dismiss-staff/dismissals-on-capability-or-conduct-grounds (accessed 12/06/2019).

4 Selling and marketing a spa successfully

After staff management and customer care, sales are the next priority. Without proper focus on the sales, revenues can easily slide, the effects of which are never pleasant.

Poor revenue performance undoubtably leads to cost cutting and given that staff costs are the largest cost segment in a spa operation, cuts often start with reducing manning hours and increasing workloads. Alternatively, if the sales results are positive, this can open up possibilities for investment, renovation and even opportunities for the staff.

Because sales are such a crucial part of the business, the spa manager needs to understand the importance they have. However, most of all, they should, as leaders, be able to sell the spa themselves effectively and be a role model for the rest of the team. Sales training or experience in selling is highly recommended for anyone thinking about managing a spa.

- **Attitude and selling**: a can-do positive attitude and belief is the starting point for any sales activity. Belief and motivation are the fuel behind the energy needed to reach sales targets.

- **Activity** is the second most important factor in selling. The more sales and marketing activities there are, statistically the higher the chances there are of meeting targets. Waiting and hoping for the business to come in, even if the spa has a super dream location and an amazing product, is asking for trouble. Continuous ongoing activity is essential.

Types of guests

In a hotel spa you normally find three types of guests:

1 Hotel guests and/or guests purchasing spa packages: in a hotel this will normally be the responsibility of the hotel sales.

2 Walk-in local guests: normally the responsibility of the spa manager or spa sales person.

3 Membership guests: normally the responsibility of the spa manager or spa sales person.

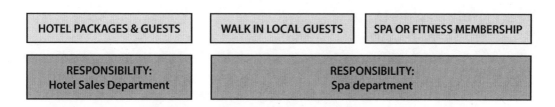

Figure 4.1: The sales responsibilities for different types of guests.

Hotel sales & marketing department

The hotel sales department is responsible for filling up the hotel rooms, and in a spa hotel or spa resort this will involve selling spa stay packages. The hotel sales department's job is to research the market (who will be the guests and where they will come from) and through various channels sell the product and collect the payment. There are two types of channels, direct and indirect:

Direct sales

■ **Website**: this is the preferred channel as it has a huge market, the client pays net rates and the hotel pays no commissions to third parties.

■ **Repeat regular guests**: again, this is a preferred channel as through regular, repeat guests good rates can be charged with no commission to be paid to third parties. In many European traditional spa hotels, up to 70% of the guests are repeat guests!

Indirect sales

■ **Travel agents**: a person or company who sells spa stays or packages (normally within a small geographical area with a low commission charge of between 7% – 10%).

■ **Tour operators**: a company or person that purchases different items in an inclusive holiday in bulk and combines them to sell a package holiday direct to the public or through travel agents (a large market, with a higher commission charge of between 15% – 20%).

■ **Wholesalers**: an intermediary between the supplier and consumer, they are involved in putting together and marketing inclusive tours and individual packages. The operation of the tour will be left to individual suppliers (a worldwide market, with a huge commission of between 25% – 40%).

■ **Specialist market tour operators**: deals with niche products to certain geographical areas (commissions of between 15% – 30%).

■ **Internet booking sites**: (e.g. booking.com, Tripadvisor etc, around 20% commission).

■   Hotel marketing

The hotel marketing will normally consist of:

- **Direct mailing**: (newsletters, special offers, promotions, greetings etc) – this will target regular guests through databases within a hotel or destination. Alternatively, the hotel can purchase databases for money and target travel professionals. The advantages of direct mailing is that it is relatively cheap and it specifically targets the right market. The main disadvantage is that it only reaches a small group of people

- **Advertising**:
  - ☐ **Newspapers**: a relatively cheap form of marketing, it is able to target a specific market, but newspaper ads have a short lifespan.
  - ☐ **Professional magazines**: they target the required market but can be expensive.
  - ☐ **Brochures**: relatively cheap to produce, easy for clients to take away, but have a huge waste potential.
  - ☐ **Ambient advertising**: advertising placed on bus tickets, till receipts and petrol pumps etc. (can be too general for hotels or spas).
  - ☐ **TV, Radio, Internet**: expensive, whilst sometimes used for spa or hotel chains, for individual hotels or spas this medium can be too general.
  - ☐ **Outdoor advertising**: billboards, bus shelters, transport, relatively inexpensive but localized only for an area with a limited time period.

- **Public relations**: PR refers to communicating to an audience an idea, a product, getting them to support a cause, or recognize an accomplishments or event. Here is what the Public Relations Society of America (PRSA) agreed upon: *"Public relations is a strategic communication process that builds mutually beneficial relationships between organizations and their publics"* (Wynne, 2016). The PR person in the spa hotel plays an instrumental role in generating articles about the spa, showing off the facilities to journalists, organising events that will spread the reputation of the spa and generally carrying out any tasks that will generate attention and interest.

- **Study tours and fam trips**: showing journalists, travel staff, famous people, writers the hotel and spa facilities in order to spread the word.

- **Exhibition and trade fairs**: hotels and spas will often attend exhibition and trade fairs to promote their products, meet potential customers or partners and/or raise the company profile. There are two main types of exhibition and trade fair:
  - ☐ **B2B** (Business to business) hotels/spas meeting travel agents, tour operators, group organisers, etc to build business partnerships.
  - ☐ **B2C** (Business to customer) promoting the hotel and spa direct to the customers.

Many spa hotels today provide great services and have a great staff, but too often they lack being unique and therefore miss out on the potential for differentiation. More and more spa menus are offering the same kind of products and services in spas with similar architecture styles. This is why I consider a well-defined brand the most important factor in successfully marketing a spa. The brand should give clear guidance on which products and services to focus on, which product brands to list and how these services should be provided. This should be the base in providing a consistent and unique experience to guests. It is important to understand that a brand is not a logo or a tagline. The brand is the most concise form of what a spa hotel stands for and of what guests could and should expect. In the end a brand is the starting point for a good reputation which is the most important 'currency' to market a spa hotel successfully today.

Tobias Bielenstein, Head of Marketing, Roman Thermal Spas.

4

Hotel sales departments

A hotel sales department generally consists of the following departments:

- **E-commerce**: responsible for generating leads and sales through the website and social media. E commerce is especially relevant to the spa department – making sure the spa facilities and services are being correctly promoted through these mediums.
- **MICE**: meetings, incentives, conferences and exhibitions. Not directly relevant for the spa department, however this department should ensure that the spa is being promoted at corporate events, wherever possible.
- **Travel trade**: travel agents, specialist and mass market tour operators and wholesalers. The sales department should be building relationships with these businesses that are specifically spa related.
- **Group sales**: group bookings. This department should be making sure that the large spa groups are properly handled.
- **Reservations**: responsible for all the bookings / reservations / packages. This department should ensure that any guests enquiring about the spa and spa stays are being given the correct information and handled properly.

Spa sales & marketing

In the spa, everyone will be expected to sell. There are three key areas of selling:

1 **Spa reception**: they will be expected to sell and promote all services to all guests, including guests staying in the hotel, walk in and membership guests.
2 **Therapists**: a less direct approach, however therapists will be expected to promote all services to all guests, including guests staying in the hotel, walk in guests and membership guests, during or after the treatments.

3 **The spa manager and/or spa sales person:** they are ultimately responsible for all revenue segments, in particular generating walk in guests, local guests on day packages, spa membership and ensuring that maximum revenue is generated from hotel guests staying on packages.

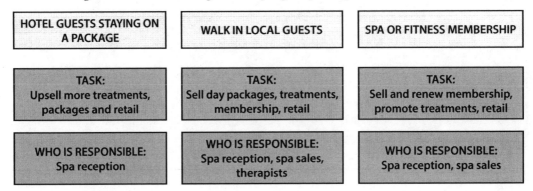

Figure 4.2: Sales tasks and responsibilities.

Planting and harvesting

Marketing and sales in spas can be compared to planting and harvesting:

- **Planting**: this is the marketing activity. In other words, actions carried out to generate interest in the spa.
- **Harvesting**: this is the activity connecting with interested guest leads, in order to build a relationship and sell the services in the spa.

In order to have successful sales results both activities (planting and harvesting) are needed. It is the spa manager's responsibility to make sure this happens and to keep the focus at all times on the revenues.

Planting (marketing)

Marketing in spas is fairly straightforward. Normally a spa will have members or regular guests, and the contact details of these will be stored in a database. This should be the starting point for any marketing or any sales activity.

> Every spa member or guest will have between 200 – 500 people in their circle of friends, acquaintances and work colleagues. The spa manager and the spa sales person and team should never forget that each contact has the potential to promote the spa within their social circle if handled correctly. Targeting the existing clients should always be the first option in a spa marketing or sales campaign, as it is the most logical and cost effective. It is also more beneficial to have members who are connected to each other as: a) they will have a better time enjoying the spa socially, b) they are more likely to repeat visit and c) less likely to go somewhere else.

Here are a number of actions that will effectively stimulate interest and generate sales:

- **Talking to the guests**: it sounds obvious to mention, but just spending time and building a relationship with the regular guests will have a positive impact on the sales. Having good customer relationships means it will be easier to promote sales actions and also persuade guests to bring their friends along to the spa. Part of the spa sales person's and spa manager's daily duty should be time out in the spa or pool area, mixing and chatting to the guests.

- **Treatment information and incentives in the spa**: sometimes the full importance of making sure that the spa information is professionally presented is not given the attention it deserves. The treatment information at the spa reception must be extremely clear, well presented, in the main languages of the guest profiles and easily accessible. If this is not taken care of (for example if price lists are running out, if the treatment information is out of date or if the language translation is poor, etc) business will be lost.

> If the spa uses more than one language, the information/promotion should be *separated* according to language and the languages marked clearly with a nationality flag. In promotions or advertising that combines different languages on one page, the information should *not* be grouped according to subject or message, but rather, grouped *according to language*, so the guest can absorb quickly and clearly the information.

Selling a club spa or membership

Let us imagine a club spa with 500 members which is looking to double its membership. As mentioned, each one of us, taking into consideration our social circle (work colleagues, acquaintances and contacts on social media etc) has a network of between 200 – 500 people approx. If the spa sales manager decides to target the existing guests, (assuming that each guest can reach out to 200 people in their social and work circle), this simple sum shows what a huge potential there is:

500 (spa members) x 200 (in each spa member's social circle) = 100,000 (contacts).

If only 1% of these 100,000 contacts express interest in the spa that is still = 1,000 potential new members. 1,000 members would more than fill up the spa!

This example shows the power of establishing strong relationships with existing clients, how important and how valuable the potential is. The secret of good marketing is to take the easiest, most economical route, using the resources at hand, in this case – using the existing clients.

The other opportunity is the staff. Each staff member will also have 200 – 500 in their social network. What staff say about where they work, and the potential they have to promote the spa positively can be a valuable part of the PR strategy. (Another reason for the spa manager to try to create a great working atmosphere).

If a spa has 40 employees x 200 in their social network = 8000 people!

An astute spa sales person will tap into this resource by creating incentives and promotions for the friends and family of staff.

Other examples of 'planting' or marketing include:

- **Social media**: making sure that the spa is visible on all the main channels and *getting the guests* to post news about the spa. An important point: it is more effective when guests share information about the spa on their *personal* social media as opposed to the spa promoting itself on their company media accounts.

- **Regular emailing to spa guests:** remembering birthdays and special events. Based on their treatment and fitness preferences (all of which should be trackable in the software system), targeting them for special interest classes, treatments or services.

- **Monthly newsletters**: with spa news, events, new services and special offers. Newsletters should have incentives to promote treatments or encourage the spa guest to bring a friend. These incentives will be more effective if tied to interesting news or information rather than cold advertising. Incentives should be offered sparingly, too many, too often will decrease their effectivity.

- **Standard letters or emails**: these should include a 'thank you for joining' letter (with maybe a free/discounted trial visit voucher for the new member to bring a friend), birthday greetings, Mother's Day, women's day promotions etc, with promotions or incentives.

- **Members evenings or events**: every so often holding an event (launching a special treatments or service, holding a unique group exercise class, celebrating spa anniversaries, personal health assessments, lifestyle lectures, etc). Events are an excellent opportunity to connect with the clients and meet potential new ones.

All the above can have a 'catch' or 'link' for the member or regular spa guest to bring a friend with them, there can be an incentive both for the friend and for the member if the friend joins or purchases a service (i.e. 'refer a friend and win…, 'refer a friend and they will receive x treatment when they join' etc. etc.) – however as mentioned, *incentives and offers should be given both sparingly and strategically.*

There are also many other marketing actions to consider:

- **Forging links with the local companies in the area**: building relationships with the HR directors, inviting them for a complimentary treatment and getting to know them.

- **Open days**: holding special events in the spa to generate PR and interest, special classes, health events, treatment try outs, charity fundraising events and local celebrities to help grab the attention. This can be combined with members events.

- **Special offers for special groups**: student memberships and offers, packages for retired people at certain times, special rates at certain times for friends and family of staff.

- **Building relationships**: with local businesses, clubs, associations and churches and religious establishments, creating special packages and incentives.

- **Flyers or leafleting**: distributed with an incentive and/or enticing offer in busy areas near the spa.

- **Advertising**: the most important advert for the spa will be the name over the spa entrance and directional signs. These must be noticeable, well presented and maintained. Placing adverts in journals or newspapers that target the spa's client base can also be effective, as can billboards/banners on routes that the client base uses.

- **E-mailing / mailshots to old expired members and cold leads**: old contacts in the sales database that have laid dormant, it is possible that circumstances might have changed and a spa membership or visit might now interest them.

Important: any promotion offering a free or discounted trial visit should ensure that the visitor has to book in advance, so that the spa sales person or spa manager can meet them and establish a relationship with them.

4

> Our spa had just opened and needed to generate revenue. Being an upmarket area with several celebrities, I found out who the local celebrities' agents and managers were. I approached them and offered four well known TV personalities a free membership and special rate for their partner. Having regular celebrities in the spa generated immediate PR. The spa guests spread the word that they were members of a spa where 'so and so' was also a member. Naturally word got around and other people wanted to join. After a period of time our spa became well known and it became the 'it' place to go to.
>
> Simon Saunders, spa and health club operator, sales expert and consultant.

■ Working with the hotel sales department

Spas in hotels have the key advantage that they will have access to the hotels database and contact lists. For this reason, the spa sales manager should do everything possible to work in close harmony with the hotel sales department. For these types of spa facilities here are some excellent marketing possibilities:

- Combining sales actions with the hotel (email blitzes to local corporates etc).

- Ensuring that local partners from companies, when touring the hotel, meet the spa manager and are given an incentive to visit and try out the facility.

- Ensuring that spa invitations and offers with incentives are visible at all corporate functions and events in the hotel. (Often it is worth having a stand outside the hotel corporate events with an attraction such as treatment demonstrations and short mini treatments to promote the spa facilities – such as 'chair' or 'head and neck' massages). Corporate functions are an excellent opportunity to collect new contacts and meet key decision makers in the company.

Other important actions for spas that are in hotels include:

- Always making sure that there is information in the rooms, lifts and in the public areas promoting the spa, and that this information is clear, attractive, up-to-date and in the relevant languages.
- Having the spa offers and events promoted in the hotel morning newsletter (if there is one), hotel information boards and at the main hotel reception.
- Making sure that the main information regarding the spa's opening times, whereabouts and main offers are available in the relevant languages at the hotel main reception.
- Ensuring the hotel reception staff are informing the guests on arrival about the spa, how to reach it and giving them the information leaflet if necessary.
- If large groups arrive, the spa sales person should make a point of welcoming them, and offering them a tour of the spa.

Promoting spa services in a spa resort hotel in Romania

The spa manager at this particular spa hotel had an imaginative approach to help fill up treatment space at the weekends. Many weekend guests coming to the spa on relaxation breaks did not book treatments in advance. Given that these guests would arrive on Fridays, the spa manager would go to the restaurant on a Friday night, introduce herself and welcome the guests. At the same time, she would take with her a list of which treatment spaces were available and whilst chatting and promoting the spa, recommend and reserve treatments for those available spaces. She also had a solution for how to occupy therapists if their treatment slot was not booked. Instead of letting them just sit waiting for clients in their treatment rooms, she encouraged them to go around the spa area and offer free 5-minute hand massages to guests relaxing by the pools. Not only did the therapists keep busy, but spa services were promoted and the guests of course appreciated the free service.

■ Creating a sales and marketing plan

A spa sales and marking plan does not need to be complicated. The starting point for the plan should be a review of the previous year's sales results and promotions and then to build on that. If something worked one year, then probably it should be repeated the next. It is advisable to break the plan into the different guest segments as their needs will vary. Figure 4.3 is a very simple example of how a sales and marketing plan for the month of January might look

This particular spa uses a new treatment a package to inject interest and life into the start of the year. It has a nice mix of events, PR, mailing, referral actions and joint promotions. Obviously, all of the actions should be scheduled into the spa calendar with dates, deadlines and the person responsible.

JANUARY		
THEME: Start the new year running and get into shape!		
New treatment: chinese cupping treatment /NewPackages: Revitalize Boost (1 or 3 days)		
Hotel guests	**Walk-in guests**	**Spa members**
Launch the new revitalization package by getting the hotel sales to include it in their e- mail blitzs to partners. Advertising in rooms for new cupping treatment .	Training for all receptionists on how to promote the new treatment. Organize large banner at reception with treatment promotion.	Special offer 'upgrade individual membership to a joint membership and receive a 10% discount and a free cupping treatment!'
Target all corporate events by having a stand & cupping treatment demonstration outside conference rooms – promote the new day package with the new treatment.	E-mail all membership and regular day visitor contacts with the new treatment.	Include in the spa members newsletter a cupping treatment article and a full promotion of the new packages.
Work with the PR manager in inviting journalists to come and try out the new cupping treatment and help with PR articles.	Advertise the new treatment in the local magazine.	Members evening. Bring a friend, if the friend joins for a year on the day, the member's membership gets a one month extension. Health lectures, special classes, cupping treatment demos, etc.
Attend B2C events with the sales department, organize free demonstrations of the new treatment and give a free revitalization package in the raffle draw.	Organise joint promotions with body product shops, with special discount coupon for the new day package and cupping treatment .	

Figure 4.3: Example sales and marketing plan.

■ Controlling the sales focus

When it comes to sales, the role of the spa manager is to ensure that they are in full control of the sales focus of the team. As a first step the manager must know the sales results in detail and on a daily basis. This should include:

- The revenue in the different spa segments (i.e. beauty, massage, retail, revenue from hotel guests, revenue from outside guests, package revenue, treatments included in packages, treatments bought on spot, etc).

- How these spa revenue segments are performing according to the budget for the month and year to date.

- Where the spa revenue stands according to last year and the budget.

The following table shows how a daily revenue control sheet should look. Many cash systems will produce a revenue report but these might not include the last year's and budget results comparison percentages. This is essential. If this information is not available automatically in the spa software system the spa manager should devise a manual system. One advantage of a manual system is that by writing in the numbers daily the spa manager will really get to know the business in detail.

Revenue Segment	1	2	3	4	29	30	31	Total	% to last year	Amount to last year	% budget	Amount to budget
Medical package revenue		€20.00						€20.00	200	€10.00	80	-€5.00
Lifestyle package revenue	€50.00	€10.00						€60.00	150	€20.00	120	€10.00
Total medical & lifestyle package revenue	**€50.00**	**€30.00**	**€0.00**	**€0.00**	**€0.00**	**€0.00**	**€0.00**	**€80.00**	**160**	**€30.00**	**107**	**€5.00**
Relaxation package revenue	€120.00	€50.00						€170.00	142	€50.00	131	€40.00
Relaxation treatments	€200.00	€100.00						€300.00	97	-€10.00	100	€0.00
Total treatment revenue	**€320.00**	**€150.00**	**€0.00**	**€0.00**	**€0.00**	**€0.00**	**€0.00**	**€470.00**	**09**	**€40.00**	**109**	**€40.00**
Beauty package		€300.00						€300.00	100	€0.00	77	-€90.00
Beauty treatment revenue	€400.00	€500.00						€900.00	129	€200.00	123	€170.00
Beauty retail sales	€100.00	€50.00						€150.00	143	€45.00	143	€45.00
Total beauty revenue	**€500.00**	**€850.00**	**€0.00**	**€0.00**	**€0.00**	**€0.00**	**€0.00**	**€1350.00**	**122**	**€245.00**	**110**	**€125.00**
Fitness membership revenue	€600.00							€600.00	120	€100.00	103	€20.00
Fitness retail revenue	€20.00	€30.00						€50.00	100	€0.00	100	€0.00
Total fitness revenue	**€620.00**	**€30.00**	**€0.00**	**€0.00**	**€0.00**	**€0.00**	**€0.00**	**€650.00**	**112**	**€100.00**	**103**	**€20.00**
SPA TOTAL revenue	**€1,490.00**	**€1,060.00**	**€0.00**	**€0.00**	**€0.00**	**€0.00**	**€0.00**	**€2,550.00**	**119**	**€415.00**	**108**	**€190.00**

Figure 4.4: Example revenue control sheet.

The above is obviously an example of a well performing spa (although it is just the second day of the month). As seen, in the 'amount to budget and last year columns' the results are both above budget and above last year. There is minus in relaxation treatments, but this is minimal. By looking at such a report the spa manager can evaluate quickly which revenue departments are up or down and how much money will be needed each day to hit the targets by the end of the month.

It must be emphasized that it is crucially important that the revenue segments are divided clearly so that the spa manager, if there is a problem, can identify where it is at a glance. In this way they can then address it with the relevant spa department.

In the above example the medical, beauty, relaxation and fitness services are separated. It is also possible to see clearly package revenue and treatments bought individually. This particular spa has decided to separate the beauty and fitness departments (so that they monitor them as mini profit centres). Retail has also been separated according to the two departments where it is sold, so that its performance can be monitored closely.

Different spas will have different segment breakdowns, but the most important point to remember is: *Clarity of revenue and financial reports is essential and must be the starting point for managing any spa business!*

Harvesting (selling)

Selling spa services or a spa club membership is relatively easy. Rather it should not even be looked at as 'selling' but rather recommending services that can benefit the lifestyle and spa experience of the spa goer.

The spa manager must ensure that all staff are focused on the sales at all times. There are certain areas to focus on:

1 The spa manager should have as part of their daily routine *communicating* the daily revenue performance with their team, both in the form of a printed report and verbally if necessary. In a large spa operation, it may be enough to communicate the revenue results to the staff of their own spa section. Therapists are in the job to deliver great treatments, not analyse to revenue reports, so it is important that the results should be presented simply and in a way that will both interest and motivate them. The more informed the team are, the more likely they are to understand the relevance of the results to take an interest.

2 The spa manager should make sure through training that all staff are able to tour a guest professionally around the spa and close a sale if necessary.

3 All staff should be recommending treatments, services and re-bookings:

☐ **Reception**: receptionists should be upselling and recommending treatments at every suitable opportunity. If a customer books a treatment, another treatment or service should be recommended. If a customer is just making an enquiry they should be asked if they would like to book a treatment, or alternatively offered a retail product or another service. The receptionists should know all of the treatments and packages in detail, and have *tried out each treatment themselves* so they know what they are talking about.

☐ **Therapy departments**: should be recommending a repeat treatment or another treatment or service at the end of each treatment.

(*None of the above should be considered a 'hard' sell, rather a polite recommendation in the interest of helping the guest to make the most out of their spa experience*).

4 All staff should know how to deal with an enquiry over the phone and to take the client's enquiries and details so that the spa sales person or another colleague can follow up if necessary.

■ Handling telephone inquiries

Telephone enquiries are potential sources of revenue and must be handled well by the staff. The aim of the person taking the enquiry should be to get the enquirer to come and visit the spa. Once they are in the spa, the visitor can see the spa and feel the atmosphere and at the same time the sales person or other member of staff can start to build a relationship with them.

In a telephone enquiry, the staff member should never attempt to sell the services over the phone. The member of staff should answer the questions but rather than focus on prices, emphasize the services and their benefits.

Club membership telephone enquiries

Often membership prices are not advertised for club spa memberships. The reason for this that it forces the client to make contact with the spa, meaning that a connection between client and spa sales person will have to take place. There are several ways in which guests will enquire:

- **Internet**: many spas and club memberships will offer a pricelist via the internet. An effective approach is to have a click box stating 'if you would like a price list please click here', by clicking the enquirer then has to fill out their contact details, after which the spa sales person can add them to their database and follow up.

- **Telephone**: if an enquirer asks for information over the phone, the member of staff should be trained on how to take their contact details – not doing so is lost business.

■ Touring potential spa clients

Every spa employee should know how to tour a guest around the spa. Rather than to give a 'standard' robotic tour, the staff should be trained to connect with the guest and adapt the tour to what the guest is interested in. The aim of the tour should be not to sell services but to build a good relationship with the potential client and make them enjoy the meeting and experience. Once the member of staff has found out what the potential client is interested in, then they can recommend and book an appropriate service or treatment. The tour should take the following steps:

1   A friendly greeting, with smile, eye contact and a handshake and introduction.

2   If the contact details of the person have not yet been taken, the member of staff should request them *before* the tour, (most spas and club spas will have a short card for the person to fill out).

3   Asking the client what in particular they are interested in.

4   If they are interested in the pool then that is where the member of staff should start the tour, if it is fitness then the fitness room, etc. Only after that should they then proceed with the other areas – if the guest is interested.

5   During the tour they should pay close attention to the body language and focus of the guest, see what catches their eye and interests them, and spend time on that.

6   They should also ask questions relating to the lifestyle of the guest; where they live, where they work, what spa services are they interested in, etc, and by carefully listening, offer and promote the services and reasons why this spa would be right for them.

7   At the end of the tour, based on the information they have gathered they should recommend and book the services that the guest has expressed interest in.

Club membership tours

Selling a club membership is normally more challenging as the money involved will very likely be much more than just a treatment, package or a product. The approach however is the same. The person conducting the tour should aim to establish a great relationship with the potential new member. Prices should be given only at the end of the tour in the following steps:

1 The staff member should sit the guest down and engage them in conversation.

2 They should show and explain the prices starting with the longer term most expensive membership options (the aim being to sell as high and as long as possible, if that will fit in with the client's demands and lifestyle).

3 After giving the prices the staff member should immediately explain the benefits and advantages of that particular membership option. It is best not to leave a pause after showing the price but to continue straight on with the benefits, particularly if the membership concerns a large amount. After explaining the benefits, the staff member can ask for the guest's opinion.

4 If one option is not appropriate then they should suggest other options that might work out for the client.

The client will have stated one of the three following options, from which the staff member should take following actions:

a) **They want to buy the membership**: the staff member should then proceed with the sale and recommend and book another service or treatment additionally if possible.

b) **They do not want to buy**: the member of staff should try to find out the reason. They should then ask if they can contact the client in the future. If the client says 'yes', a note should be made in the sales person's database, with a full description of what has been said, and with the follow up date.

c) **They want to think about it**: the member of staff should ask if they can call the person in the near future (they should suggest a date). Alternatively, they can offer a free trial for the person to try out the facility.

Selling a club membership should never be a hard sell. Ultimately, the membership should benefit the client. Pushing a client to buy when it will not fit in with their lifestyle will not be a long-term relationship.

■ The spa membership sales person

In a large club spa this is a key role. Of all the staff positions, managing sales people is the most challenging. Sales people normally have excellent communication skills, are very charismatic and, because of the nature of the job, they often have the tendency to say what the listening party wants to hear. Managing a sales person takes skill.

The spa manager should be aware that it is not what the sales person says that matters, it is the results that they generate.

Key tasks

The spa manager should be making sure that the spa sales person is carrying out the basic duties:

1   Maintaining contact with the key clients. Those clients that bring in the largest amount revenue are where the sales person should be spending most of their energy – in particular, large corporate companies.

2   Ensuring that the sales person is following up any enquiries for membership or services within 24 hours. Leaving it longer will mean lost interest and business.

3   Ensuring that the sales person is contacting members with memberships about to expire, well in advance to ensure that the member renews. Leaving it too late might result in an unrenewed membership.

4   Ensuring that they keep a well organised database (the spa manager should check this regularly), with hot and cold leads clearly marked, dates when the leads were contacted, the communication between the client and sales person clearly described and a follow up date of the agreed next action. The database should be maintained to such a level that if the spa manager gets run over by a bus then someone else can go in immediately and take over!

Telephoning and emailing: Much of the sales person's job will be telephoning or emailing. A spa sales persons should never make cold calls, but rather 'follow up' calls – calls following up enquiries generated by the marketing. The purpose of the call is to establish contact and inspire the receiver to come, meet the sales person and see the facilities – not to sell over the phone.

The sales person's working shift: Selling a spa is not a 9 to 5 job. The spa sales person should work according to the business demands. As part of the job is mixing with the guests, like the manager they should be available at busy and peak times. If Saturdays are the busiest time in the spa, then the spa sales person should be working Saturdays. If business is slow then the spa manager should prepare themselves to work longer hours, particularly towards the end of the month. If the last day of the month is Sunday and the target has not been reached, then the spa sales person should be prepared to work right up until the last minute.

Signs of trouble

Every person has their ups and downs and this is true of sales people. Selling can be a stressful job and when business is slow it can be extremely demotivating. The spa manager has to perform a delicate balancing act of giving the sales person space to do their job – nobody likes a manager breathing down their neck – but at the same time keeping a close eye on the situation. There are certain signs that should signal warning bells concerning the spa sales person's behaviour:

1   **Busy doing activities not related to sales**: long hours designing posters, internet research, chatting with people that are not likely to help with revenue, administrative duties, etc.

2 **The following statements**: 'I'm doing my best', 'the budget is too high', 'the spa is too busy', 'I don't think we are going to make it this month'

Let us have a look at each of these statements and what might be an appropriate reaction from a spa manager:

■ *'I'm doing my best'*: unfortunately, with sales performance, best does not come into it, what matters is the result. The spa manager should check the activity and all the sales processes, get the sales person to focus on weaker areas and maintain high levels of activity.

■ *'The budget is too high'*: normally the budget will be based on the year before, plus a few percent. Very rarely is it too far beyond reach of achieving. The spa manager should show the sales person the previous year, if there are no unforeseen circumstances the spa should be able to build upon the previous year's performance, period.

■ *'The spa is too busy'*: good news! A busy spa is what all spa managers want. The solution is not to stop selling, but consider increasing prices and look at filling up the quieter hours.

■ *'I don't think we are going to make it this month'*: this is perhaps the most manipulative of statements. It is the sales person letting the spa manager know that they have given up. By saying they will not make it, they can feel that they have been honest and can now relax having let themselves off the hook. The spa manager should ensure that the sales person puts in more effort and works right up until the last minute till the end of the month. They should do their best to make the sales person sustain belief that hitting the target it is achievable no matter how grim the prognosis. Miracles can happen!

> On several occasions I can remember being well below budget on the last day of the month, but through sheer determination and calling around every possible client and just believing we could do it, like a miracle the money came in at the last minute!
>
> Simon Saunders, spa and health club operator, sales expert and consultant.

Problem solving sales performance

In a hotel spa if the results are not coming in the problem will lie in one of two areas:

1 The hotel guest or package sales

2 The membership or walk in guests.

If the problem is with the hotel guest or package sales, the spa manager should meet with the hotel sales manager urgently, review all the activity that has taken place in the various channels and work together with them on solutions to rectify the problem.

If the problem is in membership sales or walk in guests, the problem can be will be found in the attitude, sales focus or level of activity in the spa department:

- If the spa is continually reaching 70 – 80% of its targets, it means there is a serious problem – a major restructuring concerning the marketing approach, product or even staff organisation may be required.

- If it is reaching 80 – 90 % of the results, it means whilst there are issues, with some good marketing and lots of action the situation can be turned around.

- Hitting between 90 – 100% of the target means with a little push exceeding budget can be achieved.

It is worthwhile for the spa manager to keep a track on the average revenue performance that the spa sales person achieves, more often than not a down turn in sales will be reflected in their motivation and focus.

Problems

Problems can be broken down into three categories. Let us have a look at what is behind the problems and how to rectify them:

1 **No or few enquires/interest**: either the marketing is not working, or the staff are not taking down the enquiries at the reception, or both. Another marketing approach and more activity is needed. The spa manager should also check the handling of the enquiries by phone and if the walk-in guest's and telephone enquirer's details are being taken.

2 **Interest/enquiries but low number of tours/visits**: the obvious problem here is that the sales person or reception is either not following up the enquiries, or not handling them effectively. The spa manager should check the database system is tight and in order, and listen to how the sales person is handling the enquiries and check the activity of the sales person. They should check the ratio of enquiries to booked visits or tours. It should be about 1 to 5 at least.

3 **Tours, walk-ins but low sales**: here the spa manager needs to check the quality of the tours and sales closing techniques, of all involved. For each five tours there should be a sale. If the quality of the tour and closing techniques are satisfactory, then it would worth checking the competition and their pricing.

To sum up: results require motivation, activity and belief. The spa manager should be constantly focused on motivating the staff, focusing them on the sales, ensuring the right activity is being done and plenty of it, but must of all that there is belief within the team that are able to achieve the results!

■ Emergency sales actions

A spa manager is going to experience those months when the business is slow and even seems to dry up. Panicking and getting despondent will not help the sales to come in. Thankfully there are some tried and tested actions that can bring in interest almost immediately:

- **Flyer distribution**: Flyers will have an almost immediate effect. Getting a therapist, student or another member of staff to go to the nearest travel hub (metro station, bus, station, high street) and hand out flyers with an incentive which has a short validity and involves personally visiting the spa. Flyers can also be dropped off in local cafes, businesses, shops etc.

- **Using the existing members and members**: Giving a voucher to each guest in the spa with a special incentive and offer (i.e. "bring a friend"), with a short validity date.

- **Members referrals**: launching an immediate offer that if a member brings a friend before a nearby date, they and the friend receive an incentive.

- **E-mailing**: sending a blitz email to all members and all leads in the database.

- **Advertisement**: advertising in local papers and blitzing local businesses and shops with news about the spa and an incentive to visit and purchase before a certain date.

4

Feedback from the interviews – what the experts say

The most important elements for the respondents are related to the quality of products, services and facilities, as well as to the range and effectiveness of treatments and therapies. It is mentioned that there should also be a clear and ideally unique concept which is somehow connected to the local context. Innovation is important, as stated by Elena Bazzocchi, Global Hospitality Manager "being trendsetters and not followers".

Important factors also include the skills, qualifications, professionalism and motivation of staff. They should be friendly, competent, caring with a positive attitude. Knowledge of the product and brand is essential in order to create customer trust.

Knowing and understanding the customer base or profile(s) is fundamental, including segmentation, mix of guests, as well as targeting new markets. It was thought that facilities and treatments should be aligned with customers' needs and also exceed their expectations, as stated by one respondent "Promise less, deliver more". It was deemed important to create tailor-made experiences, for example, "Personalized rituals and treatments" as suggested by Nataša Ranitović, CEO of Sunny Ltd. Wellness Consulting. Alastair Graham, Consultant, made the following point: "Recognise that whilst someone may just be another customer to you, to the customer their visit to your facility is a meaningful event". Several respondents stressed the importance of loyal customers and the importance of good feedback and reviews from customers.

The location and environment are also important, including accessibility, architecture and design. Good management (e.g. cleanliness, hygiene, safety), maintenance and renewal of the facility are also cited as being necessary.

Attractive, informative and truthful marketing and promotion are highlighted too. As stated by Chris Theyer, Training and Development Director of LivingWell Health Clubs "Pictures sell on line - people buy with their eyes".

Economic success is also referred to and the importance of being 'revenue driven' and dynamically adapting offers and prices to different markets and target groups.

Research and further reading

Tezak (2012) produced a very practical book that included chapters about merchandising and marketing. He emphasises the need to know one's customers well and to launch and maintain active programmes that attract new customers and retain them. He highlights the importance of branding and using multiple marketing tools, but concludes that word-of-mouth is the most effective. Navarro (2014) emphasised the importance of innovation in the spa industry, arguing that most innovations relate to the customer and are of a 'demand-pull type'. He discusses product innovation, marketing innovation, organisational innovation and process innovation. This includes cost reduction and revenue management strategies as well as the designing and marketing services. The importance of social media marketing for the spa and wellness industry was noted by Lagrosen and Grundén (2014). Their research findings show that a dedicated staff are needed for social media marketing, but that more training is needed; traditional marketing may still be used for older clients; the tone and register of the social media posts is important, as well as the time of day of postings; it is also essential to create interest, through competitions, for example. Buxton (2017) focuses on selling experiences and the maximisation of retail sales to boost a spa's revenue. Staff reluctance and motivation are addressed and the benefits for guests are also highlighted. Michopoulou (2017) examines the multi-faceted and complex nature of spa marketing using the 4Ps model, as well as discussing pricing issues.

References

Buxton, L (2017) 'Selling the total spa product', in S. Rawlinson and T. Heap (eds) *International Spa Management*, Oxford: Goodfellow Publishers, pp. 99-113.

Lagrosen, S. O. and Grundén, K. (2014) 'Social media marketing in the wellness industry', *The TQM Journal*, **26** (3), 253-260, Doi: 10.1108/TQM-12-2013-0129

Michopoulou, E. (2017) 'Marketing for the Spa Industry', in S. Rawlinson and T. Heap (eds) *International Spa Management*, Oxford: Goodfellow Publishers, pp. 114-129.

Navarro, J. V. I. (2014) 'How Innovation Shapes the Spa Industry and Determines its Evolution', *Global Journal of Management and Business Research*, **14** (2), 6-23.

Tezak, E. (2012) *Successful Salon & Spa Management*, Boston: Centage Learning.

Wynne, R. (2016) 'Five things everyone should know about public relations', *Forbes*, 21 January, www.forbes.com/sites/robertwynne/2016/01/21/five-things-everyone-should-know-about-public-relations/#4123f1c2a2c1 (accessed 29/06/2019).

5 Financial management in spas

Because of the number and complexity of the various different spa sub departments, spa financial reports can appear daunting at first glance, which is one of the reasons that many spa managers put off giving financial management its necessary focus. Financial acumen and a basic understanding of spa financial reports is a weakness affecting many spa managers. According to Loynes and Rosamond (2017:146) "The current employment market reflects the spa industry's growing need for higher academic levels of business acumen which will enable the industry to fill the gaps in middle to upper management positions". In short, financial business acumen in spas is both a weakness and a key skill that spa managers must have.

Once a spa manager understands what financial areas to focus on, the main priorities and where to look, spa monetary management is relatively straightforward. This chapter explains the basics of how a manager should approach reading a spa P&L (a profit and loss statement) and the processes of preparing a budget. It also covers some of the main key performance indicators which are useful in managing a spa business.

> Managing a spa today requires an extensive range of skills, the most important being leadership and having the ability to build a solid team. It is also important to have an awareness of the global wellness trends and to have global understanding of their influencing factors – socially, economically and politically. All of the above needs to be combined with knowledge of how to prepare budgets, reports, marketing and sales skills.
>
> Stavros Mavridi, Wellness and Spa Director.

Financial basics

When looked at objectively, the process of making a profitable spa operation (or any operation for that matter) is very simple (Figure 5.1). As this flow diagram shows, the aim of any business is to generate a surplus or profit. In simple terms, profit equals net sales revenue minus cost of goods sold (Loynes and Rosamond. 2017). This, in essence, is what the spa manager should be striving to achieve – always.

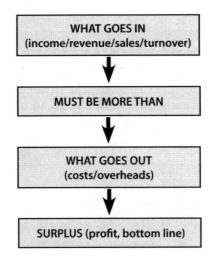

Figure 5.1: The basic rule of any business.

The report in which the monthly and yearly results are communicated is called a P&L (profit and loss) statement. Generally, there will be three sections:

1   What goes in (the income, sometimes referred to as *revenue, income, sales* or *turnover*).

2   What goes out (the *costs*, sometimes referred to as *expenditure* or *overheads*) .

3   The *profit* (sometimes referred to as the *bottom line*, as this is the final line in the P&L statement).

The aim of the spa manager is to generate this profit, which will normally exceed what has been set in the target or plan (also referred to as the budget). The budget will normally be set at more than the previous year's results by a few percent.

The revenue figures in the P&L will be NET (total amount after deductions, normally sales taxes such as VAT – value added tax).

In a well-run spa operation, part of the profit or surplus should be reinvested back into the business (Figure 5.2). However, in many companies this is not the case. It is not uncommon for spa facilities to be underinvested in, and allowed to run down, with the owners/directors still insisting on a growth in profit each year – a challenging situation for a spa manager to find themselves in!

Ideally what is reinvested back into the spa should improve the facility and generate more revenue which, in turn, should lead to more growth. For large developements, additional loans may be taken out to invest and improve the profit further.

Examples of areas where spas reinvest their profits include:

1   **New services**: introducing a new treatment or product brand.

2   **New equipment**:

  ☐ Upgrading equipment to ensure a better-quality product that will attract more guests.

☐ Introducing a totally new piece of equipment into a department that will bring in more revenue.

☐ Changing an existing piece of equipment to something more fashionable and in demand (i.e. getting rid of an out-dated sunbed and exchanging it for an infra-sauna or floatation tank instead).

3   **Creating new spaces**: i.e. turning an unused space into another treatment room (for example designing a nail bar station underneath an unused stairwell) or constructing additional new spaces onto the building.

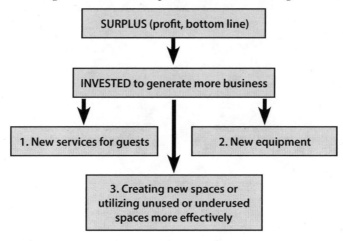

Figure 5.2: Part of the profit should be reinvested in the business.

Clarity of financial reports

In Chapter 4, it was emphasized how important it is to have a well laid out revenue report so that the different revenue streams can be seen in clear, separate segments. This is not just true for revenue but also for costs – and indeed for the entire financial reporting system. When starting out in the job, before embarking on any other activity, as a first step, the spa manager should do everything possible to ensure that they are able to see the revenue, costs and profitability figures clearly. Figures sloppily grouped or poorly laid out will mean that the spa manager will not be able to identify problematic areas quickly and efficiently.

The financial report should also be laid out in such a way that the spa manager can see exactly what is going on in each area and sub-departments of the spa. Wherever possible, the separate spa departments should be sub-grouped into their own little mini profit centres, with their relevant revenues and costs. In this way, if there are discrepancies in the bottom-line results, the spa manager will be able to see exactly where the problem lies at glance.

If the financial reports are poorly laid out and not grouped logically, then the spa manager should speak to the financial department (or whoever is responsible), and do everything in their means to make sure that reporting layout structure is revised. This may mean restructuring a system that may have been in place for years – a restructuring that the financial department will most likely resist. Given also that a comparison between the current year's results to the previous year is an important factor, it might mean that it could take more than a year after the report has been restructured to have overall clarity. However, having clear, easy to read reports is absolutely essential if the business is to be well run and for the spa manager to be able to see and investigate reasons for underperformance and take corrective action.

Put simply, a good financial spa report should contain:

- **Net revenue**: divided into the various different spa departments in the spa with a total sum of net revenue.
- **Costs**: also divided into the various different spa departments (wherever possible) with a sum of total costs.
- **Cost / revenue percentages**: the percentage of the costs to the revenue.
- **Profit / revenue percentage**: the percentage of the profit to the revenue.
- **Percentage comparison**: to the last year's performance and the budget.

■ Revenues

In Chapter 4 an example of a spa revenue daily report was given. Ideally the revenue section in the monthly profit and loss statement should have exactly the same layout as in the daily revenue reports. This will make it easier to compare and check the official figures released in the official P&L report with what has been reported in the daily results.

In a P&L statement, the revenue will appear at the beginning of the report, and as emphasized earlier, it is essential that the revenue segments are divided clearly so that if there is a problem, the spa manager can quickly see where the problem lies.

The layout will follow the structure in Figure 5.3:

- There will be three columns of *monetary numbers*:
  - ☐ **Last year**: these will be the numbers achieved in the previous year for that particular month in the monthly figures and from January up until the current month in the year-to-date figures.
  - ☐ **Budget**: these will be the numbers targeted/planned for that particular month in the monthly figures and the period from January up until the current month in the year-to-date figures. (Generally, the target/plan or budget will always be a few percent higher than the previous year).
  - ☐ **Actual**: these will be the actual numbers achieved in the spa in the current month and period from January up until the current month in the year-to-date figures.

- There will then be two columns of *percentage numbers*:
  - ☐ One will be the **percentage performance of the current year compared to the last year**. Obviously, the spa manager will want to see an improvement of **over** 100% in the revenue segments and **under** 100% in the costs.
  - ☐ The second column will be the **percentage performance compared to the budget.** Again, the spa manager will hope to see that the figures are **over** 100% in revenue and **under** in costs.

When faced with 10 or more columns of detailed numbers it can appear confusing. The trick is to know where to look and what to focus on.

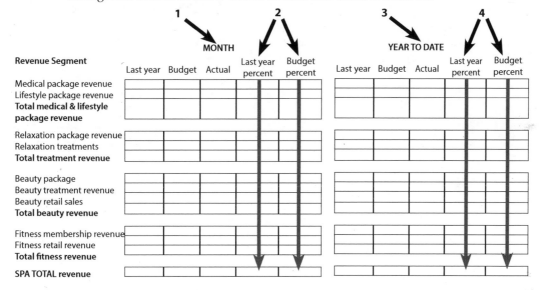

Figure 5.3: Example revenue section of a P&L statement.

1 Generally, the spa manager should start by looking at the performance of the *month* that has just passed.

2 They should do a quick skim down the report looking at the *percentages* achieved according to the last year and the budget. The last year's percentages are important as these will indicate whether or not the business is improving. The budget is important because that is what will have been agreed as a target (in many companies the spa manager will have to have signed their agreement and confirmation that they will be able to achieve this target!).

3 The spa manager should then look at the *totals* of revenue starting with the largest numbers first (i.e. the total spa revenue, followed by the various departments with the largest revenue generators taking first priority).

4 Finally, they should analyse each individual revenue lines, starting with the largest numbers first.

The manager should be keeping an eye out for any decrease in the largest revenue segments compared to both the budget and last year columns.

All of these steps should be repeated for the next set of figures in the year-to-date section. The year to date section being a culmination of all of the months in the year up until the present month. At the beginning of the year, these figures tend not to be so important but as the year progresses, particularly by October / November, the year-to-date figures are critical as they will show whether or not the spa is going to achieve budget and/or exceed the previous year.

The manager should make notes whilst going through the accounts. It is not necessary to deal with the small ups and downs. What is needed is to prioritise and focus on the important, larger amounts, to search for any trends or threads that stand out and to come up with effective solutions.

If the spa manager has been keeping a daily sales report and a close eye on the day to day sales performance, then they will already be one step ahead and already have anticipated what will be in the monthly P&L before it is released. In this way, hopefully, corrective action will have already been taken. However, if the spa manager has not been keeping an eye on the day to day performance, this will put them at a disadvantage as often the monthly P&L is only published around half way through the next consecutive month, meaning that valuable time to combat any problems will have been lost or it might be already too late!

■ Costs

In a spa department there are minimal number cost segments with some costs having more of an impact than others. As a spa manager it is important to know which costs to keep a close eye on – for example the staff costs (also referred to as manning) and energy costs, which will normally count for the largest expenditures (Loynes and Rosamond, 2017).

Manning costs

Costs	MONTH					YEAR TO DATE				
	Last year	Budget	Actual	Last year percent	Budget percent	Last year	Budget	Actual	Last year percent	Budget percent
Salaries & wages										
Accrued salaries										
Bonuses										
Subcontractor costs										

Figure 5.4: Manning costs.

- **Salaries and wages:** These will more than likely be one of highest cost expenditures in a spa. Controlling these costs is imperative in ensuring that the spa reaches its profitability targets. In some smaller spas this cost can account for up to 70% of the total costs!

  □ **Therapists' salary costs**: Making sure that staff time is fully utilized is key to ensuring manning cost efficiency. For therapists, this means ensuring that their work time is filled with treatment bookings. The spa software system must be able to see clearly the exact amount of time a therapist is occupied and the times they are not. If the master data in the software system is well constructed the spa manager will be able to see these statistics clearly and be able to monitor them daily. There will be times when the spa treatment schedule is busy and the whole team are needed on deck, in which case, staff could be required to put in extra hours. At other times there may be empty gaps in the schedule. In such cases staff can be asked to take holidays or use up their overtime hours. For the spa manager, managing the staff workflow is a delicate balancing act between respecting the private lives of the staff, but at the same time ensuring that there are enough staff to deliver the necessary treatments. This requires a diplomatic but firm approach. If there is an automatic booking system the system should be programmed to reserve treatments to minimize worktime gaps.

☐ **Reception salary costs**: a well-run spa reception should be operated so that guests rarely have to queue. This means having enough staff on the desk to deal with the peak traffic flows, but at the same time avoiding a situation where staff are unoccupied and sitting doing nothing. Ways to manage traffic peaks and troughs include the use of part-time staff or for existing staff (such as the spa manager/spa sales person/unoccupied therapists), to be rostered onto the desk at peak times. The number of full-time receptionists should be kept to the bare minimum and topped up with internal or outsourced solutions when necessary. The layout design of the spa should also take into consideration manning costs, with as few permanent manning stations as possible (i.e. spa reception with visibility to spa pools, spa reception combined with spa bar or café etc).

■ **Accrued wages:** "this is the amount liable at the end of a reporting period for wages earned by hourly employees but not yet paid to them. Accrued wages are recorded in order to recognise the entire wage expense of the spa during a reporting period and not just the amount actually paid" (Accounting Tools, 2018). For example, a yoga teacher is paid 20 Euro per hour and is paid on the 25th day of the month, but has taught an additional 5 classes during the period from the 26th to the 30th days of the month. This unpaid amount will be recorded as accrued wages as of the month end.

■ **Bonuses**: these are hard to anticipate, particularly if these are tied to sales performance. If the spa is having a weak period, obviously these will be lower, however if the spa has had a bumper month, then a large increase in this particular cost can be expected. The bonus structure should be constructed in such a way that it takes into consideration the bumper months' payments and at the same time ensure that these payments cannot negatively impact the bottom-line/profit.

■ **Subcontractors and outsourced staff**: the question for spa managers concerning outsourced staff is to ask whether this person or service is really necessary? If it is an outsourced therapist, for example, the spa manager should be asking themselves if this particular treatment or person is really required, or with a readjustment of the schedule can an existing full-time employee replace them?

One position which is normally outsourced are exercise class teachers. The importance of these teachers is often underestimated. A good teacher can generate a popular following which, in turn, will help create value for the spa guests and contribute to a positive spa atmosphere. The spa manager should not underestimate the importance of such teachers. However, if cost cutting is required, training up the fitness staff on how to teach classes and/or only employing fitness staff who have teaching X number of classes written into their contract can be a solution. It should be pointed out that finding fitness staff who are able to do both classes and instructing to a high level is not easy. Some fitness clubs and spas nowadays are introducing virtual reality classes with no live teacher at all.

Ways to cut manning costs

- **Multi-skilling:** the most effective way to reduce employment costs is to employ staff who have a wide range of skills and through additional training, are able to widen their professional capabilities. In this way, staff can be moved around departments according to the business demands. This is not only financially beneficial for the business, but it makes the work routine for staff more interesting, helping to improve motivation and reduce staff turnover.

As a busy thermal medical spa, our masseurs were expected to do back to back massages all day. We decided to train them up to be able to work in different spa departments and organised for each one of them to undertake a lifeguard qualification. We found that by circulating them to different departments (one day in the massage department, the next hydrotherapy, the next mud packing and one day a week as a pool lifeguard), both costs were saved and motivation improved. Our therapists appreciated the change in routine and in particular their day on lifeguard duty as it gave them a much-needed rest from the physical demands of the other departments. This did not only have a positive effect on the staff, but on the quality of treatments too.

Viktor Marsalla, Spa Manager.

- **Staff performing treatments simultaneously:** one of the reasons Central European thermal spas have such a low cost/revenue ratio per treatment is because many treatments are carried out where one therapist will perform treatments on up to four or five guests simultaneously (for example, mud packing, electrotherapy treatments and hydrotherapy). This dramatically reduces the employment cost per treatment. Spas that do not offer simultaneous treatments should consider incorporating them into their spa menu as it can greatly increase the profit margin in the department.
- **Are staff required at all?** Sometimes, for some departments it may not be even necessary to employ staff at all. Many spas are now designed (dependent on pool depth and local health and safety regulations) in such a way that a

lifeguard may not be necessary. In some situations, the lifeguard position can be substituted by CCTV or by designing the reception with a view to the pool.

Another solution is to offer some treatments which do not require staff. This may seem contradictory given that the 'human touch' is a key reason why guests visit spas, however certain treatments (hydromassage beds as one example and salt caves another), can often play a valuable part in the treatment schedule. Having one or two unmanned treatments not only saves costs, but on days when spa therapists may be fully booked, such treatments can be offered as an alternative option to guests.

Virtual reality exercise classes are also an option. Whilst there is some investment for the technology and licences, it has far less overall expenditure, is easier to coordinate and in many cases the quality of classes is better than employing local outside teachers. A good solution is to have a mix of both ongoing virtual reality classes, peppered with high quality live classes at peak times.

5

Making better use of staff in a Central European health spa chain

This particular company had a policy of manning their fitness centres with full time staff, however, for most of the time the instructors would just sit around with little to do. A decision was made that they no longer would employ full time fitness instructors. Instead the group exercise class teachers were asked to stay one hour after their classes to provide advice or write out a fitness program for any guests who required individual instruction – otherwise the fitness room remained unmanned – a huge cost saving for the company and more motivated group exercise class teachers.

Costs of sales

Costs of sales refers to the cost of the products (spa, beauty or retail) compared to how much they have been sold for. This is an important number. There are often two or three lines with cost of sales in a spa P&L for example;

- **Retail**: there will most likely be two forms of merchandise sold in the spa:
   - ☐ items like T-shirts, swimwear, slippers etc., and
   - ☐ spa and beauty products.

Some spas will split the costs of sales according to these two areas, the reason being that the spa and beauty products can then be easily identifiable and linked to the treatment and therapist performance.

Retail merchandise cost should be around 50% of the total selling price, and the spa and beauty retail products should cost no more than 60% of the selling price in the worst-case scenario (Tezak and Folawn, 2011).

- **Treatment cost of sales**: this is the cost of the products used on the guests during the treatments. Normally, for a high-end product, this should be no more than 10% –15%, though in some spas this can go up to 20%,

■ **Food and beverage**: if there is a food and beverage department, this should be separated from the other cost of sales in the spa. Food costs should be around 30% of the sales.

Ways to control product costs

Strict inventories are needed to ensure that a) stock is not going missing, and that b) stock is not sitting in cupboards for long periods of time – stock in storage is lost money. Here are some ways to control cost of sales:

■ *Ensuring that the selling price of the treatment justifies the product brand cost*: western product brands can be expensive and the spa must be able to charge a high enough treatment and retail price able to absorb these costs. Many spas in developing countries are just not able to charge the treatment prices needed to justify for the cost of an international product brand. In this case they should consider using local products instead.

■ *Going local:* Often procuring local product suppliers will be much cheaper, however these will not have the kudos of an international spa or beauty product brand and often quality training is not included.

■ *Negotiating a 'purchase when sold' contract with the supplier:* This means that the retail products are only paid for (to the supplier) once the spa has sold them. An excellent solution as it means no holding stock overheads!

■ *Keeping stock secure and regular inventories:* stock should be securely locked and inventories taken at least once a week.

Other costs

The other main costs include:

■ **Marketing**: these costs relate to the marketing activity in the spa – adverts, promotions etc. Around 2%–4% of the total costs. (Tezak and Folawn, 2011)

■ **Materials**: this will relate to all the materials required for the operational running of the spa from toilet rolls to cotton pads for the treatments. Some spas divide their material costs between treatment related and general operations. This is advised as it is possible to see exactly the material costs for each treatment, and a cost per treatment can then be calculated.

■ **IT and licences**: this relates to any IT expenditures and licences such as music, permissions, etc.

■ **Cleaning**: this applies if the cleaning is outsourced through an external company. If not, the cleaning staff costs will be included in the manning section and the cleaning products in the materials section – if this is the case it is advisable for a separate cost centre, so the cleaning expenditure can be clearly identifiable in the accounts.

■ **Maintenance**: this can be a substantial cost in the spa operations, particularly if the spa has a fitness centre and many spa pools. The older the spa is, then clearly the higher these costs will escalate. These costs can range from 4% of total costs to much higher, particularly in thermal hot spring spas (Tezak and Folawn, 2011).

- **Laundry**: this is another large cost for a spa. Each guest will have towel (or two!), possibly a robe, not to mention the towels used treatments. Laundry will either be done in-house or as is more common these days – outsourced. Controlling the laundry costs is not easy. Theft of towels is also common. Some spas or health clubs may require a deposit or some form of control to ensure towels are returned.

- **Energy and/or utilities**: gas, electricity, water, etc. In a spa, particularly one with an extensive pool and sauna area, these costs can be extremely high. Water and drainage costs will also be a factor. In thermal spas, it is common for the supplier of the thermal water to charge per flow rate of thermal water to the spa by cubic metre. In a hotel spa, often energy and utility will not be visible in the spa accounts. This is because often it is not always possible to split the usage between the hotel and spa. To compensate, the hotel may not add a revenue allocation for spa usage by hotel guests. At a minimum these costs will be at around 5% of total costs, but in thermal spas and spas with large pool areas, energy costs can be much higher (Tezak and Folawn, 2011).

■ Depreciation and amortization

In the account report there might be two lines for amortization and depreciation.

- **Amortization**: …"is the practice of spreading an intangible asset's cost over that asset's useful life" (Investopedia, 2019). Intangible refers to assets such as trademarks, patents, copyrights and also relevant to spas – franchise agreements. It is fairly unusual to have an amortization line in the spa accounts.

- **Depreciation**: …."is the expensing of a fixed asset over its useful life" (Investopedia, 2019). By fixed assets, this refers to something physical, like a piece of fitness equipment or a new jacuzzi. Common assets depreciated in spas will be any equipment, spa furniture, machinery and even the building itself. The cost of the asset is allocated into the accounts and evenly spread over the expected life span of the asset. This means the depreciated amount is in fact a tax deduction for the company until its lifespan has expired. Different items will have different lifespans. For example, a building might be depreciated over twenty or more years, its fixtures and fittings ten years and equipment five years. Some fixtures and equipment might be depreciated at an accelerated rate, meaning most of the cost is allocated early on in its usage. The idea of depreciation is that once the asset has come to the end of its depreciated life, it can be sold or disposed of and replaced by a similar valued asset. Unfortunately, however, in reality this often does not happen. Many owners and companies will be happy to retain the depreciated asset as long as possible. Depreciation costs are normally around 10% in spas (Tezak and Folawn, 2011).

■ ## Profit

At the bottom of the financial report will be the following information or similar:

1 A total *summary* of the *spa sales*

2 A total *summary* of all of *the costs*

3 The *profit*

4 *The profit margin* – this is the percentage of the profit to the sales. This is an important figure – in a well-run spa the profit percentage should be above 20%. The smaller the spa, the harder it can be to have a higher profit percentage margin. This is because proportionally, the wage and utilities cost will tend to outweigh the guest revenues. The larger the spa (providing there is a healthy revenue and the maintenance and energy costs are controlled) the easier it should be to reach a relatively high profit margin.

		YEAR TO DATE			
	Last year	Budget	Actual	Last year percent	Budget percent
Total spa revenue	750,000	800,000	820,000	109	103
Total spa costs	500,000	525,000	527,000	105	100
Spa profit	250,000	275,000	293,000	117	107
Spa profit margin	33	34	36	107	104

Figure 5.5: The key figures at the end of the financial report.

This particular example shows a well performing spa at the end of the year, exceeding both the previous year and budget. Note how the spa profit margin has also increased.

Summary of reading a spa P&L

The steps in reading a P&L are simple. With practice and familiarity, the spa manager should be able to spot discrepancies fairly swiftly. Here is a quick summary:

1 Look at both the actual month then the year to date figures. Remember, the further on in the year, the more important the year to date figure becomes.

2 Check the percentages compared to the last year and to the budget.

3 Check the monetary figures of the sales, the costs, the profit, profit totals and margins – *focus on the large amounts first*.

4 Go into detail.

5 Make notes.

6 Take corrective action focusing on the main areas of concern.

Preparing a budget

Unless there is a crisis or major impact on the spa operation (for example, part of the spa being closed for refurbishment), the spa manager will be expected to make more profit than the previous year. Preparations for the next year's budget normally start around September/October. This is to ensure that the budget is finished and agreed before the start of January of the next year. By autumn, enough of the year has passed from which the spa manager can estimate what results will be achievable for the upcoming year's budget. Here are some of the simple steps taken in creating a budget:

1 The spa manager should gather all of the costs and sales from the current year's results.

2 If they are doing the budget in September, then they will also need to estimate what will be the predicted results for the remaining months of the current year. There are two ways of doing this:

☐ By looking at the previous year's performance from September to December, adding the current year's inflation figures, and based on this, estimate what is likely to happen in the current year.

☐ Calculate an estimate month based on an average of all of the months up until September of the current year and put that in for October to December.

3 The predicted inflation figure for the upcoming year should then be added onto the costs.

4 Costs should be analysed to see if there are any that can be reduced.

5 Sales revenues for the upcoming year should be increased to ensure there is growth in the profit compared to the current year's forecasted performance. This can either be achieved by raising the selling prices and/or coming up with imaginative ways to increase the revenues.

> The spa manager will need to justify HOW they are going to increase the performance. Ways in which sales revenues can be increased may include price increases (the competition spas should be checked as if the spa is already charging higher prices than the local competition, this could be unrealistic), putting together marketing actions, introducing new services, etc. They will need to show imagination and creativity when it comes to cost controls.

Generally, depending on the company's strategy and market situation, the spa will be expected to make a few percent more than the current year. The owners or company will naturally push for the highest growth possible whilst the spa manager will try to keep the expectations as realistic as they can (partially due to the fact that their bonuses will normally be tied to the budget!). Budget negotiations can be tense, but usually end in a compromise – though more in favour of the expectations of the owner or directors than the spa manager.

Forecasting

Short term forecasting is generally done for operational reasons, with revenue forecasts helping to direct adjustments in staff levels and stock holdings to minimize waste. One of the most common approaches to forecasting is known as the Time Series Forecasting which uses historic data to predict future demand (Loynes and Rosamond, 2017). In high street spas, or spas dependent on daily walk-ins, forecasts will rely on historical trends and data, but whilst they can give an indication of what might happen, they are not a definite prediction. In hotel spas and spa hotels where the bulk of the revenue is dependent on hotel bookings, forecasts can be fairly accurate as it is possible to see the pre-booked rooms and guest numbers.

Benchmarking and KPIs

Benchmarking is a way of comparing one spa's performance with the general industry trend performances. Benchmarking can be defined as follows: "A measurement of the quality of an organization's policy, products, programs, strategies, etc., and their comparison with the standard measurements, or similar measurements of its peers. The objectives of benchmarking are (1) to determine what and where improvements are called for, (2) to analyse how other organizations achieve their high-performance levels, and (3) to use this information to improve performance" (Business Dictionary, 2019).

■ KPI stands for 'key performance indicator'

Key performance indicators and benchmarking are useful ways of measuring the spa business and can help to dramatically improve the operational and financial performance. There are many KPIs and benchmarks that a spa can use. It is important to note that the KPIs useful for one type of spa might be irrelevant for another – in other words a spa should compare itself like with like, for example: city day spa with city day spa, cruise ship spa with cruise ship spa.

Some common KPIs

- **Number of USP treatments sold**: if the spa's most important and popular treatment is the local mud pack and this is what is attracting guests to the spa, then the spa manager should be watching the trends of these treatment numbers closely. If one particular treatment or service is the core attraction of the spa and these numbers start to decline then this could mean trouble for the overall business. By keeping a close eye, the manager can be one step ahead and come up with an emergency plan if necessary.

- **Number of USP packages sold**: USP package statistics are also an important KPI. This is particularly true for thermal medical spas where often the main revenue earner is a medical rehabilitation package which will account for most of the spa revenue. In cases such as this, this particular statistic is one that the spa manager would want to watch closely.

- **Repeat guest ratio:** (the number of guests who return to the spa for treatment stays). This statistic is also extremely important for medical or destination spa hotels, where most of the business is dependent on guests returning regularly or year after year. In thermal spa facilities the repeat guest ratio can be as much a 70%. However, in an airport spa, which derives its business from transient traffic, such a figure would not be relevant. Also important for medical and destination spa hotels are the market(s) or countries the guests (and repeat guests) are coming from.

- **External guest ratio**: (the number of outside guests coming into the hotel spa). This particular KPI is useful for a hotel spa which is hoping to attract a local market from the surrounding area, for example a city hotel or club spa. In such cases measuring the number of external guests and watching whether these numbers increase or decrease is important. Alternatively, for a spa hotel in the middle of the mountains or wilderness spa in the desert, where there is little if not any opportunity to attract local guests, such a KPI would be irrelevant.

- **Hotel capture rate**: (the number of hotel guests visiting the spa). In a hotel spa this is an important KPI as it shows how popular and necessary the spa actually is for its guests. By seeing these statistics, the spa manager can then examine ways to increase the traffic flow of hotel guests into the spa. In a spa - hotel however, this number is not so necessary as it is a given that most, if not all of the guests in the hotel will be staying on a treatment package in the spa.

Treatment and room utilization KPIs

- **Cost percentage per treatment**: this is an essential statistic. The costs (staff, products used, utilities) should be calculated and based on this (and an evaluation of the local competition prices) the actual selling price decided. Ensuring that this percentage remains the same or decreases each year should be the goal of the spa manager.

- **Room utilization**: (the actual occupied room time divided by the total available room time). This is a popular KPI used in many spas. However, it is more relevant for some spas than others. For example, in a cruise ship or small high street spa, every treatment room and every square metre has a considerable value, therefore revenue per treatment room and room utilization are critical performance indicators. At the other end of the spectrum however, a large thermal hotel spa operation where the aim is to fill up the hotel rooms first and then afterwards ensure that there are enough treatment spaces to meet the peak periods of the year, such a KPI would be less relevant compared to, for example, staff occupancy.

- **Revenue per available treatment room (RevPATR)**: (total spa revenue divided by the number of treatment rooms). As with room utilization this would be an important KPI for spas where space is at a premium.

- **Average treatment rate**: (revenue divided by the number of treatments — this will give an average rate of each treatment). The trends and the ups and downs of the average revenue per treatment are a useful statistic. However, if the spa is offering a combination of various different treatments such as beauty and medical, then the average treatment rate should be separated according to segment. Mixing diverse treatment departments can dilute this statistic distorting benchmark comparisons.

- Other useful treatment and room KPIs include:
  - ☐ Profit per available treatment hours GOPPATH (Gross Operating Profit Per Available Treatment Hour) – more critical than RevPATR.
  - ☐ Treatment utilization – occupied treatment hours per available hours (as opposed to treatment room utilization, as sometimes more than one treatment is carried out in one room).
  - ☐ Revenue per available treatment hour.

Staff KPIs

Given that staff costs are such a large overhead, measuring staff utilization and the effectiveness of the team is critical.

- **Staff utilization percentage**: (occupied hours divided by total employed hours) – this is *the most important statistic and KPI* that a spa manager should be looking at. As mentioned earlier, one of the main tasks of the spa manager is to check that the staff's employment time is as occupied as much as possible, with duties essential to the operation. The spa manager can only do this if they can see clearly the number of hours where the staff have been actively working as opposed to being unoccupied. Unoccupied can mean anything from a therapist having empty treatment spaces in their shift to having too many staff at manning points such as the spa reception.

- **Payroll cost percentage and payroll amount**: (payroll cost compared to total costs). Obviously, the payroll amount is what matters the most, but this can be more effectively monitored, particularly when it comes to seeing operational trends, by looking the percentage of the payroll cost compared to the overall costs.

Retail KPIs

Retail in most spas is an important part of the revenue, particularly in spas more focussed on beauty and wellness. Here are some useful spa retail KPIs:

- **Spend per guest**: this is the retail revenue generated divided by the number of guests who have visited the spa.

- **Percentage of revenue**: this is the percentage of retail revenue compared to the overall revenue. In a spa focused on beauty treatments this can reach 25% of the total revenue, whereas in a large medical thermal spa focused on large volumes of simultaneous treatments, this can drop to 5% or less.

Summary

As has been described, there are many tools and KPIs to analyse the financial operations of a spa. However, it must be emphasized that the role of the spa manager is to be out with the guests and staff, not sitting poring over accounts in the office. Focusing on the main numbers, in addition to one or two critical KPIs relevant to their type of spa and being one step ahead by taking corrective action should be the goal of the spa manager when it comes to financial management.

Feedback from the interviews – what the experts say

Spa managers were asked what measures would they recommend in order to control their costs more efficiently?

- Spa managers need good bookkeeping and financial planning skills, a clear awareness of profit and loss management, a focus on increasing revenues and ideally, forecasting skills too. Chris Theyer, previously Training and Development Director, LivingWell Health Clubs states that "Financial skills are imperative. A spa manager should have his/her eyes on the day to day financial performance of the business. Team managers need also to be financially aware and regular management meetings to review performance, along with planning future activity are essential."

- Several managers emphasise daily cost control. It is especially important to control consumption and wastage and to monitor product sales. Searching for the best suppliers and buying in bulk were recommended, but only if the products can easily be shifted.

- Energy efficiency was emphasised including educating employees about it.

- Staffing was cited as a big factor especially in terms of "manpower optimisation". Staff should be trained to multi-task and cover each others' tasks. They should also be trained in upselling.

- According to an editor from a spa industry magazine "As always it really comes down to optimisation – how many staff, how many rooms vs forecast of customers".

- Managers should keep a grip on membership retention, sales and promotion. They need a knowledge of demand, the market and the competitors. Attention should be paid to occupancy rates too, especially during quiet periods and out-of-season.

- Spa software was recommended as a way of helping with daily, weekly and monthly reports as well as incentivizing on a metric like GOPPATH (Gross Operating Profit Per Available Treatment Hour) a great way to ensure all are motivated to maximise profits, not just revenues"

- Processes as well as the use of machinery should constantly be monitored, and investments and reconstructions should be planned ahead.

- Stavros Mavridis, Wellness and Spa Director, suggests "Keep inventory in low levels by creating sustained spa menus....Keep daily reports of revenues and ratios. Evaluate monthly all ratios, so yearly the orders and elastic expenses can be controlled more effectively."

Research and further reading

A few past studies focused on spa revenue management, e.g. Kimes and Singh (2008) provide a detailed analysis of different tools and techniques. Madanoglu and Brezina (2008) suggest that using a specific technique can mean that a well-operated spa can make a significant contribution to resort revenues. However, some of these tools may now have been superseded by newer methods. Tezak and Folawn (2011) provide chapters on how to finance a spa business, as well as examining how to calculate and control operating costs. Loynes and Rosamond (2017) emphasise the importance of profit maximisation in the spa context and identify several tools that can be used for its measurement and management. This includes calculating profit and loss, controlling expenditure, budgeting and forecasting, optimising revenue through sales and increasing productivity. Guo, Guillet, Kucukusta and Law (2016) undertook a study in Hong Kong which segmented spa customers based on their preferences for spa rates and restrictions. They identified four clusters, which were treatment-oriented spa goers, guarantee-sensitive spa goers, price-sensitive spa goers, and fewer days advance booking seekers. It is thought that the findings could be useful when designing rate fences preferred by different types of customers in spas, which could eventually increase spa revenue.

In countries with state supported medical spas (e.g. many Eastern European countries like Hungary, Slovakia, Czech Republic, Poland), the financial situation is somewhat different. Guests who are referred for treatments by their doctor will have their costs reimbursed by health insurance. However, in recent years, many governments are starting to cut down the length of stays in medical spas or to limit the treatments that are reimbursed. Many spas have run into financial difficulties and increasingly have to abide by the rules of a free market of health services. Detailed studies of this phenomenon in Slovakia can be found in the work of Derco (2017) and Derco and Pavlisinova (2017) and in Poland by Dryglas and Salamaga (2017) in Poland.

References

Accounting Tools (2018) 'Accrued wages', https://www.accountingtools.com/articles/2017/5/7/accrued-wages (accessed 14/12/2019)

Business Dictionary (2019) 'Web Finance', http://www.businessdictionary.com/definition/benchmarking.html (accessed 11.07.2019).

Derco, J. (2017) 'Impact of health care funding on financial position of Slovak medical spas', *Tourism*, **65** (3), 376-380.

Derco, J. and Pavlisinova, D. (2017) 'Financial position of medical spas – The case of Slovakia', *Tourism Economics*, **23** (4), 867–873, Doi: 10.5367/te.2016.0553

Dryglas, D. and Salamaga, M. (2017) 'Applying destination attribute segmentation to health tourists: A case study of Polish spa resorts', *Journal of Travel and Tourism Marketing*, **34** (4), 503-514, Doi: 10.1080/10548408.2016.1193102

Guo, Y., Guillet, B. D., Kucukusta, D. and Law, R. (2016) 'Segmenting spa customers based on rate fences using conjoint and cluster analyses', *Asia Pacific Journal of Tourism Research*, **21** (2), 118-136, Doi: 10.1080/10941665.2015.1025085

Investopedia (2019) 'Amortization vs Depreciation. What's the difference?' https://www.investopedia.com/ask/answers/06/amortizationvsdepreciation.asp (accessed 14/07/2019).

Kimes, S. E. and Singh, S. (2008) 'Spa revenue management', *Cornell Hospitality Quarterly*, **50** (1), 82-95, Doi:10.1177/1938965508324868

Loynes, T. and Rosamond, V. (2017) 'Finance for the spa industry', in S. Rawlinson and T. Heap (eds) *International Spa Management*, Oxford: Goodfellow Publishers, pp. 146-155.

Madanoglu, M. and Brezina, S. (2008) 'Resort spas: How are they massaging hotel revenues?', *International Journal of Contemporary Hospitality Management*, **20** (1), 60-66, Doi: 10.1108/09596110810848578

Tezak, E. and Folawn, T. (2011) *Successful Salon and Spa Management*. 6th Edn, Boston: Cengage.

5

6 Quality management in the spa environment

According to Matthews and Wells (2008: 169) "If quality is to be delivered in the operations, then the 'systems must fit the philosophy' of the spa". In other words, the spa's mission, vision and values should be the starting point for producing a quality guest experience.

- **The mission statement** is the reason for the organization's existence. A mission statement does not describe a specific outcome and should contain no time limit or measurement. The mission statement provides the basis for the setting of the company's goals.

- **The vision statement** should define what the organisation seeks to become. It should generate human energy and engagement. In other words, it should provide direction and a focus for the organisation.

- **The values** are the beliefs behind the organization's vision and mission. Values give dignity and direction to the mission.

   (Wittington, 2016)

In short, a mission states what a company is about, a vision where that company wants to go in the future, and its values are the beliefs. Figure 6.1 is an example of a typical spa mission and vision statement.

Elements of the mission, vision and values statements are then combined to provide a more detailed statement of the company's purposes and goals. Some of these goals will be actualized through integrating them into the quality systems, others will be incorporated into the developmental strategy of the spa – "the role and function of operations management involves a broad range of spa processes and procedures in an effort to meet the needs and interests of the consumer" (Samkange, Simba & Baker, 2017: 83).

If the starting point for a spa quality system is the mission and vision, there are certain systems that are essential in both the delivery of quality service and the continuous and ongoing improvements needed to meet the expectations of the spa goer.

MISSION

"Our mission is to provide our guests with first class relaxational spa treatments and services to satisfy their needs, through carefully listening to their feedback and providing them with sensitive, high level customer service that continually exceeds their expectations."

VISION

Our vision is to grow the number of our spa resorts in locations of outstanding natural beauty. We believe in using the local expertise and knowledge, protecting the local identity, customs and traditions and growing the business with a long-term sustainable strategy."

VALUES

- To protect our environment.

- To be true to our word, honest, open and fair.

- To respect all people – our customers, our staff and our community.

- To deliver high quality.

- To enhance the lives of everyone that comes into contact with our business.

- To be authentic.

Figure 6.1: Example of a typical spa's mission, vision and values.

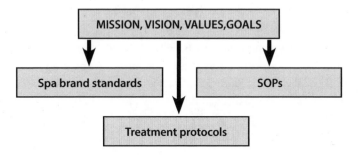

Figure 6.2: Spa brand standards, SOPs and treatment proptocols are all derived from the mission, vision and values.

Spa brand standards

The mission, vision, values and goals are the building blocks for a spa brand, but for the brand to have meaning there must be clear, concise standards to ensure that the services deliver a consistent and uniform spa experience. Brand standards are normally written, then approved by the directorship and released to the team in the form of a brand manual. What has been written into the brand standards and manual is expected to be realized in the operation.

Brand standards are essential as they:

- **Ensure operational and brand continuity**: this means that in each department the guest should experience the same level and quality of services and treatments. If it is a spa chain with several locations, the brand standards will ensure that the level of quality in spa X will be the same as in spa Y.

- **All staff are clear on what is expected**: once the standard has been written, approved and communicated, it is then set. For example, if it is written into the standard that all therapists must wear their name badge on the right-hand side of the chest, from that point on there is no need for any discussion or debate about it. On the other hand, if this is not written into the standards, then staff will have free range to make their own choices. A name badge is just one small example, but when it comes to room presentation, guest communication etc, the necessity for logical and uniform standards becomes essential for both the service delivery and smooth communication between the manager and staff. The more detailed and specific the standards the higher the chances of a quality operation.

- **Ensure that the operation is being checked according to the set standards**: brand standards will set the expectations for what should be delivered in the operation. There will also be a regularity of when these standards are checked. By having regular checks that are written and recorded, the management can be assured that the operation is being run professionally. Of course, the level to which these standards are delivered will depend on the quality of the standards and the checks themselves (for which there are control systems which will be discussed later in the chapter).

- **For training purposes**: lastly, the spa brand standards will form the backbone of what will be delivered in the staff training. Training courses will be built around the various standards and incorporated into the staff induction, orientation and ongoing training.

Maintaining the brand standards

Sometimes the brand standards will just provide a written expectation of what should be delivered at a specific moment in time in a specific location in the spa. Other times they might include work processes as well or they may be a combination of both.

Figure 6.3 shows the brand standards of a treatment room. In this particular example, at any time of the day, the treatment room in this spa should be adhering to the points listed in the figure. The standards have been broken down into what is expected with regards to the staff, the technical elements, the state and maintenance of the fixtures and fittings, the cleanliness and the presentation.

TREATMENT ROOM STANDARD	Maximum Points	Points Achieved	Comments	Deadline	Whom
STAFF					
1 Is the therapist in the correct uniform?	8	8			
2 Is the therapist groomed according to company standard?	8	8			
3 Does the therapist have a clean undamaged namebadge on their right chest?	6	0	Name badge missing	Immediate	Therapist
4 Has the therapist completed all training necessary for the position?	8	6	Complaint handling training required	30 days	Spa Trainer
TECHNICAL					
1 Is the room lit with indirect lighting?	6	6			
2 Are all the light bulbs should be working?	6	6			
3 Is the room ventilated and at a temperature of between 21-24 Celsius?	8	8			
4 Is there spa music playing via the approved central system?	6	0	Music not working	24 hours	Technical
5 Is all the treatment equipment in working order?	8	8			
6 Is the daily equipment checklist being carried out and signed?	4	2	Today it wasn't signed for	Immediate	Therapist
FIXTURES & FITTINGS MAINTENANCE					
1 Are all walls clean with no grubby marks or scuffs?	6	6			
2 Are all fixtures in a good state of repair?	6	6			
CLEANLINESS					
1 Are floor walls and fixtures clean and free from marks or dirt?	8	6			
2 Is the waste bin no more than 30% full?	4	0	Waste bin full	Immediate	Therapist
PRESENTATION					
1 Is there standard approved decoration on the treatment room shelf?	6	6			
2 Is the therapist using the bed decoration before each treatment?	6	6			
3 No personal items on view (coffee cups, mobile phones, personal pictures etc)	8	4	Small picture of therapist's baby to be removed	Immediate	Therapist
TOTAL NUMBER OF POINTS	110	86			
PERCENTAGE		78			

Figure 6.3: Example of a brand standard treatment room checklist.

The scoring system in this example is based on each standard having a maximum number of points divisible by two (2, 4, 6, 8), which can be graded according to how much a particular standard is being adhered to. The auditor or checker will then check the room according to the standards listed, giving them an appropriate score. Where the maximum points are not achieved, the manager or auditor will then write a comment as to what action is required, where the action needs to take place, who is responsible for carrying out the action and by when. This is important, as tasks or action points that do not have deadlines or responsibility are not likely to get addressed.

The action points will automatically be summarized in the final report and totalled up into a grand percentage for the entire spa. In an example such as the one above, a spa should be achieving at least 90%. 90% means that most of the deliverable standards are being completed (give or take a few discrepancies). 80%–90% means that the spa is falling short of adhering to the brand standards and below 80% would be unacceptable. Below 80% the spa should be given deadlines to rectify the faults and be rechecked at a date in the near future.

Of course, there are many different scoring systems and percentages and this is just one example. Whichever system the spa manger or company decides to implement, it should contain:

- **Clear written standards** – normally one standard for one set of points.
- **A grading system** to score to what level the standards have been achieved.
- **What** points to action.
- **Where** the action needs to take place.
- **Who** is responsible.
- **When** – a deadline.

Without consequences or incentives, audits will have little effect. Alongside the creation of the standards, there should be incentives for the manager and team to inspire them to achieve high scores and consequences if they do not.

The newer, more effective systems are not paper based. Nowadays it is not complicated to create a simple software quality audit program which can be completed by tablet. The advantage of this is that at the same time as checking the spa, the spa manager can be inputting their comments and scores. When the audit is finished a summary report can then be automatically generated and sent to the relevant staff members immediately. As the action points get completed, these can also be automatically updated into the report. The next brand standard check should be based on the previous report and should highlight which action points have been resolved and which not.

An audit program on a tablet is clearly much faster and more effective than making handwritten notes on paper, typing them up and manually monitoring the progress. The larger the spa or group of spas, the more reason there is to digitalize the audit process.

The most important aspect of any spa quality assurance program is that it should focus on the service quality experience from the *visitors' point of view*. Since service quality has a high impact on the emotions of the consumer, it must be managed professionally and given the attention it deserves. Instilling confidence in the clients that the property is committed to a high-level standard of care is not just a marketing issue but should be the basis for the very profile of the spa. Furthermore, a consistent quality control system is a tried and tested means to verify that the processes, workflows, products, physical facilities, pricing, distribution, and procedures meet current industry standards and best practices, which is becoming more and more important in today's well-informed, worldwide-travelling online society. In my experience, audits are best carried out by independent third parties and/or external professionals to ensure an objective and up-to-date view of the entire spa product.

Dr Anke Zeqiri, University of Milan, Global Hotel and Spa Auditor

Daily checks

Normally such brand standard detailed checks will be carried out periodically (i.e. every couple of months or even quarterly or annually). A brand audit, dependent on the size of the spa, may contain hundreds of standards. It would be both impractical and impossible for the spa manager to check them on a daily basis. For this reason, the spa will also have a daily check list – this daily check list should be based on and contain the most important brand standards, in addition to any other items essential to the safe and effective running of the daily operation. The purpose of the daily checklist is:

1   To ensure that a responsible member of staff is checking the facility, minimum once a day if not more.

2   To ensure there is a written account of what has been checked and what issues need to be addressed.

The daily check list should be as simple as possible – Figure 6.4 gives an example. The daily checklist should include:

- The most important health and safety standards – i.e. fire exits are unblocked and functioning, water hygiene, pool plant room safety, electric cupboards locked, protective gear to standard etc.

- General maintainance – equipment, including all lightbulbs working, ventilation, music, temperature.

- Cleanliness, tidiness and presentation of areas, including back of house.

- Staff attitude and customer focus.

DAILY CHECK LIST		NAME OF CHECKER: ....
		DATE: ....

THE FOLLOWING SHOULD BE CHECKED IN ALL AREAS

1	CLEANLINESS: Floors, carpets, sinks, mirrors, doors, windows, air vents and all fiittings should be clean
2	MAINTENANCE: Lightbulbs all working and are matching, all technical items are working, music, ventilation etc.
3	PRESENTATION: All areas and surfaces tidy, appropriate decoration, waste bins
4	STAFF: All staff are in uniform with name badge, well presented, customer focused

	RECEPTION	COMMENT	FOLLOW UP ACTION
1	Cleanliness, maintenance, presentation, staff all to standard		
2	Treatment information is available in all languages		
3	There is enough space in the schedule for selling extra treatments		
4	Retail space is stocked appropriately		
5	Other		
	POOLS		
1	Lifeguard is in attendance		
2	Cleanliness, maintenance, presentation, to standard		
3	Water tests are being carried out and are within correct parameters		
4	There is no pooling of standing water		
5	Other		
	TREATMENT ROOMS		
1	Cleanliness, maintenance, presentation, staff, all to standard		
2	Equipment checked and signed for in checklist		
3	Water tests are being ca rried out and within correct parameters		
4	No pools of standing water		
5	Other		

Figure 6.4: Example of a daily check list.

Customer focus is particularly important. Often check lists tend to focus on inanimate objects, but the energy and customer focus of the staff should be checked in the same way as a light bulb is – but of course customer service being more important than the light bulb!

The daily check list is the most important tool in maintaining the day to day operations. The quality of how these checks are done and how the items are followed up, will determine the quality of the operations as a whole.

Whilst the spa manager should be taking a lead in checking the spa, it is not essential that they complete the daily check themselves as stated by Samkange, Simba & Baker (2017: 93) "…management need to engage employees productively and research often links employee engagement to productivity…". In fact, involving responsible members of staff to check the spa on a daily basis can be a way to improve the overall quality by focusing and educating the team as to what is expected. If the spa manager knows that they have trained up a pool of staff who are able to check the spa competently, this can be of great help to the manager, especially if they are away from the operation (for example, on days off or on leave).

■   # How to check a spa

Checking a room in a spa (such as a treatment room) is fairly straightforward. As shown in the checklists, the person checking should focus on four areas:

1   Cleanliness
2   Maintenance
3   Presentation
4   Staff.

A recommended format for checking a room

1   Check the staff first, that they are in uniform, with name badge, well-groomed, smiling and with good energy.

2   Look up and check the ceiling – check for stains on ceiling tiles, dust or grime in the air vents, cobwebs etc.

3   Look down and check the floor – for cleanliness, stains on carpets or tiles, dirt under furniture such as massage beds.

4   Look around the room in a clockwise direction – marks on walls, chips on fittings, tidiness, presentation.

5   Check the maintenance – light bulbs, temperature, music, any equipment and equipment safety checklists.

6   Look in drawers and cupboards – check any cleaning materials are safely stored and have the correct documentation.

Following such a protocol not only ensures that the check will be thorough, but the person doing the check will look professional too – for the audit to have a positive effect, how the auditor conducts him or herself is as important as what they check!

Common areas and what to check daily

■   **General**: fire/emergency exits should never be blocked or used as storage; the fire safety system should be working; electrical cupboards locked; cleaning and storage cupboards locked; back of house areas clean and tidy

■   **Spa entrance**: cleanliness (no rubbish near the entrance, an inviting first impression, doors polished, signage clean and working); maintenance (all lights working, doors, welcome mat etc. in good condition); presentation (plants, signage attractive etc).

■   **Spa reception**: cleanliness (floors, surfaces retail cabinets not dusty); maintenance (all light bulbs working, music on, fittings not damaged); presentation (reception desk tidy and free from clutter, attractive retail display, treatment information available and neatly presented, cupboards and back of house tidy); administrative (treatment spaces available – normally there should be 20% availability on the day, cash till is correct), staff (in uniform, well presented and customer focussed).

6

- **Treatment rooms**: cleanliness (air vents, floors); maintenance (walls, fittings, music, lighting, any equipment working and checked); presentation (no personal items, decoration, towels folded neatly, treatment bed displayed correctly); staff (in uniform, well presented and customer focussed).

- **Pool area**: cleanliness (scum line on pool sides cleaned, no body fat layer in showers, sauna glass, under sauna benches, floors, ceilings, air vents); maintenance (all water tests to standard, all equipment working, ventilation); presentation (beds laid out neatly, decoration); staff (lifeguard on duty, in uniform, well presented, attentive).

- **Changing rooms**: cleanliness (ceilings, air vents, floors, no body fat in showers, no dust on top of lockers, lockers clean, mirrors polished); maintenance (all light bulbs working, temperature correct, showers working, shower heads and taps free from limescale, toilets working and clean and hair driers checked and working); presentation (decoration, coat hangers in each locker).

Standard operating procedures (SOPs)

A standard operating procedure in a spa is a set of written instructions describing how a work process should be followed. In many companies, standard operating procedures can become over complicated and bureaucratic. To be effective and user-friendly, the standard operating procedures should be as simple and as short as possible, covering the main steps in a process. Similar to the brand standards the SOPs will:

- Ensure consistency in the operation.
- Give clear guidelines for the various business and customer related interactions.
- Provide a basis for training.
- Hold the spa staff accountable.

In a spa, often the standard operating procedures will be split into two areas:

1 SOPs for the **business/operational** procedures (mainly concerned with the operations and spa desk financial and customer interactions).

2 SOPs for carrying out the treatments or **'treatment protocols'**.

SOP business/operational procedures

SOP business procedures will cover all of the main administrative work processes taking place in a spa. Examples include:

- Changing or cancelling treatments
- Day opening, day closing
- Cashing up the cash machine
- Creating a bill
- Booking a treatment
- Procedure for changing shift on reception

- Ordering of materials
- Booking, creating and scheduling packages
- Staff timetable
- System down procedures
- Emergency procedures
- Enquiries over telephone
- Dealing with theft
- Lost property.

DEALING WITH TREATMENT ENQUIRY ON THE TELEPHONE

PROCEDURE CODE NUMBER: 05

ISSUED BY: Spa Manager

APPROVED BY: Resort Director

VALID FROM: 01.01.2020

STAFF RESPONSIBLE: All spa receptions and any staff answering the phone to a guest

1. The guest calls the spa.

2. The spa receptionist or member of staff should pick up the receiver within four rings and say"... Spa Resort (hotel name) Spa ....(Name) speaking, how can I help?' with a smile.

3. The receptionist or staff member should listen carefully to the enquiry and answer the questions accordingly.

4. They should ask if there is any particular service they are looking for.

5. The receptionist or member of staff should recommend the services they think would suit the guest's needs. They should recommend that the guest should visit the spa personaly, where it will be easier and more effective to communicate the information that the guest wants. It also will give more of an opportunity to upsell.

6. If the guest is a hotel guest and would still like to book by phone, the receptionist or member of staff should book the treatment into the software. They should ask the guest to arrive ten minutes before the treatment and come to the reception to sign for the treatment. They should also explain cancellation policy, if the guest does not show up for the treatment or wishes to cancel less than four hours before.

7. If the guest is not staying it the resort but would still to book by phone, the receptionist or member of staff should book the treatment into the software, however payment must be taken. They should ask the guest to arrive ten minutes before the treatment and come to the reception to sign for the treatment. They should also explain the cancellation policy, if the guest does not show up for the treatment or wishes to cancel less than four hours before.

8. When booking the treatment the member of staff should try to look for a time that is most suitable for the guest.

9. Depending on the treatment they should ask whether the guest would prefer a male or female therapist.

10. The receptionist should enquire if there is any else that they can do for the guest, then thank the guest for calling.

Figure 6.5: Example of a SOP for business procedures.

6

SOPs for treatment protocols

These follow the same guidelines as an SOP, but often in a different format.

DE-LUX HEAD AND FACE MASSAGE

TREATMENT PROTOCOL CODE NUMBER: 08

ISSUED BY: Spa Manager

APPROVED BY: Resort Director

VALID FROM: 01.01.2020

LENGTH OF TREATMENT: 30 minutes

STAFF RESPONSIBLE: All therapists

TREATMENT DESCRIPTION AS ADVERTISED IN SPA:

This wonderfully relaxing massage begins with gentle pampering and stroking movements to the face, forehead, nose, eyes and ears. A deeper more intense technique is applied to the nape of the neck and top of the shoulders. This massage is extremely effective in reducing stress and tension – an excellent way to de-stress after a long day sitting at the computer or commuting in the car.

---

*All staff should be familiar with the treatment descriptions so that they know what the guest is expecting!

SUITABLE FOR:

1. Stress
2. Stiff neck and tension

NOT SUITABLE FOR:

1. Certain skin conditions
2. Injury to face, head or neck

TREATMENT PROTOCOL

Check your Presentation

1. Check your hair is tidy and groomed, hands are thoroughly washed and nails clean.
2. Check uniform is clean, in accordance with the standards and that you are wearing your name-badge.

Room Preparation

1. Check that the room is tidy and free from clutter, any decoration to be of quality and displayed attractively.
2. All linen to be folded neatly.
3. Check room temperature – adjust if necessary, and possible.
4. Check lighting - adjust if necessary, and possible
5. Check music - level adjust if necessary, and possible
6. Check you have an aroma lamp and a full-sized towel to cover the guest.
7. Check the bed display is prepared (if applicable).
8. Check if there is drinking water available.

Treatment Preparation

1. Bed should be covered with a clean sheet
2. There should be a display cover for the bed with the standard bed decoration.
3. Prepare the anti-allergic oil facial massage oil.

Guest Welcome and Introduction

1. Walk out confidently with a smile to the guest waiting area and welcome the guest personally with a eye contact.
2. Introduce yourself by your name.
3. Guide the guest into the treatment room, walking a couple of inches behind their left shoulder.
4. Ask the guest if they have had this treatment before?
5. If needed describe the main points of the treatment
6. Ask the guest to lie down on the bed on their back.
7. Cover the guest with a sheet from the chest down.
8. Ask the guest if the temperature and music are alright.
9. Ask the guest if they have any health problems – particularly regarding facial skin or injuries to the face, head or neck.
10. Ask the guest if they would like an aroma lamp. If so set one up and light it.
11. Ask the guest if they are happy for them to start the treatment.
12. Tell the guest that starting from now the treatment will last 30 minutes.

Key points when carrying out the treatment

1. Start from the top of the chin stroking upwards towards the forehead on either side of the nose.
2. Go on to massage the temples.
3. Use a stroking action around the eye, going out under the forehead and going inward under the eyes.
4. Using your fingertips proceed from the temple to the forehead in three strokes starting from the eyelashes to the edge of the hair.
5. Stroking the two sides of the face at the same time loosely horizontally, starting from the root of the nose to the parotid region, from the lips to the parotid region and from the top of the chin to the parotid region.
6. Rub the top of the head / scalp from the nape to the forehead.
7. Stroke the neck from the shoulders. To do this lift the patients head a bit from the table.
8. Carry out a short massage on the shoulders.
9. Finish the massage with lengthwise action from the top of the chin to the forehead.

Ending the treatment

1. Thank the guest and tell the guest the treatment has ended.
2. Ask them if they were satisfied with the treatment.
3. Offer them a glass of water or a herbal tea.
4. Recommend them another treatment or service.
5. If they require it help the guest up from the bed.
6. Give the guest a towel or their bathrobe. If they need assistance, if so assist them in dressing
7. Thank them once more and wish them a pleasant spa stay.

Figure 6.6: Example of a SOP for treatment protocols.

A good treatment protocol, in addition to stating who is responsible, validity dates etc., will also contain the following information:

1 The **treatment description** as read by the guest in the brochure on the website. This is vital as the therapist should know what has been sold to the client –

naturally, what has been written in the description should be the same as what is delivered in the treatment room!

2   **Contra-indications** – i.e. health conditions which should be taken into consideration prior to giving the treatment. For example, if someone has had an operation on the vertebrae in their neck, are they able to have the treatment? The therapist should know exactly what conditions and health problems are not conducive to the treatment they are about to perform. In the consultation before the treatment they should enquire if the guest has any health issues.

3   The protocol should then be divided into the various steps; **preparation** (for the person doing the treatment), the **welcome,** the **treatment**, and **ending** the treatment. The beginning and end of the treatment are as important as the treatment itself.

The protocol should be short and to the point, and a copy of all relevant treatment protocols should be kept in the treatment room so that the member of staff has them to hand to refer to if necessary. The protocols should form the basis of any treatment training.

The importance of checking

As was highlighted in earlier chapters, the staff are more likely to do what the boss does. Sometimes it is not enough just to set an example and instruct the staff. The manager does need to actually check! Whilst this may seem obvious, many spa managers, particularly if they have been in the position for a long period of time, will make assumptions rather than check. Even when they do check, over time they may become what is known as 'operationally blind' – becoming too accustomed to the operation to see the faults. This is another reason to delegate a second person to support in checking the quality systems.

The art of checking a spa effectively is a balancing act. Excessive checking can generate a resistance, whereas too little checking can encourage a lax atmosphere. Moderate checking which is focused and prioritizes the important aspects of the operation, if it is carried out politely and professionally will focus the team and at the same earn the spa manager respect.

When checking the spa, the manager needs to take into consideration two points:

1   The items that need rectifying (prioritizing them and ensuring they are written down with deadlines and persons who are responsible).

2   The communication style with which the audit or check is done.

Knowing what to check and where to focus is key as this will directly impact on the standard of operations. During a check or audit is advisable to focus on a few but important shortfalls and afterwards address them effectively, as opposed to producing a long, detailed audit report and lists.

The style in which the audit is conducted is even more important. An audit carried out with an abrupt, superior, aggressive manner will spark resistance –

people expect respect and not to be belittled. At the other end of the spectrum, checking too slowly and fastidiously can also cause a negative impact – particularly if staff are busy. Having a manager taking up time unnecessarily will not endear a team to an audit. The manager should therefore aim to be quick, polite and to the point.

Dealing with resistance

Nobody likes being checked and nobody likes being corrected. Resistance is likely to come in three forms:

1 **Passive resistance**: where the therapist or member of staff being corrected just nods and says "yes", but clearly has no intention of rectifying the problem or changing it.

2 **Aggressive resistance**: showing anger – anger can be justified (but normally this is rare); in most audit cases, anger will be a tactic to ward off being given extra tasks or criticism.

3 **Diverting**: diverting will take the forms of excessive talking (providing excuses to take up time and wear the auditor down) or acting occupied or busy.

Having good brand standards and SOPs are tools that can help minimize the above. If the standards and work processes have been devised well (and have had input from the staff in their creation) and if the audit is carried out in a professional style, the chances of such resistance will decrease. Whatever level of opposition, the goal of the manager should be to manage it effectively, not be drawn into a side-track of discussion and analysis, and focus on what needs correcting.

Managing guest satisfaction

The mission, vision, goals, standards, SOPs and protocols are the building blocks to ensure a quality spa experience for the guest. These tools/systems are dynamic, in the sense that they are constantly changing and evolving. A standard that might have been appropriate for ten years, may suddenly need to be rewritten. Knowing what and when to change quality standards and systems will be based on feedback from the customer. Guest feedback can be collected in many forms:

Direct feedback

This is perhaps the most effective form of feedback. Simply by talking and mixing with the guests the spa manager can find out what the opinion is of their services and where are the problem areas. Just wandering around the spa chatting to the guests and asking 'how are you enjoying the spa?' or 'is everything ok?' can unleash a wave of information.

Inhouse questionnaires

These can be placed either at the spa reception and (if it is a spa hotel), in the guest rooms. Paper questionnaires are useful tools to gather information. They will normally consist of a scoring system for the relevant spa departments and, more importantly, space for the guest to write their opinion on the various services. In a paper questionnaire each spa department should be clearly separated with its own scores and space for comments. This means if one department (for example, the hydrotherapy) is consistently receiving lower marks then it can be identified clearly. The scores will then be uploaded into a report and measured over time.

- *Advantages of paper questionnaires*: a lot of detailed information can be collected.
- *Disadvantages*: being paper based, it is a time-consuming system to operate, adding to the administrative paperwork of the spa. Also, areas of concern and complaints may not be discovered until after the guest has left and the questionnaire has been inputted.

Alternatively, questionnaires can be sent in the form of an e-mail link to the guest after the stay. Although this approach is superior in the sense that it is less bureaucratic and statistics can be generated automatically, again as the information is sent after the guest has left, the manager may not be able to resolve the problem in time. Some spas will send the questionnaire during the guest's stay, but there is a hit and miss chance that the guests will read the email and fill out the form, as opposed to a paper questionnaire left in the guest room or on the reception.

For both systems, gifts or vouchers may be offered to inspire guests to give their feedback. The more feedback there is, the more information and the more realistic the statistics become.

Feedback tablets

More and more paper feedback systems are being replaced with tablets in treatment waiting areas and spa receptions. Tablets have some distinct advantages over paper-based feedback systems, yet they are not without their disadvantages;

- *Advantages of touch tablets*: instant feedback. Statistics and comments from guests can be received in real time. This means that if a guest is unhappy with a service or treatment, the spa manager is able to react immediately. Guests also enjoy using these systems.
- *Disadvantages:* only a limited amount of information can be collected, particularly if the tablet is in a common area. Guests are only prepared to fill out a number of questions in a short amount of time, with a limited number of clicks. If it is too long, they will get bored or frustrated and give up. Given the difficulty and speed many people have typing into a table, feedback opinions tend to be minimal. Unfortunately, also, adults and children like to play on touch tablets, putting in jokes and wrong information, which can further distort the statistics. There is also a cost factor, as such feedback systems will normally incur a license fee.

When designing tablet-based feedback questions, these should be extremely simple and focus on specific areas – reception, treatment and spa facilities, aiming for a minimum number of questions and clicks.

Mystery customers

Mystery customers are an excellent tool for gathering detailed information on the quality of services and facilities in the spa. There are many professional mystery customer companies with experience in the hospitality sector. They can help the spa decide on the areas and points to be checked in the mystery customer audit. These should be based around the spa's brand standards, SOPs and protocols.

- *Advantages of professional mystery customers:* the audit will give a detailed professional insight into the operations and at the same time will focus the staff on the standards and SOPs. Because the audit is being carried out by experienced professionals it will give both a guest's and a professional's opinion, highlighting not just problems but often giving practical solutions as well. The mystery checkers will also have checked competitor spas, so they will be able to compare the current spa's service levels with other operations. All of this information is summarized in a detailed and professional report

- *Disadvantages:* the report will depend solely on the abilities, experience and professionalism of the auditor. Managers and staff are extremely sensitive to any criticism and if there are mistakes or faults in the audit, then there will be a tendency to discredit the entire audit. The audit can also fail, because either through common questions asked by the auditor or suspicious behaviour, the staff discover who is the mystery shopper. Once the mystery customer has been recognised the whole purpose of the audit is defeated. Finally, outsourcing audits through a third party is expensive. For this reason, such audits may only be carried out once or twice a year and therefore will just provide a snapshot of the operation on a particular day. If the day of the audit happens to be one where there is a virus and half of the staff are off sick, then this would not be reflective of the operation in general. This is why the questionnaire results and other quality measuring systems should be taken into consideration when reaching a conclusion regarding the entirety of the operation, not just the mystery shopper report.

Using mystery customers to improve services in a spa chain

This particular spa chain's official mystery customer visits kept highlighting the same problems – therapists not asking guests about their health problems before each treatment and reception staff not upselling. These two areas of weakness were evident right across the chain. The spa director then implemented a new policy, that spa managers should be sending in their own mystery customers to check these and other key areas at least twice a month. These 'mini' internal mystery customer visits were put into the brand standard system and checked in the company audits to ensure that they were happening. Almost immediately there was an improvement, and in the next 'official' mystery customer reports, most of the spas saw dramatic improvements in their results.

Internal mystery customers

This is an effective checking mechanism which is not often used. This is where the spa manager organises a friend or colleague, who is not known by the staff, to go in and check specific areas of the spa.

- *Advantages of internal mystery customers:* it focuses the staff on particular points in the quality standards and if there is a weakness in one area of the operation, a check can be designed to focus purely on that particular area (or selected standards or work processes). Since the spa manager is organising it themselves, they feel more responsible and more in control of the outcome as opposed to an outside person checking them. There is also little or no cost which means that such checks can be carried out regularly.

- *Disadvantages:* this is not a professional audit therefore there may be weaknesses and biases.

External quality audits

Many spas will pay for the use of an external company's standards and use such a company to audit them. Examples include ESPA'S (The European Spa Association) quality accreditation systems and TÜV Rheinland's wellness standards. Many national spa associations also have their own standards and auditing services. Whilst these come at a cost, they often have particular benefits:

- *Advantages of a partnership with an external quality organisation:* often such organisations will have a reputable name, for example TÜV Rheinland. An accreditation by such an organisation can lift the guest's trust in the spa services and the prestige of the operation, particularly if the spa is promoting itself to European or German speaking markets. Because of their wide experience in auditing, a relationship with such a provider can improve the quality systems in the spa and the quality of service as well.

- *Disadvantages:* such a partnership comes at a cost, often promising more benefits than they actually deliver. Ultimately having a stamp of approval has little market value unless it is promoted and made use of actively by the spa, through its own PR and marketing efforts. It is also important for the quality systems to be appropriate to the type of spa – for example, a wellness standard accreditation will not be suitable for a medical rehabilational spa.

Third party booking sites

Nowadays most third party booking sites will have a score for the spa based on the feedback from customers who have visited. The score itself has a considerable value as do the comments from the customers. Most people booking a spa stay will take note of both and read the most recent feedback. The aim of the spa is to have as many customers leaving positive scores and comments as possible. Often spas will give incentives to get customers to give positive feedback on such sites and will put up signs in the spa reception saying that if guests enjoyed their stay to please leave a positive comment.

Summarized guest feedback website reports

There are also companies who offer a service collecting all of the data feedback from the internet and collate it into one report. In addition, they can provide and analyse comparisons and trends with local competitor spas and spa hotels. This comes at a cost, but it will give valuable information and save a lot more time than if the spa does this themselves.

Creating beautiful and welcoming spa environments is an important element of spa success, but spas cannot succeed without busy treatment rooms. Clients don't return because the spa is attractive; the treatments, the staff and the overall experience are what compel them to return. Yes, you've trained your staff, more than once, but a spa or wellness facility that expects to grow will need to have systems in place that manage the quality and consistency of the client experience on an ongoing basis.

It's always helpful to ask guests about their experience during the checkout/departure process, but they'll usually just say everything was fine. Maybe they'll even say it was great! But that's just anecdotal. Placing comment cards in a prominent place at the front desk, and also in the lounges/locker rooms, will invite more detailed responses, especially if you ask specific questions. Make sure you have a secure place where the cards can be dropped. Many operations software systems now support the emailing of a survey once the client has checked out; these can be simple, 3 or 4 questions, and many won't be answered, but those that do will give you more specific feedback, and you can even apply scoring metrics for your team. Sending out an email survey to your entire database, once or twice a year, will give you the opportunity to ask more direct questions about the relationship the spa has to the guest as well as the experience that is provided. Employing a mystery shopper is always an excellent way to learn what is really going on behind closed doors, ensuring that your staff is as welcoming, and rapport and retail focused, as you hope. One of the best ways to get a sense of your performance is MBWA – Management By Wandering Around. Make sure you are not sitting in your office behind closed doors all day; getting out and about, poking into corners, chatting with guests, peeking in at the laundry and break areas, and even working an hour at the front desk will be very revealing. It's not one solution or another, it's really doing everything you can to ensure your spa maintains its stellar reputation.

Lisa Starr, Principal, Wynne Business Consulting & Education

■   Quality ambassador

Managing all of these systems and ensuring that the relevant guest feedback gets communicated to the staff can be a complex task. In larger spas, the role of 'quality ambassador' can be delegated to a member of the team who has a passion for quality management and an eye for detail. The role is normally an additional task given to a member of staff and will involve:

- Assisting in the creation, updating and implementation of new standards, procedures, checklists and audit forms.
- Collating all of the guest feedback.
- Making sure the information from the feedback gets communicated to the right people and that areas requiring improvement are rectified.

Summary

Here is a summary of some of the main components that make up an effective quality system in a spa:

Figure 6.7: The main components of an effective quality system.

Whilst all of these actions and systems will contribute to ensuring that quality is delivered, ultimately what is important is not the systems themselves but the effect that they have on the ground. A spa can have the best mission, vision and standards, but if the management are not listening to the feedback from the guests and are not flexible in adapting their approach, then such systems are worthless. The result is what matters when building up and implementing a spa quality system – the system itself is secondary. However, if all of the quality components are put together thoughtfully and audits are conducted to a high level then this will undoubtably have a positive effect on the spa services.

The spa mission, vision, values and quality system are vital tools, but in some operations, they almost become like a religion. Even though they may be helpful for the operation, the spa manager should not forget that they are just tools and nothing more.

As has been emphasized in earlier chapters, what matters most is the energy and atmosphere in the spa – a positive energy from the manager will trickle down to the staff and guests – as is described in this popular quote by Richard Branson:

"Happiness is the secret ingredient for a successful business. If you have a happy company it will be invincible."

In short, the manager should ensure that the spa has excellent quality management systems, but not forget that in the end, it is the energy and happy working culture that they inspire that will have the greatest impact on quality.

Feedback from the interviews – what the experts say

Spa managers were asked what they would recommend in order to manage quality in their spa.

- The most common suggestion is for mystery shopping as well as internal and external audits and quality control. This can include self-quality audits like ISO or accreditation by associations like the European Spa Association. Quality Management Systems (QMS) were mentioned as well as up-to-date, relevant Standard Operating Procedures (SOP). As stated by Chris Theyer, previously Training and Development Director of LivingWell Health Clubs "Setting standards for every aspect of the business from uniform to operating procedures ensures high delivery of product and service for customers".

- Emphasis was placed on the communication with employees as well as regular checks and training. Employees should be clear on expectations and rewarded for good performance. Patricie Irvelková, Director of Marketing & Sales from Mariánské Lázně, refers to "Properly set and achievable goals for the team members and reasonable reward for achieved goals".

- The importance of customer feedback was recognised, either in the form of customer surveys or guest reviews. One respondent stated "Listen to customer feedback, especially on sites like Trip Advisor – a Harvard study once showed that a half-point rating can make the difference between a business being successful or going bust!"

- A few respondents referred to the quality of the environment and facilities. These included cleanliness, hygiene, health and safety, air and water temperature, as well as atmosphere and appearance of staff.

Research and further reading

A few studies have been undertaken on service quality in spas and wellness hotels. Blešić, Čerović, and Dragićević (2011) used the ServQual model to analyse five spa hotels' service quality in Serbia. They noted that there were negative gaps between customer expectation and perception values. Albayrak, Caber and Öz (2017) undertook a study of spa and wellness services in a five star hotel in Antalya using the ServQual model and found that 'Tangibility' was rated highest which they explain by customers' sanitary and hygiene concerns, followed by 'Credibility & Safety' then 'Competence & Courtesy' of the staff. Lo, Wu and Tsai (2015) undertook research in Southern China on the impact of spa service quality dimensions on customers' positive emotions. Their research showed that responsiveness (attitude and behaviour of employees) and reliability (e.g. timing, pricing) are the most significant factors in influencing positive emotions, followed by empathy (i.e. responding to customer's personal needs) and tangibles (physical environment, appearance of facilities). Vryoni, Bakirtzoglou and Ioannou's (2017) study in Greek spa centres showed that employees' commitment to the comfort of their customers and honest and empathic treatment of customers had the strongest relationship with customers' satisfaction. Another study in Greece showed that factors such as cleanliness of the spa influence customers' choice of spa (Trihas and Konstantarou, 2016). Lagrosen and Lagrosen (2016) undertook research with customers in Swedish spa hotels. Their findings showed that the main determinants of service quality according to customers were physical effects (e.g. feeling physically better after their treatments); mental effects (i.e. feeling more relaxed and less stressed); experiencing pleasure (including a nice environment, enjoyable treatments and friendly staff); smoothness (i.e. flexibility with booking treatments, minimum hassle, uncrowded, reasonable price). All respondents ranked the following items very highly: calm atmosphere (the most important), possibility to relax in pools, delicious food, friendly staff, availability of spa treatments and well-cleaned premises.

References

Albayrak, T., Caber, M. and Öz, E. K. (2017) 'Assessing recreational activities' service quality in hotels: an examination of animation and spa & wellness services', *Journal of Quality Assurance in Hospitality & Tourism*, **18** (2), 218-234, Doi: 10.1080/1528008X.2016.1208550

Blešić, I., Čerović, S. and Dragićević, V. (2011) 'Improving the service quality as a socially responsible activity of hotel companies', *Economic Interferences*, **13** (29), 273–286.

Lagrosen, Y. and Lagrosen, S. (2016) 'Customer perceptions of quality – a study in the SPA industry', *European Business Review*, **28** (6) 657 – 675, Doi: 10.1108/EBR-05-2016-0070

Lo, A., Wu, C. and Tsai, H. (2015) 'The impact of service quality on positive consumption emotions in resort and hotel spa experiences', *Journal of Hospitality Marketing & Management*, **24** (2), 155-179, Doi: 10.1080/19368623.2014.885872

Matthews, J. and Wells, D. (2008) 'Spa chain operations: the experience of the Mandara Group, a division of Steiner Leisure Limited', in Cohen, M. and Bodeker, G. (eds) *Understanding the Global Spa Industry*, London: Routledge, pp. 151-170.

Samkange, F., Simba, A. and Baker, L. (2017) 'Finance for the spa industry', in S. Rawlinson and T. Heap (eds) *International Spa Management*, Oxford: Goodfellow, pp.83-93

Trihas, N. and Konstantarou, A. (2016) 'Spa-goers' characteristics, motivations, preferences and perceptions: Evidence from Elounda, Crete', *Alma Tourism Journal of Tourism, Culture and Territorial Development*, **7** (14), 17-38, Doi: 10.6092/issn.2036-5195/6300

Vryoni, S., Bakirtzoglou, P. and Ioannou, P. (2017) 'Customers' Satisfaction and Service Quality of Spa Centers in Greece', *Acta Kinesiologica*, **11** (1), 12-18.

Wittington & Associates (2016) 'Vision, Mission, Values, Goals, and Objectives', https://www.whittingtonassociates.com/2016/12/vision-mission-values-goals-objectives/ (accessed 18/07/2019

7 Health and safety and water handling

Spa facilities are associated with serious risks and hazards, so it is therefore essential that a spa manager has sound understanding of health and safety systems and regulations, in addition to knowledge of the fundamentals of pool plant operations and water handling.

Each country has their own health and safety regulations which may differ, however, there is generally a commonality in their approach. Because this book is aimed at a wide international readership, this chapter focuses on these commonalities rather than specific legislation(s). For a more detailed overview, the WHO "Guidelines for safe recreational water environments" is recommended.

There are three main goals of health and safety in the spa:

1 To ensure that the spa facility is as safe as possible – 'facility' refers to the building, the equipment and the people in it.

2 To ensure that the staff, guests and premises are supervised properly – through systems and control measures (i.e. checklists, audits, Hazard Analysis Critical Control Points, Control of Substances Hazardous to Health etc.).

3 To ensure that the staff are following health and safety regulations and that they are trained in health and safety procedures (i.e. emergency action plans and procedures)

(Crebbin-Bailey, Harcup and Harrington, 2005).

Aside from the water handling itself, there are certain health and safety areas which require an active participation on behalf of the manager. These are:

■ Risk assessments.

■ Health and safety procedures to reduce risks (including emergency action plans).

■ The safe handling and storage of pool and cleaning chemicals (Control of Substances Hazardous to Health – COSHH) and as well as agents and oils for massages and other treatments.

■ The safe and hygienic handling of food & beverages (Hazard Analysis Critical Control Points – HACCP).

Risk assessments

A risk assessment "entails a careful evaluation of all of the aspects of a spa that could cause harm to employees and to persons using the spa, in order to determine whether sufficient precautions are being taken to minimize these risks or whether more measures need to be put in place" (Crebbin-Bailey, Harcup and Harrington, 2005: 144).

A risk assessment on the spa will normally be carried out at least once a year:

1 To review recent *precautions* put in place.

2 If there has been any change to the *physical structure* of the spa facility.

3 If there has been any change in *tasks* or *workflows*. (For example, the introduction of a new treatment, cleaning agent or procedure.)

4 If there has been an accident and any *weaknesses* have been uncovered.

5 If there has been any *change to health and safety legislations* – a review to ensure that the systems ensure compliance.

Risk assessment forms will differ from country to country but all risk assessment forms should contain the following:

- A list of the potential hazards. (This might be anything from slippery water pooling around the side of the pool, to an unlocked electrical cupboard.)

- Who may be affected – guests and/or staff.

- The chances of an accident – ranging from hardly likely to extremely likely.

- What action has been taken to resolve the hazard – (e.g. for the slippery water pooling, maybe a slip mat has been ordered; for the unlocked electrical cupboard, maybe the lock has been replaced and a sign placed inside the door telling staff to lock the cupboard after use).

- All actions should be recorded in the risk assessment and should include the *name* of the person responsible for supervising the rectifying of the hazard (or potential hazard), the *deadline* for the action and the *date* of completion.

Emergency action plans

An emergency action plan is a written document concerning how to handle emergencies that have a reasonable possibility of occurring in the spa. The action plan will include:

- The *procedure(s)* to be followed in the case of an emergency.

- The *evacuation plan* (if needed), with evacuation routes.

- Procedures to account for employees and staff after the emergency has taken place.

- *Telephone numbers* of who to contact.

- What *reporting procedures* are required.

■   The main areas of risk

There are three main areas of risk in a spa: drowning and injuries, microbial hazards and chemical hazards (WHO, 2006: 2).

Drowning and other injury risks

- **Drowning:** is the biggest serious risk in spa facilities, particularly if children are permitted to use the pools or alcohol is served on the premises.
- **Slips:** in pool areas are likely to be the most common form of accident experienced.
- **Impact injuries:** from hitting hard or sharp surfaces.
- **Burns:** particularly from touching the coals in the sauna or from the steam jet.
- **Overheating from the heat experiences:** fainting and adverse circulatory and heart reactions can be common.
- **Suction forces in the pool:** that might trap people in the water by a body part or hair.
- **Reactions to treatments:** Adverse reactions to certain treatments or creams.

Microbial hazards

- **Infection and water related diseases**: from unclean or poorly treated water vomit, faeces, blood.

Chemical hazards

- **Chemical and water handling:** if pool chemicals are not handled according to instructions, they can cause gas leaks and even explosions.

In addition, there are other occurrences which also should have emergency action plans:

- **Fire:** saunas pose the highest risk for possible fire outbreaks in spas. These can be caused by electrical malfunction, oils, newspapers or towels left on or near the coals.
- **Other:** power outages, damage to the building by weather or natural forces, leaks, theft, death, etc.

■   The plan's contents

The emergency action plan should consist of:

- The *title* of the emergency
- The *department* it affects
- Important *telephone numbers* and *contact persons*
- *Steps of action* (normally in the form of a flow diagram)
- *Who* to inform.

■ Reporting

All incidents large or small should be recorded in an emergency action report, the reason being, if there are further consequences (i.e. such as an investigation or court action), there will be a detailed record to refer to. Figure 7.1 is an example of a typical incident or accident report form.

ACCIDENT OR INCIDENT REPORT FORM

Person involved in the accident or incident: (Name address, contact details)

Person completing the accident or incident report: (Name address, contact details, position, department)

About the incident   **Incident Number:**

Time incident occurred: Date of incident:

Where the incident occurred — Department / room / area:

Details of the incident including cause if known [use additional page if required]

Details of any injury suffered:

Is a risk assessment required following this incident?   YES / NO

The person involved in the accident or incident: Signature .... Date: ....

Figure 7.1: Example of a typical incident or accident report form.

In serious cases such as a death, a major injury (i.e. broken bones, fainting or hospital admission) or a dangerous incident (i.e. fire, gas leak, electrical failure) the local health authority would be informed and, in addition to the accident/incident report, dependent on the local regulations an official form may also be required to be filled out.

Spa managers are used to having a lot of initiative to get things done, often alone, however health and safety is a vital topic which requires a different level of knowledge and overall team engagement. From infection control, food safety, water quality testing, to risk assessments and Fire Warden training – there is a considerable need for 'depth of knowledge' that may be lacking, particularly with small teams of dedicated spa specialists. Health and safety knows no boundaries however and applies to all.

It is worth spa owners and managers budgeting very carefully to ensure they allocate for the right level expertise and service contracts to support facility management (HVAC, refrigeration, swimming pools, sauna/steam) and equipment servicing. I also strongly recommend investing in safety training that extends beyond the minimum mandatory compliance. Training helps to embed a culture of 'safety as a priority' within the team. When the business takes health and safety seriously and management involves staff through training and exposes them to 'good governance' practices and supportive safety systems, management, staff and guests all benefit. The industry is also less likely to be tarnished by media stories that may portray all by the poor practices of the few.

Sheila McCann, General Manager, Lanserhof U.K.

Hygiene, chemicals and water handling

■ Hygiene

Now more than ever cleanliness is essential in any spa operation and this will involve the handling of chemicals and cleaning agents. Every spa should have written and visible hygiene rules and procedures. These rules and procedures should describe:

- The *area(s)* to be cleaned
- The *frequency* of the actions
- Which *cleaning agents* are required
- The *concentration* of the agent needed
- *How* to prepare it, how to use it and how often
- The *person(s) responsible*.

The above instructions should be accompanied with the cleaning agent delivered by the supplier. It is the spa manager's responsibility to ensure they are acquainted with the handling and use of the cleaning products, that a copy of the documentation is kept with the products and that the cleaning staff have been trained appropriately in their usage according to these instructions. With straightforward cleaning agents, if the rules and procedures are in place, there will normally be no issues. One common discrepancy often highlighted in many spa audits, is cleaning chemicals being poured into unmarked containers by the cleaning staff – all cleaning agents should be in their correct, labelled containers and stored and administered according to the usage guidelines.

Pool chemicals

The biggest area of risk concerning chemical handling will be the pool plant room and the chemicals that are used for treating the pool bathing waters.

In terms of health and safety (in addition to the sauna and pool areas), pool plant rooms pose the most risks in a spa facility. Dangerous fumes and gases can be emitted through leakage or when certain chemicals are mixed together, in the worst-case scenario, even explosions can occur.

COSHH – Control of substances hazardous to health

COSSH regulations describe which substances are dangerous to health and how they should be used and stored (Crebbin-Bailey, Harcup & Harrington, 2005: 152). As with cleaning agents, the manufacturers must issue clear guidelines and instructions with the chemicals covering labelling, safety, delivery, storage and emergencies. Only trained staff should be allowed to handle chemicals. The names of the staff and the training that they have received must be kept on record.

Not only is it necessary to control the handling of the chemicals, but also, how the chemicals are stored is integral to the safety of the spa:

- There must absolutely be no smoking in or near the pool plant room or chemical storage area. (This seems obvious to mention, however, storage areas are often out of the way places where staff go to sneak a cigarette break – spa managers should be vigilant!)

- All chemicals must be labelled – sometimes the chemicals will not be utilized from the container in which they arrived. Any container which is holding a chemical *must* have a label clearly stating what the container contains. Safety handling instructions should be fixed adjacent to the chemical.

- Different types of pool chemicals should be stored separately, locked if possible, in separate rooms or in clearly separated areas of the pool plant room.

- Chemicals should not be stored on the floor but in trays chemically resistant to acid (so if there is spillage it does not spread).

- Chlorine is often stored in gas cylinders. If exposed to heat they can become a serious fire risk, therefore they should be kept out of direct sunlight and away from heat sources such as radiators. Only trained personnel should handle the cylinders, which should be fixed in an upright position to prevent them from falling over. Filled and empty cylinders should be kept separately.

- Dangerous or inflammatory chemicals should be stored in a fire-resistant room.

What to do in the event of a chemical spillage

If chemicals leak or spill normally there will be two courses of action, one for a minor spill and one for a major spill (i.e. in the pool plant room):

7

- **Minor spill**: (e.g. a cleaning agent): the member of staff should notify others in the area that a spill has occurred, put on the protective gear, isolate the area, control the spread of the liquid by containing the spill by placing an absorbent material from the outer edges in towards the centre at the same time as neutralizing acids. The absorbed material should then be collected, disposed of safely and the area cleaned. Finally, the management should be notified and a report filed.
- **Major spill or chemical leak**: e.g. in the pool plant room, the area should be evacuated, all doors closed, management notified, the supplier company and/ or emergency services called and people prevented from entering the area.

What to do in the event of a gas leak

Gas leaks are extremely serious and are normally caused by wrongly mixing two chemicals together. In the case of a gas leak or explosion in the pool plant room, the following action should be taken:

- Leave the area
- Close all doors
- Evacuate the entire spa
- Call the fire brigade.

Tidiness and cleanliness in the pool plant room

Pool plant rooms are often not checked as thoroughly or as regularly as necessary. There are several reasons for this. Often the spa manager will assume this is being taken care of and is the responsibility of another department (e.g. maintenance), or their lack of knowledge in pool plant operations will deter them from wanting to get involved.

If not checked and monitored, a pool plant room can quickly become an alternative storage area or dumping ground for old or broken equipment for the spa or hotel, turning it into a dangerous hazard. As part of their daily check routine the spa manager should be checking the pool plant room, even if the direct responsibility of its operation lies with another department, the reason being that it is too important an area to assume or hope that it is being maintained by somebody else. The pool plant room(s) must be kept clean, tidy and organised like any other room in the spa department – the spa manager must play their part in enforcing this.

Protective equipment

Each country will normally have legislation concerning protective equipment for staff to minimize their chance of injury. Personal protective equipment is essential when dealing with chemicals. Each plant room should have:

- Goggles to protect the eyes
- Apron or chemical protective clothing

- Gauntlets/gloves for handling the chemicals
- Rubber boots
- Potable water for cleaning and neutralizing acid.

A respiratory mask should be placed outside the pool plant room in case of a gas leak. Often in spas, the mask can be found stored with the rest of the protective gear inside the pool plant room. This is a serious mistake. The mask must be stored outside the pool plant room, so in case of a gas leak it can be put on outside of the contaminated area.

Pools, water handling and safety

Whilst spa managers are not expected to be technical engineers, they do need to have a basic understanding of how pool systems work, particularly when it comes to water hygiene. In countries where manning costs are high, spa managers may be expected to play an active role in water management and pool plant maintenance.

Water quality can be impacted by micro-organisms, dirt from guests and by products from disinfection. If the pool happens to be outside, dust, algae and dead insects can also affect the safety of the water. There are four ways to ensure good water quality:

1   Adding more fresh water into the pool

2   Increasing the flow of recycled water

3   Ensure that the water is properly filtered

4   Disinfection. (Von Storch, 2016: 61)

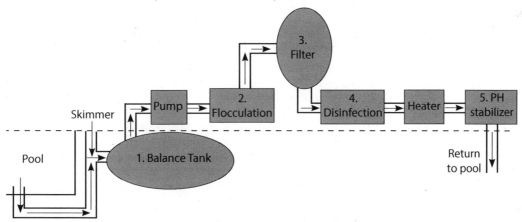

Figure 7.2: A simple diagram showing the main points in pool plant system.

The water flows out of the pool either via a skimmer at the top and/or drain at the bottom. It then goes into a *balance tank*. A *balance tank* is to ensure that the water in the pool remains at the correct level to compensate for people going in and out of the water. In pools with deck level drainage, a balance tank is essential because the water is continually flowing into a drain.

Balance tank

The balance tank can cause a risk of germs, therefore the volume of water in the tank needs to be changed at least once per day. It should have no edges but be rounded and should have a continuous flow (Von Storch, 2016). (In fact, any water holding a tank or filter in the system should have no edges and be rounded).

The **pump** pushes the water around the pool plant system.

Flocculation

This is the process by which a coagulant agent such as aluminium sulphate is added to the water. This binds together the small waste particles in the water so that when they enter the filter they are big enough to get trapped and not be recirculated back into the pool.

The filter

The water with the large waste particles goes through the filter (a tank normally filled with sand). These large waste particles will get stuck in the sand and the clean water with a significant reduction of waste particles then proceeds to the heater. Over the course of a couple days there will be a build-up of dirt in the filter. This dirt will need to be cleaned out. To do this the water flow is reversed through the filter to push out the dirt, this dirty water is then redirected to the drain – this procedure is called *backwashing*. If filters are not backwashed regularly there can be a risk of microbiological contamination.

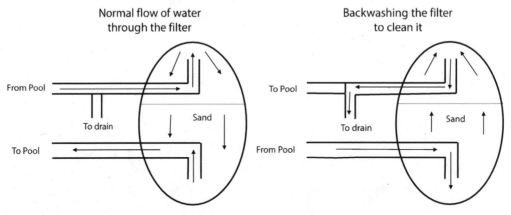

Figure 7.3: Normal flow and backwashing through a filter system.

Disinfection

Next the water is disinfected. There are a number of common disinfection methods, these include:

- Chlorine: this can be used either as a gas, a liquid or tablet (tablets are mainly used in pools with lower bathing loads, such as private home swimming pools) (WHO, 2006). There are three measurements used:

☐ *Free chlorine*: this is the type of chlorine that is still active in sanitizing the water that has not interacted with any contaminants. Internationally there will be variation regarding the exact levels permitted, but generally speaking the free chlorine should be between 1 and 3 parts per million (PPM).

☐ *Combined chlorine*: this is the type of chlorine that has been used in disinfecting the water and its ability to sanitize the water is limited. Combined chlorine is the result of a chlorine and molecules combining with ammonia and nitrogen to form chloramines which lose most of their sanitizing power. This is the chlorine that will cause the bad smell, red eyes and irritated skin. Combined chlorine should be between 0 and 0.5 parts per million PPM.

☐ *Total chlorine*: is the sum of both the combined and free chlorine

Above 5 PPM chlorination should be stopped and above 10 PPM guests should be evacuated from the pool.

Other disinfection methods:

■ **Bromine**: is a tablet, it does not admit gas, it has no smell, but it is expensive and is very caustic therefore needs special measures for protection particularly for the staff who are handling it.

■ **Ozone**: is a gas is made up of oxygen molecules, which oxidizes particles in the water. Alone it will not be sufficient sanitation and will not eliminate all contaminants, so bromine or chlorine should be added.

■ **UV**: is a light which destroys 99% of pathogens but only at the point of treatment, after this point the water may need further treatment.

PH Stabilization

After disinfection it is necessary to balance the PH level in the water to maintain the effectivity of the disinfection. The lower the number of the PH, the more acidic the water and the higher the number, the more alkaline. The PH level should be maintained between 7.2 – 7.8 for chlorine pools. (WHO, 2006: 20). There are chemical agents to raise PH levels (such as sodium hydroxide) and agents to lower PH levels (sodium hydrogen sulphate/sulphuric acid).

■ **Testing**: the chemical level testing procedures of the water will be dependent on the size and type of spa pools and the local regulations. Normally there will be automatic testing and manual testing carried out in the pool plant room and manual testing direct from the pools themselves, carried out at least three times per day or every couple of hours. Tests will be carried out on the free and fixed chlorine levels, PH levels and water temperature.

■ **Bathing loads**: there will be a maximum number of people per cubic metre allowed in the water at any one time, but this will vary dependent on local regulations. If the maximum number is exceeded this will have a negative effect on the hygiene and chemical balance of the water.

Thermal pools

These are either pools with artificial heated water, pools with natural mineral artificially heated water or thermal/mineral water which is naturally warm or hot.

Water in natural thermal/mineral pools will have a continuous flow and for this reason may not be recirculated or even treated. This is often deliberate, as treating/disinfecting the mineral water will alter its chemical composition – the main motivation for people wanting to bathe in the water in the first place.

Natural thermal/mineral water will either be pumped up from an underground thermal water source or directed from a natural spring into the pool and filled up at the beginning of the day. During the day, enough fresh water will continually replenish the pool, so by the end of the day (at a minimum) the entire water in the pool basin has been replaced. Once the spa closes the basin will be emptied, scrubbed with disinfectant, rinsed and filled up for the next day. Dependent on the size of the basin this can take up to several hours.

Some spas may recirculate their thermal mineral water (or a part of it) in the same way as a normal pool and use a chemical agent and/or UV as a precautionary form of disinfection. However, as stated, UV only kills the germs at the point of the UV treatment and not thereafter.

Other risks

■ Physiological risks

Aside from the hazards and risks associated with handling chemicals there are also risks of injury and infections from contaminated water.

Drowning

The spa manager is responsible for ensuring that the spa pool areas are properly supervised at all times. Depending on the size and depth of the pools a lifeguard, (fully or partly supervising the pools) may or may not be required. However, if there is an accident or fatality, the pool supervision policies of the spa (in normal cases), will be investigated by the authorities to check if the spa management have taken adequate measures to ensure the safety of their users. If it is decided that inadequate measures were in place, then the spa and management will be liable for negligence. For this reason, it is safer to err on the side of caution and employ lifeguards whenever possible. If children under the age of 15 are using the pools and/or alcohol and food is served in the pool areas, lifeguard supervision would be required (HSE, 2003). Bathing rules, that clearly describe the regulations for which the pools are to be used, should be clearly visible to bathers.

Slips

In pool areas, slips are likely to be the most common form of accident experienced. Slip measures such as plastic slip prevention matting over main walkways, attendants regularly mopping up pools of water and visible signage asking guests to wear indoor footwear in the pool area, can help to minimize this risk.

Impact injuries

Impact injuries are normally caused by slippery surfaces, running or jumping in the pool area or are related to alcohol consumption. The risk of injuries can be minimized through proper supervision and signage in the spa areas. In addition, there should be actions to reduce slippery or sharp surfaces and rules to deter guests from jumping or diving into pools and consuming alcohol or food whilst bathing (Crebbin-Bailey, Harcup and Harrington, 2005).

Injuries from heat

Heat from thermal pools or heat experiences from saunas and steam rooms can result in fainting and/or adverse circulatory or heart reactions. Clear signage with usage instructions should be visible next to the heat experiences. These instructions should advise guests on the recommended length of time and how to use the heat experience, and list any contraindicatory health conditions. Staff should be regularly checking the saunas and heat experience facilities during operational hours and testing water temperatures. The saunas should have guards around the coals, and hot steam jets in steam rooms should not be positioned in places where guests can get burnt.

Suction forces in the pool

These can trap body parts, jewellery and hair under the water resulting in serious injury and even death. Drain covers can break or be removed by guests unaware of the potential dangers. Certain actions can be taken to reduce this risk, such as avoiding the use of drains and using gutters or overflows instead, increasing the number of drains, installing anti-entanglement hair drain covers and safety vacuum release systems so that drainage will stop if there is any obstruction. Finally, checking to see that all drain covers are in good condition should be a part of the daily check list.

Adverse reactions to treatments

Adverse reactions to certain treatments or creams can be avoided by properly consulting the guest beforehand, enquiring if they have any health problems or allergies and following the treatment protocols correctly.

■ Risks from infection from faeces, blood or vomit in the pool

There are several guidelines of what action to take if there is faeces, blood or vomit in the pool. These will vary according to different health authority guidelines and the size and type of spa bathing pool.

Normally if the faeces are solid and of a small amount, it should be removed quickly and discarded. The scoop used to remove it out of the pool should be disinfected. Chlorine will kill the bacteria and viruses so there should be no reason to close the pool if the amount is not excessive and the chemical levels are correct.

If there is a large amount of solid faeces or vomit, the pool should be cleared of people, as much of the substance should be removed as possible and the scoop or the equipment used to remove it disinfected. Then the chlorine level should be raised to at least 2 PPM for 25 minutes, to kill any possible germs.

If there is diarrhoea or excessive blood the pool should be cleared of people, closed and the chlorine raised to 2 PPM for over 12 hours, after which the filters should be backwashed. *

(*These instructions are based on different recommendations from different sources. Spa managers should check the health and safety procedures in their location).

Precautionary measures

In addition to administering stringent disinfection procedures, certain precautions can be taken to avoid contamination in pools. These include:

1 Ensuring that all spa goers shower before swimming.

2 Toilets and showers situated within easy access of the pools.

3 Designing separate pools for children in the spa concept.

4 Clear signage to deter people from running, jumping etc, and advice for how to use the different experiences.

■ Water related diseases

Water related diseases will come in the form of bacteria (single celled organisms that get their nutrition from the environment), viruses (which need another cell's structures to reproduce) and protozoa (single celled organisms living in damp environments). Here are some common waterborne infections to be aware of:

Bacterial diseases

- **E-coli**: spread by contaminated water, theis is an intestinal infection that produces a toxin that damages the lining of the intestines, resulting in hemorrhagic colitis, causing abdominal pain, diarrhoea and fever. It is killed by chlorine.
- **Leptospirosis**: normally carried via animals, characterized by jaundice, meningitis and kidney failure. It is killed by chlorine.
- **Shigella**: also called bacillary dysentery, is spread from faeces, causes stomach pain, fever and diarrhoea. Shigella is transmitted directly or indirectly via the fecal-oral route and may occur due to the ingestion of contaminated food or water. It is killed by chlorine.
- **Pseudomonas**: can infect any part of the body depending on which area has been infected. If it is on the skin it can cause skin inflammation, if it is in the

ears then pain and swelling, and if it is in the digestive tract stomach pain and diarrhoea. It is killed by chlorine.

Viruses

- **Adenoviruses**: common in poorly disinfected pools causes fever, red eyes and sore throat. Chlorine is effective in killing the virus but not immediately.

- **Papilloma virus**: warts contracted through contact with inadequately disinfected floors or surfaces.

- **Hepatitis A**: a potential problem when large numbers of people congregate and where overcrowding, inadequate sanitation and drinking supplies exist. It is a virus causing infectious inflammation of the liver. It is killed by chlorine though not immediately.

Protozoa

- **Cryptosporidiosis**: caused by parasites, this is the commonest cause of diarrhoea in pools, with fever, cramps, nausea and vomiting. It is resistant to chlorine, but not filtration. Ozone and UV are effective.

- **Giardiasis**: is primarily an infection of the small intestine in which a microscopic parasite causes fever, nausea, diarrhoea and cramps. It is resistant to chlorine, so promoting proper hygiene (i.e. showering before swimming etc) can help stop the germs getting into the water in the first place.

(WHO, 2006 and Crebbin-Bailey, Harcup & Harrington, 2005).

The above diseases demonstrate:

1   How important it is to reinforce good hygiene practices, both in terms of keeping the spa facilities and services as clean as possible, but also promoting good hygiene habits with the staff and guests.

2   As can be seen from this list of diseases, chlorine and effective filtering will minimise the risk of infection. All it takes is for one pool to have poor disinfection, or not maintaining a clean filter and one guest to be infected. The result can be catastrophic for the spa and particularly for a spa that is in a hotel, as in such environments diseases can spread like wildfire.

> A spa hotel that attracted seniors was hit by an infection of E-coli. The infection resulted in over 40 infections. By analysing the pool records it was discovered that the chlorine levels in one pool had been extremely low due to a fault in the automatic dosing system. The levels had been recorded, but because the spa manager was not checking the record sheets, no follow up action was taken. The hotel had no option but to close the spa, carry out a thorough disinfection of all the spa pools and offer a rebate to the guests. The negative PR fallout was highly damaging to the business. As a result of the accident, a new policy was put in place that all spa managers in this particular hotel spa chain had to check and sign the pool water testing sheets twice a day, more signage was put up asking guests to shower before using the pools and in the spa café and restaurant entrance a disinfectant hand gel was placed asking all guests to use it.

■   Fire

Each country will have their own fire safety regulations and guidelines, these should include:

Checks that the fire safety standards are in place:

This will include ensuring that:

- Emergency exits are clearly marked.
- Emergency exits are not blocked and doors all work.
- Alarms are tested regularly and are in working order.
- The sprinkler system has been tested and is working.
- The electrical system and in particular the sauna and other electrical equipment has been checked for safety.
- Fire extinguishers are approved and checked that they are within their validity date (this date can range from between one to two years).

Ensuring that there are fire emergency action plans:

These should be in all areas, positioned by the fire alarms and exits. The emergency action plan should contain the following steps:

- Containing the fire by closing off the area.
- Notifying by calling the emergency numbers, stating who is calling, what happened (fire, explosion etc), where it is, how many injured (if any).
- Evacuating the area – ensuring all guests leave via marked escape routes, closing the doors behind and assembling at the evacuation point.
- Small fires can be extinguished with hoses or extinguishers, providing the person doing the extinguishing is trained and is at no risk.

Training

All staff should have had training in fire safety and emergency procedures. In normal cases this would be repeated on an annual or twice-yearly basis.

Practice drills

Most spas would test the alarm weekly and carry out a practice drill twice a year.

■   Other risks

- **Power outages:** blackouts in spa pool areas can particularly be a problem in spas with no natural outside light or if a blackout occurs after dark. Checking that the emergency exit signs function at all times regardless of power outages, that torches are available in all departments, and that staff are trained in how to handle the event of a blackout would be part of the emergency action plan.
- **Damage to building by the weather or nature:** the chances of damage caused by heavy rain or storms should not be underestimated and there should be a

plan of action for such an event. In certain geographical areas, earthquakes should also be listed as a potential risk.

- **Leaks**: spas focus on water experiences; water entails piping and plumbing, the more pipes, the greater the chances of leaks occurring. Checks of the piping and plumbing should be included in the daily checklist, with an action plan of what to do and who to contact in the event of an emergency.

- **Theft**: a particular concern for day spas and hotel spas in towns, cities and built up areas. In such spas, safes should be available at reception for valuables and signage in the lockers advising guests to use safes. In addition, there should be a protocol of how to handle missing, lost or stolen items and who to contact dependent on the situation.

- **Death**: many spas, particularly thermal spas in Central Europe will attract senior guests. These guests are normally visiting with (or to be treated for) health conditions. It is not uncommon for a guest to pass away on the premises. The spa manager should have a protocol of what to do in such a circumstance so that the situation can be dealt with both professionally and sensitively.

Common health and safety regulations

7

Depending on the country of the spa, there will be other health and safety regulations which the spa manager needs to be aware of, these include:

- **Workplace regulations**: health and safety in the workplace, relating to physical conditions such as temperature, ventilation, lighting, cleanliness and waste, staff changing and washing facilities, facilities for rest and eating.

- **Equipment**: regulations to ensure that all equipment is suitable, correctly maintained and that staff are trained and competent in using it. A common standard in spas is for every piece of equipment in the spa (i.e. from a manicure equipment sterilizer to a hydro-bath) to have a daily equipment checklist. The piece of equipment will be checked and tested by the user, who will then sign to confirm the test has been completed. Any discrepancies and/or repairs will be recorded on the check sheet. In addition, all devices should be listed on an inventory sheet containing the following information:

  ☐ Identification, type of equipment, serial number, year of purchase.

  ☐ Name of the equipment and model, name of company and the name of the person responsible for the equipment.

  ☐ Location it is used in.

  ☐ Safety controls in place (i.e. the daily checklist). (Storch, 2016)

- **First aid qualifications**: each country will have their own regulations as to the minimum number of first aid qualified people necessary – this will be dependent on the size of the spa and number of employees. As a bare minimum there should always be one person on duty at all times who is qualified in first aid, however in a well-run spa it should be mandatory for all spa staff to be first aid qualified.

- **First aid boxes**: in each main area of the spa there should be a clearly labelled first aid box containing: a guidance card, sterile dressings in various sizes, adhesive dressings, eye pads, safety pins, triangular bandages. Medications should not be kept in the first aid box and only administered by qualified personnel. In many countries now it is also mandatory for the spa to have a defibrillator.

HACCP (Hazard Analysis Critical Control Point system)

Spa managers who are responsible for food and drink sales in their operation will need to be familiar with HACCP. HACCP is process control system that identifies where hazards might occur in the food production process and puts in place actions to prevent hazards from occurring. There are seven principles that serve as a foundation for HACCP, these are:

1   Conducting a hazard analysis.
2   Identifying the critical control points (CCP) in the food production process.
3   Establishing critical limits for preventative measures for each critical control point.
4   Establishing monitoring requirements to ensure that each critical control point stays within its limits.
5   Establishing corrective actions if the critical control point is not within its limits.
6   Establishing effective record keeping, concerning monitoring, verification and deviation.
7   Establishing procedures to ensure that the HACCP system is working properly. (HACCP Alliance, 2019).

Ensuring staff are trained in food safety would also be part of a HACCP system.

Liability insurance

There are two types of liability insurance that spas will have:

- **Employers liability**: in case of employees being injured or becoming sick as a result of their job or workplace.
- **Public liability**: this covers operator against claims made by members of the public .

(Crebbin-Bailey, Harcup and Harrington, 2005).

Ensuring accident/incident reports are filled out for any occurrence are of special importance when it comes to liability and liability claims.

■ ## Medicines

In many thermal or medical spas there will also be medications kept and stored on the premises. There are certain rules that the spa manager should be aware of regarding the storage of pharmaceuticals:

- No medication on the premises should be stored over its date of expiry.
- Opened pharmaceuticals should be marked separately with their sell by date.
- All medications should be stored securely and locked.
- Narcotics should be stored in a safe.
- The temperature of the refrigerators where the pharmaceuticals are stored must be monitored periodically.
- Patients' medication should be marked separately as opposed to the medication prescribed through the spa.

■ ## Air hygiene

Air is normally circulated in the spa area and treatment rooms by clean air being fanned in from outside and old air from inside being extracted out. Air pipes that are not clean can be a breeding ground for Legionnaires disease (a bacterial pneumonia). Spas have a strong risk of harbouring this bacterium as it likes to live in damp and water between 25 – 55°c. Periodically (at least once every 2 years) air circulation pipes should be cleaned and sprayed with a disinfectant which is not harmful to humans, such as chlorine.

Children in spas

The presence of children in spas is a contentious issue, not just with respect to health and safety but also the effect that children have on the spa environment. Whether to allow children in the spa or not will depend on the spa concept design. Some spas will deliberately target families and children, some will be strictly for adults only. Either way, it should be a conscious, managed decision and preferably planned right from the conception.

Regarding health and safety, children pose a serious risk. They are more likely to be involved in a drowning or accidents. In pools and jacuzzis, they are more suspectable to diseases due to a less developed immune system and the fact that the core body temperature of a child increases faster than an adult, meaning they have less ability to cool down. For this reason, allowing children into very hot pools and environments like saunas is not advised.

Given that most people visit spas to relax, if spas do welcome children, the facilities should be designed to cater for them (i.e. separate pool and recreational areas).

Feedback from the interviews – what the experts say

The subject of health and safety was mentioned several times by the respondents during the course of the interviews. Here is a brief summary of the points made:

- Hygiene and cleanliness are mentioned as a critical part of the customer experience. This includes the facilities themselves as well as the appearance of the spa manager and employees. Regular monitoring is deemed essential.

- Risk assessments and logging are key to ensure that health and safety issues are properly identified and dealt with. This includes infrastructure, procedures, equipment and spa products.

- Several respondents stated that the spa should be both up-to-date and modern with safe with fully functioning equipment which is checked regularly and maintained properly.

- Those respondents who work in medical thermal spas emphasise the need for special training in the use of waters and muds as well as other treatments and therapies. More research is needed to provide evidence-based reports on the safety and effectiveness of treatments

Research and further reading

Much of the further reading with regards to health and safety in spas tends to focus on managing recreational waters. In addition to the World Health Organisation (2006) guidelines for safe recreational water environments, Giampaoli and Spica (2014) discuss some of the more recent developments including the new technologies being used to control and manage water hygiene and sanitation. Margarucci et al. (2019) suggest that alternative and more sustainable approaches need to be taken to manage hygiene in natural spa pools, such as photocatalytic nanotechnologies to enhance the native antimicrobial properties of spa waters. They also suggest that users should be educated and managed properly. Valeriani, Margarucci and Spica (2018) discuss the challenges of leaving medical or healing thermal waters untreated as far as possible to ensure the mineral composition remains while avoiding risk of infection. For example, a young boy died in Costa Rica because of a parasite present in hot springs (Abrahams-Sandí et al., 2015). Silva et al. (2013) warn that the radon found in thermal mineral spas could also pose a threat to human health.

References

Abrahams-Sandí, E., Retana-Moreira, L., Castro-Castillo, A., Reyes-Batlle, M. and Lorenzo-Morales, J. (2015) 'Fatal meningoencephalitis in child and isolation of Naegleria fowleri from hot springs in Costa Rica', *Emerging Infectious Diseases*, **21** (2), 382–384. Doi:10.3201/eid2102.141576

Crebbin-Bailey, J., Harcup, J. and Harrington, J. (2005) *The Spa Book*, Atlanta: Thomson.

Giampaoli, S., & Romano Spica, V. (2014) 'Health and safety in recreational waters', *Bulletin of the World Health Organization*, **92** (2), 79. Doi:10.2471/BLT.13.126391

HACCP Alliance (2019) 'Questions and answers', http://haccpalliance.org/alliance/haccpqa.html (accessed 04.08.2019).

HSE (2003) *Managing Health and Safety in Pools*, 3rd Edn, Sudbury: HSE Books.

Margarucci, L. M., Spica, V. R., Gianfreschi, G. And Valeriani, F. (2019) 'Untouchability of natural spa waters: Perspectives for treatments within a personalized water safety plan', *Environment International*, **133**, Part A, 105095.

Silva, A. S, Dinis, M. L. and Diogo, M.T. (2013) 'Occupational exposure to radon in thermal spas', in Arezes, P. M., Baptista, J. S., Barroso, M. P., Carneiro, P., Cordeiro, P., Costa, N., Melo, R. B., Miguel, A. S. and Perestrelo, G. (eds) *Occupational Safety and Hygiene*, London: Taylor and Francis, pp. 273-277.

Valeriani, F., Margarucci , L. M. and Spica, V. R. (2018) 'Recreational Use of Spa Thermal Waters: Criticisms and Perspectives for Innovative Treatments', *International Journal of Environmental Research and Public Health*, **15**, 2675, Doi: 10.3390/ijerph15122675

Von Storch, K. (2016) *Quality in Wellness and Spa*, European Spas Association.

WHO (2006) *Guidelines for Safe Recreational Water Environments*, Geneva: WHO.

7

8 Spa definitions, history, facility types, challenges, treatments and trends

In addition to understanding the management practicalities of leading a spa operation, spa managers should have a basic knowledge about health, wellbeing and spa products. The next four chapters are focused on essential product information which all spa managers should be aware of.

What is a 'spa'?

The word 'spa' generates a certain amount of confusion. The International Spa Association, (an American organization set up to 'advance the spa industry') defines 'spa' as a place "devoted to overall wellbeing through a variety of professional services that encourage the renewal of mind, body and spirit" (ISPA, 2019).

According to this definition, anybody who offers a facility that provides services in this very broad spectrum can call themselves a spa, and they do! In the last 20 years, thousands of beauty salons and treatment centers have capitalized on the spa trend and re-branded themselves as 'spas', but the question is: just because they offer a few mind, body or soul services does that mean that they are really spas?

Better dictionary definitions define a spa as "a town where water comes out of the ground and people come to drink it or lie in it because they think it will improve their health", or "a place where people go in order to become healthier, by doing exercises, eating special food, etc" (Cambridge Dictionaries Online, 2019).

These definitions help to better clarify the spa product in its entirety as they encompass both the European traditional spa product as well as a more international perception of a spa. The first definition refers to its European, historical roots while the second refers to what many spas have evolved into today.

Where does the word 'spa' come from?

There are several opinions on this. It is thought that it is either an acronym for the Latin phrase 'sanus per aquam' ('health through water'), or alternatively it comes from the town of 'Spa' (in Latin Aquae Spadai) – a spa town in Belgium. If you attend any spa conference, it is almost guaranteed that 'sanus per aquam' will be the opening slide in many a power point presentation!

The origin of the word 'spa' is perhaps not so important but, for a spa manager, understanding clearly what constitutes a spa is. First, it is necessary to understand why spas evolved in the first place:

1 **Heat and water**: In water, the body's weight reduces by 90%, which immediately alleviates pressure on the bones and joints, as well as giving a sensation of weightlessness. In addition, the range of motion of the joints also increases. When exposed to heat, initially the body tries to regain its original temperature with an increased heart rate and blood pressure, however as the temperature of the body rises, in turn the blood vessels dilate (expand). As the resistance to the blood flow decreases, the blood pressure and heart rate lower. More oxygen is delivered to the organs and there is an increase in the removal of CO_2 gas, lactic acid and other waste products. This is one reason why after having a hot bath the body feels so relaxed. Of course, when soaking in hot water if it is combined with massage jets and minerals the feeling of relaxation is intensified.

2 **The 'wonder-drug' syndrome**: The quest for a 'magic bullet' solution to give super health or cure an illness (either in the form of a diet or other one-stop solution) seems to be a recurring trend every few years. People of no matter what era, are willing to buy into and invest in 'quick fix' promises. Spas, particularly in the 19th century, capitalized on this, aggressively promoting their treatments and natural resources as a cure for everything from tuberculosis to even venereal diseases. Even today many spas will tend to over-exaggerate the benefits of their unique therapies and/or natural resources.

3 **Pampering**: In the 19th century (the golden age of spas) the aristocracy and many of the upper middle classes, in particular women, did not work. Spas, which were mainly facilities and resorts for the upper echelons of society became destinations in which to recuperate and be treated for a range of maladies, in particular melancholia and anxiety (often caused by a lack of occupation) – places to retreat from everyday life and be nursed and pampered.

4 **Social**: In past eras, spas were also just as much about socializing as they were about health, offering programs such as concerts, lectures, theatrical events and even gambling. Visiting a spa offered excellent opportunities for social interaction and advancement as well as excitement and a diversion from the tedium of everyday life. Whilst the social element of visiting a spa is perhaps not what it was a century ago, it still plays an important part in the spa experience.

8

A brief history

In order to understand today's spa product, spa managers and indeed anyone delivering spa services or therapies should have some knowledge of how spas have evolved.

■ Prehistory

Hot springs, played an important part in the establishment of many of the first human settlements and are on the path of some Nomadic routes. These were in essence our first 'spas'. Several painted caves in France and Spain are in walking distance of natural hot springs and we can safely assume that pre-historic man-made use of these natural resources for bathing and cleaning.

Aside from bathing, the first spa treatment is believed to be the 'sweat hut' – the remains of which are to be found across the globe. Sweat huts, heated with hot coals to induce sweating were common throughout Africa, the Americas and were particularly favoured in the cold northern zones of Western Asia (Finland, Russia, Poland, Denmark, Sweden, Norway and Celtic regions). A few ancient Irish sweat huts still existed in the 19th century! (Smith, 2007).

One of the earliest pieces of evidence we have of man-made baths is from the Eshnunna Palace in Babylon dating from 2300BC and we know that the Egyptians practiced forms of water therapy and herbal remedies. Alongside sweat huts, hot springs and bathing, grooming and touch were our first spa treatments.

■ The Greeks

The Greeks laid the foundation for our modern spa product, giving us the word 'cosmetic' (derived from 'kosmos' meaning adornment and 'kosmetikos' meaning having the skill to adorn or beautify). Greek public baths consisted of a large rectangular hall with seated baths in recesses and domed hot sweat baths at one end; the domes circulated heat given off by a brazier in the middle. The other rooms were heated by hot air from under the floors. Outdoor pools were often found adjacent to the baths, though swimming for the Greeks was not strictly a sport – but more of a form of therapeutic exercise (Smith, 2007).

■ The Romans

The Romans took the Greek tradition of bathing and expanded on it and because of their ability to use concrete to construct aqueducts built magnificent and massive bath complexes.

The remains of famous Roman baths are to be found all over the Roman Empire (for example Baiae near Naples with its hot sulphurous thermal springs which became a fashionable Roman spa resort with its bathhouse and villas). Rome itself also boasted several magnificent bath houses, such as the Diocletian baths which in their day, spanned more than 13 hectares and could accommodate up to 3,000 people at the same time, containing a pool with a water surface of more than 3,500 square metres. (National Roman Museum, 2014) As the Roman Empire slowly fell into decline so did the bathing culture.

■ The Turkish Baths

Following the Muslim conquests of the seventh century across the East Roman Empire, the Middle East and North Africa, Islamic builders took the bathing culture from where the Romans left off and adapted it, although on a much smaller scale. The layout of the hammam was similar to a Roman bath, with some minor differences. The town baths and private baths of the Islamic Empire were a central part of the culture. For example, in AD 900 there were 1,500 bathhouses in Baghdad (Smith, 2007). Hammams can still be found all over North Africa and Arabia, both in towns and in the deserts as resting and hygiene facilities for caravans and traders.

■ The Middle Ages

There is a misconception that people in the Middle Ages did not bathe. This is untrue. Bath houses were common in most towns and were normally built next to the bakery, using the same fire to heat the water as bake the bread. Through paintings of that era. it appears that communal bathing combined with eating a meal was something of a weekly ritual in Medieval Europe. Of course, where the sexes were mixed and naked, there was an increased likelihood of sexual activity and prostitution. In the 1490s, syphilis erupted and spread across Europe and the trend for communal bathing stopped. The fear of syphilis may not have been the only reason, the depletion of Europe's forests meaning the price of firewood/ fuel increased could have been another factor. This was also the start of the reformation and a new puritanical trend was spreading across Europe; modesty, hard work and devotion went against the hedonistic pleasure of bathing naked. Some public baths did remain open, but with continual epidemics of syphilis and plagues, they never regained their previous popularity.

Carlsbad (Karlovy Vary) in the Czech Republic was a popular spa destination by the middle of the 14th century. The most famous health center of the middle ages was Salerno in Italy which was renowned for its medical school and healing facilities.

■ The 16th and 17th centuries

In the 16th and 17th centuries, whilst bathing and public bathing in Europe had gone out of fashion, we have some evidence that bathing for medical reasons was practiced. The resort of 'Spa' in Belgium became the focus of English Catholic dissidents. To counteract this the English Protestant monarchy began promoting bathing for medicinal purposes in England, in such towns as Bath, Buxton and Harrogate (Crebbin-Bailey, Harcup and Harrington, 2005). In Central Eastern Europe, due to the Turkish invasion of Hungary in 1526, superb hammams were constructed. The magnificent thermal baths of Budapest constructed in a Hammam style (the Rácz, Rudás and Király) are still in operation today.

■ The 18th century

Queen Anne visited Bath at the beginning of the 18th century and subsequently Richard (Beau) Nash, a socialite and fashion leader, and the architect John Wood transformed Bath into England's most fashionable resort. England was about to become the world leader in industry, commerce and culture. What happened in Great Britain would be replicated elsewhere, and the concept of a spa resort like Bath was no exception. The 18th century saw a revival in the medical use of spring and thermal water across the continent and the fashionable trend of visiting a spa destination. The 18th century was also the Age of Enlightenment, when the health benefits of bathing, hygiene and a healthy diet started to be discovered. As part of this trend, thalassotherapy took off in Brittany, France. In Central Europe, Empress Maria Theresa ordered a registry of mineral and thermal water springs throughout the lands controlled by the monarchy, including a chemical analysis and a description of which water was appropriate for specific diseases.

■ The 19th century

The 19th century was the golden age of spa resorts and the era of the hydrotherapy trend. A key figure in starting this movement was Vincent Priessnitz, a peasant farmer from Grafenberg in Austria, who healed himself after an accident through a regime of wrapping cold wet sheets around his body. He developed his therapy into a popular 'cure' regime by incorporating healthy food, air, exercise rest and cold-water bathing.

Priessnitz's concept was taken up and further developed by Sebastian Kneipp, a priest, who also ill and claimed to have cured himself with a cold-water cure. Similar to Priessnitz, he promoted healthy nutrition, fresh air, exercise such as walking barefoot and further developed the cold-water hydrotherapy treatments by combining alternative hot and cold water 'pourings'. Kneipp's treatment was so effective and popular that its center still exists today in Bad Wörishofen in Southern Germany.

The 19th century saw the expansion of the health and hygiene trend. This was the age of Semmelweiss (who discovered that mortality in midwifery wards could be reduced by washing hands in lime solutions), Louis Pasteur (famous for his discoveries on the principles of vaccination and pasteurization) and Joseph Lister (who established the link between lack of cleanliness and deaths after operations). Cleanliness in hospitals was further promoted by Florence Nightingale, the founder of modern nursing, who was also a pioneer of the concept of medical tourism and a great supporter of the hydrotherapy movement. Combined with this, an outbreak of cholera in Liverpool ignited a sanitary revolution in Great Britain via a series of laws collectively known as 'The Baths and Wash-houses Acts'. At the same time, the middles classes were exposed to a barrage of health information on the benefits of cleanliness and exercise.

As part of this trend, in America, Sylvester Graham a Presbyterian minister, combined hydrotherapy with a vegetarian diet and sexual restraint; likewise Ellen

White (the founder of the Seventh Day Adventists) promoted clean living and hydrotherapy. By the 1850s, the USA had 27 hydrotherapy centers built around different hot springs (Smith, 2007), the first indoor bathroom had been built and by the end of the century, middle-class homes, schools, institutions and army barracks in the UK all had hot and cold water. For those without plumbing, a strip wash in a hip bath was the norm and bathing children in cold water was thought to be healthy. In Britain, the sea-bathing craze continued and, by the middle of the century its coastline was full of seaside resorts accessible by train.

It was 'gymnastics' from Per Henrik Ling's Gymnastika Centalinstitut in Stockholm, later complimented by Friedrich Ludwig Jahn's 'Turnplatz' ('turning' equipment, with wooden beams, bars and benches) which was introduced into Britain and America, that became the foundations of our modern fitness clubs. Massage for rehabilitation was also introduced at this time by a Dutch physician, Johan Mezgner (1839-1909).

On the European continent, the invention of artesian drilling meant that spas could be built, not just over natural springs, but anywhere over underwater mineral reservoirs. Health retreats for the aristocracy, rich and upper middle classes were established all over Europe, the most famous being Baden-Baden, Aachen, Spa and Weisbaden in Germany, Karlsbad, Franzensbad, Marienbad (frequented by Edward VII) in today's Czech Republic and Vichy in France. The spas of the 19th century promoted themselves as being able to cure almost any disease and were frequented, not just by the bored upper classes, but by people seriously ill with diseases such as tuberculosis and cancer. Today's traditional European spa routine has changed little from the 19th century and consisted of:

- An early rise.
- A light breakfast then a stroll to the pump house to drink the water (In many European spas guests had and still do have their own allocated 'cure' cup, with a special spout, kept especially by the spring).
- A morning of treatment regimes, mainly baths, wraps, mud packs and massage.
- Lunch and rest.
- A promenade or sightseeing.
- Dinner.
- Entertainment (e.g. a concert, performance or lecture) in the Kurhouse or casino.

The 20th century

By the beginning of the 20th century, spas had become incredibly popular and a seasonal visit was now embedded into the European culture. The hydrotherapy trend continued and was further complemented with additional treatments (such as the newly discovered electrotherapy). As medicine became more advanced, spas slowly stopped promoting themselves as a panacea for all illnesses and instead began to specialize in specific diseases, especially mobility diseases like arthritis and rheumatism, and lifestyle disorders such as gout and obesity.

Naturism evolved out of the hydrotherapy principles and Adolf Just, a German naturopath, wrote his book *Return to Nature* (1896), promoting all the values of hydrotherapy but with an emphasis on nudity and exposure to the elements. He revived the 'earth bath' from its 18th century roots, where a patient would be buried naked up to their neck in earth, in the belief that the body would absorb the minerals from out of the ground. He opened two centers; one in Austria and one in the USA.

In the US, John Harvey Kellogg, the maker of cornflakes, opened a sanatorium based on similar principles to those of Sylvester Graham, with a focus on nutrition, enemas and exercise, combined with the American puritan influence of sexual restraint. The health farm was born, and in 1925, Champneys in Hertfordshire opened its doors; it is now one of the UK's top health spa brands.

In 1906, Dr. Max Bircher-Benner founded his privat-klinik outside Zurich. He promoted a detoxification nature cure of exercise, bathing, a raw fruit diet and fasting. He also invented the famous Birchermuesli of porridge oats, milk or yoghurt, honey, nuts and raw fruits – hence the detox trend.

In the 1920s, naturism, naturalism and healthy living became a major trend and the free body culture (Freikorperkultur) in Germany gathered pace. It is estimated that, by the 1930s, there were three million nudists in the country (Clapham and Constable, 1982). Since Germany was Europe's leading power, naked swimming and sunbathing became popular right across Central Europe, explaining why nudity is still so embedded in many European cultures today.

The period after the Second World War saw a dramatic change. In Britain, the new National Health Service withdrew from supporting hydrotherapy treatments meaning that the traditional spa resorts went into decline and with Europe split by the Iron Curtain, many of its spa resorts became inaccessible.

By the 1970s in Western Europe, there was both public and private investment into spa facilities, particularly those using a natural resource such as thermal water. Now affordable, these newly expanded spa complexes opened their doors to the mass market, some countries subsidizing spa treatments through state insurance schemes.

Socialist governments in Czechoslovakia, Hungary, Romania, Russia, Poland and the Balkans constructed huge sanatorium spa complexes offering patients long-term, two and three-week stays combining the natural resources with medical physiotherapy treatments, stays covered by their state insurance system – many of these such spas are still in operation today. Meanwhile in Britain and America, the health farm was in vogue, offering crash diets and slimming programs for its wealthy customers.

■ The 1980s and 1990s

This era saw the introduction of the health and fitness clubs. Prior to this, body building had been in existence, primarily for men. Health clubs, unlike body building gyms, also offered pools, saunas, beauty and treatments. Also, at this time Yoga and Eastern holistic therapies became popular through personalities such as Pattabhi Jois and B.K.S. Iyengar and found their way into the new spa product. Ayurveda was a part of this movement.

With the lifting of the Iron Curtain, many Eastern European spas, which up until the 1990s, had been run more or less as sanatoriums, were privatized and started to see the subsidization of their state insurance guests reduced. Those that adapted, modernized and found new markets for private paying guests survived; those that did not fell into disrepair. It was at this time that 'Wellness', which had been in existence for several decades, became the new buzzword. These traditional medical spas introduced wellness, beauty and fitness into their portfolios and began to also cater for local markets and short stay guests. With an aging population in Europe and new markets from Russia and the Middle East, the medical rehabilitation product in these spas continued to have some demand.

In Western Europe, in countries such as Austria and Germany, councils invested in expanding their public spas to attract a local market and private hotels (which linked themselves to the public spas via corridors) were developed. Guests, however, also demanded spa facilities in the hotels as well, so these destinations morphed into massive (sometimes with ad hoc planning) spa resort destinations. Bed and breakfasts also began to spring up around them to catch some of the business.

Elsewhere in the world, fitness was becoming part of mainstream lifestyles. Hotels, which had started to add fitness facilities in the 1990s (often selling local memberships to increase revenues), by 2000 were starting to cash in on the word 'spa' adding relaxation treatments and facilities as well. Beauty salons also inserted relaxation treatments and facilities; they too re-branded their facilities to 'spa'. Now the world 'spa' has become common place – in hotels, high streets, shopping centers, remote wildernesses and cruise ships.

Spa facility types

As we have seen throughout history, different spa cultures have influenced one another, whilst at the same time modern wellness trends have slowly integrated themselves into historical traditional spa concepts. This melting pot of spa ideas and trends is continually producing new and exciting spa treatments and concepts. Because of this, it is becoming more and more challenging to box spas into specific categories. In addition, different cultures use similar words and terminologies which may have completely different meanings (the word 'spa' itself is just one example). In their *Health and Wellness Tourism* book on spas and hot springs, Cooper and Cooper list 49 types of spas! (Cooper and Cooper, 2009: 35). For the purposes of simplicity, Figure 8.1 shows just some of the main spa facility types as defined by ISPA. (At the moment, these are the only mainstream international definitions.)

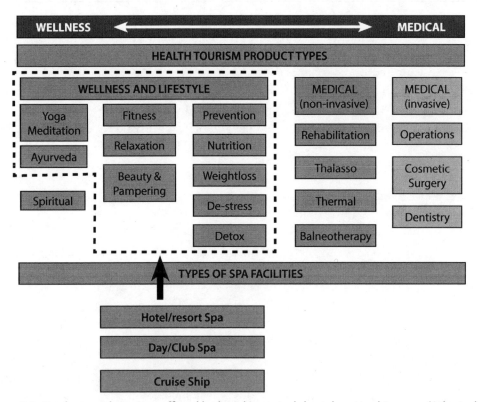

Figure 8.1: Products and services offered by hotel/resort, club and cruise ship spas. (Adapted from Smith and Puczkó, 2009).

■ Day spas, cruise ship spas, club spas and hotel resort spas

Hotel/resort spas, day/club spas and cruise ship spas can be grouped together as they tend to offer similar products and services:

Day spa

A spa offering a variety of professionally administered spa services to clients on day-use basis (ISPA, 2019). Day spas may offer spa relaxation facilities (i.e. saunas/steams/water facilities, such as a hydro pools/relaxation rooms etc, though it is worth mentioning that in the USA few spas have water facilities), spa relaxation, skin and beauty treatments. Day spas are normally located in more populated areas and may also be connected to a hotel (a cruise ship spa is essentially a day/hotel spa on board a cruise ship). Day spas are to be found worldwide from London to Lagos.

- **Challenges:** Because these are small operations, the owner will often also be the manager (in a cruise ship spa the treatment facility is normally outsourced). These types of spas are normally small, local, operations. Because of their size, cost margins will be tight, meaning that filling up every treatment space, upselling and controlling costs will be a key focus.

- **Management**: To run a day spa (or cruise ship spa), previous reception and/
  or therapist experience would normally be required – if one of the team are
  sick, then the manager is able to step in quickly. The manager may also be
  expected to cover shifts either on the desk or in the therapy department. The
  team will be made up of receptionists, therapists (beauty and massage) and
  hair dressers (for hair, the chairs or room will often be rented out as opposed
  to employing staff directly). Duties include quality checks, organising the staff
  timetables, customer relations, hygiene/health and safety, selling treatments
  and products, ordering supplies, creating marketing plans, monitoring and
  improving the business whilst leading the team. Organisation, attention to
  detail, customer service, sales skills and some business acumen are needed in
  what is a very hands-on management position.

Managing a day spa effectively

Day spas, with their extensive reach into communities, are primary gateways for consumers into the wellness world. According to the 2017 Global Wellness Economy Monitor from the Global Wellness Institute, day spas (including club spas) comprise almost half of all of spas globally. As the spa industry has grown and morphed into wellness, interest from consumers has never been higher. This is great for business, but also a challenge; the more people travel and are exposed to stories about spas in the media, the more they expect from their local day spa. Globally, day spas are challenged to employ enough staff to meet the demands of the public, which is fueling a movement into offering therapies and treatments that don't required a hands-on licensed practitioner. These services, such as halotherapy, LED treatments, cryotherapy, and sensory-deprivation experiences including floatation, are gaining in popularity as guests become more experiential. However, there will always be a demand for therapies delivered by skilled practitioners. Day spas that can keep their labor costs under control, and are well-marketed, can typically achieve profit margins of 5-10%, beyond salaries for owners.

Lisa Starr, Spa Expert – Principal, Wynne Business, USA.

Club spas

A facility whose primary purpose is fitness and which offers a variety of professionally administered spa services on a day-use basis (ISPA, 2019). In a typical club spa, you would expect to find a fully-equipped fitness facility (equipment and classes), pool(s) with relaxation facilities (saunas/steam rooms/relaxation rooms etc.) spa relaxation and beauty treatments. Club spas are mainly located in cities/towns as stand-alone operations with a local membership and are sometimes connected to hotels. Club spas are common worldwide and are especially prevalent in major urban areas and cities where they may be part of a chain.

- **Challenges**: Club spas are often sizable operations with several large departments; fitness (instructors, outside exercise class teachers), spa therapy (masseurs, beauty therapists, hair dressers, sometimes physiotherapists), pool areas, a sales department, technical and cleaning. Dependent on their size such spas may have sub-department managers or supervisors for each of these areas. The main challenge in operating these types of spas revolves around people management – hiring, dealing with staff turnover, training and motivation. Some club spa facilities can have several thousand members, so sales, maintaining guest satisfaction and guest retention is a key part of the role. Controlling costs should not be underestimated – in such facilities, equipment numbers can be extensive and their usage high, not to mention the cost of operating pools, saunas etc.

- **Management**: To operate one of these spas, therapy and/or fitness knowledge/experience would be required, in addition to reception and supervisory experience. Duties include: people management (holding meetings, appraisals, interviewing etc), audits and quality control, ensuring that customers satisfaction and health and safety is of a high level, cost control, meeting sales targets and coming up with plans and strategies to develop and grow the business. This is very much a leadership role where organisation, attention to detail, strong staff management, customer service, sales and business skills are essential.

Resort / hotel spas

A spa located within a resort or hotel providing professionally administered spa services, fitness and wellness components (ISPA, 2019). In a hotel or resort spa the spa facility is an additional attraction and revenue source. However, this does not mean that all guests in the resort will visit the spa. Operationally resort and hotel spas are similar in many instances to club spas, particularly if they also offer an outside membership, in which case, they will also have similar department structures, fitness, relaxation facilities, spa, beauty and pampering treatments being the key products offered. Many resort/spa hotels offer also prevention products, wellness programs and retreats (i.e. detox, de-stress, weight loss) as well as Ayurveda, yoga etc. Resort/Hotel spas are now common place globally.

- **Challenges**: Often in a resort the spa will be separated from the resort's pool and leisure areas, making it a smaller, easier to manage operation than a club spa. The main challenge in operating resort spas is finding suitable staff (particularly if the resort is in a secluded location), maintaining consistent high quality of treatment service levels, ensuring that customers from the resort actually do visit the spa facility, finding ways to increase the time the guests spend in the spa and increasing their spending when they do.

- **Management skills and duties**: Skills and duties will be similar to a club spa and will include – quality checks, organising the staff timetables, customer relations, hygiene/health and safety, sales, ordering supplies, monitoring and improving the business. Organisation, attention to detail, customer service, sales skills and business acumen are required.

Destination spas

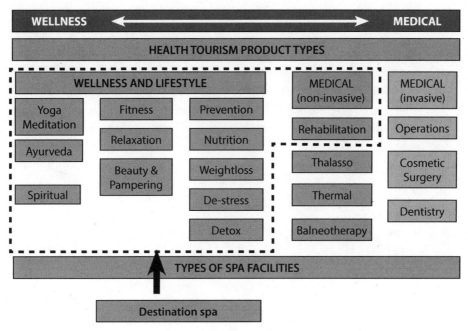

Figure 8.2: Products and services offered by destination spas. (Adapted from Smith and Puczkó, 2009).

A destination spa is a facility with the primary purpose of guiding individual spa-goers to develop healthy habits. This lifestyle transformation can be accomplished by providing a comprehensive program that includes spa services, physical fitness activities, wellness education, healthy cuisine and special interest programming (ISPA, 2019). The focus of destination spas is to offer services and treatments which are designed to improve quality of life and longevity. These facilities offer basic wellness and preventative programs (weight loss/de-stress/detox/nutrition/fitness/relaxation/pampering) and diverse products such as Ayurveda, Yoga, life coaching and workshops, spiritual treatments etc. Destination spas are now extremely sophisticated with a wide range of self-improvement programs including brain fitness, relationship-building, and programs aimed at helping people deal with life's changes such as divorce, bereavement, etc. Destination spas are popular in Western Europe and, in particular, America. They are often located in remote areas with tranquillity and scenic beauty so that their clients can really escape. A destination spa provides lodging, and most guests spend their entire visit on the premises.

■ **Challenges:** Given the diversity of services and treatments, destination spas are extremely complex operations to manage, and they are also often in remote and isolated locations. The main challenge is to find suitable, highly educated and experienced staff to deliver the wide range of complex services offered. This means sourcing, recruiting and retaining not just therapists and fitness trainers, but dynamic counsellors, lifestyle coaches and even doctors and, of course, since it is also essentially a hotel, challenges in finding housekeepers, cooks, etc, as well as attracting guests. The other challenge is ensuring that the services offered have an ongoing market demand, that they are promoted and sold effectively and are delivered to a level that will contribute positively to the reputation of the spa.

- ■ **Management skills and duties**: Managing a destination spa requires extensive experience in hospitality and/or health operations, in addition to having detailed knowledge and experience in health, wellness and complementary medicine and therapies. The role involves all of the operational duties pertinent to the other spas, but with an additional focus on developing and implementing complex health, wellness and spiritual spa programs.

■ Medical spa

A facility that has a full-time, licensed, health care professional on-site, which is further defined as a health professional who has earned a degree of Doctor of Medicine (M.D.) as defined by AMA. All applications are reviewed individually and international standards are taken into account when applicants from outside the U.S. apply for membership (ISPA, 2019).

Medical spas, also called 'medi' or 'med' spas are a combination of a day spa and medical clinic. The treatments offered will range from pampering treatments (such as massage, wraps and facials) to treatments more commonly found in a dermatology or plastic surgery medical centre (light and laser treatments, botox, chemical peels, hair implantation and other cosmetic surgeries etc.) Medical spas are generally popular in the USA, South America and in Asia. Given that these are medical facilities, they will normally be operated by a doctor or health professional depending on the local legal requirements.

Medical spas in Europe

Many European thermal spas refer to themselves as medical centers or medical spas, since they offer a full medical team, balneotherapy and medical non-invasive therapies – these are described in detail in another chapter. Whilst the term medical spa applies to thermal spas in Europe, in the US and other countries it normally refers to aesthetic cosmetic invasive and non-invasive treatment centers.

Common spa treatments

In wellness spas the most popular spa treatment is massage, followed by beauty treatments like facials and body treatments such as wraps and scrubs. Most spas will also offer manicures and pedicures. It would take another book to cover the main popular treatments found in spas today, however here is a summary of the most common treatments:

- **Heat treatments**: as seen from the history, heat was the basis of our first spa treatment; the aim – to relax the muscles and joints. Heat also helps cleanse the skin and the sweating helping to flush out waste products (sometimes called toxins) from the body.

- **Saunas**: A wood panelled room with a specially designed heater, constructed of, or filled with, rocks at a temperature of 70°C to 100°C. A sauna experience consists of repeated cycles of exposure to heat and cold, the length of duration is normally between 5 and 20 minutes. During the sauna the heart rate and blood pressure accelerate initially then as resistance of the blood vessels decreases the diastolic blood pressure decreases. It is thought that the increased body temperature also tricks the body into thinking it has a fever, which in turn stimulates the internal organs and immune system.

- **Infra-red sauna**: An infra-red sauna uses light to create heat which warms up the body internally inducing a sweat, but without the discomfort of a normal sauna. This is an advised alternative for people who cannot tolerate a normal sauna either through preference or health reasons.

- **Steam**: A steam room is normally at a temperature of 40°C and humidity of 100%. Although the temperature is lower than a sauna the humidity makes it feel quite hot. Like the sauna the steam room is good for blood circulation, easing muscle tension and creating a feeling of relaxation. The steam room has the extra benefit of having a positive effect for persons with respiratory problems such as asthma and allergies.

- **Hammam**: A typical hammam consists of three interconnected rooms: hot, warm and cold. The person initially relaxes in the warm room that is heated by a continuous flow of hot, dry air allowing the bather to perspire and acclimatize, before moving into the hotter room. Here, the bather may have a massage on a large marble stone, wash themselves or be washed by an attendant from water taps at the side. Once this is finished, they retire to the cooler room for a period of relaxation and refreshment.

- **Aroma cabins**: These are steam rooms or saunas into which aroma essential oils are added, offering the double benefit of heat and/or and aromatherapy. When inhaled in the steam, the different scents send messages to the brain through the limbic system, and have a physiological effects on various organs and systems in the body, specific to each type of oil. Popular oils include lavender, orange, marjoram, tangerine, peppermint, eucalyptus, chamomile etc.

- **Ice rooms, snow rooms and cold experiences**: Different cold experiences are often introduced alongside heat experiences. If the body is exposed to cold water immediately after a heat treatment, the dilated blood vessels contract, pressurize and squeeze the blood to the periphery blood vessels. It is this that gives the body a tingling relaxing effect as the blood circulation is stimulated.

- **Laconicum**: Typically, the laconicum was visited after the hot steam room before the person went into the warmer or colder baths, designed as a room

8

where the body can return to its normal temperature. Laconicums are used as relaxation areas maintained at temperatures of between 34 – 38C, often with heated lounge beds where guests can relax as long as they like, between or after their spa therapies.

■ Water treatments

- ■ **Jacuzzi and whirlpool baths**: A jacuzzi has all the benefits of relaxing in hot water, with the additional advantages of the effect of water currents on the body. These currents relax tight muscles and joints as well as release endorphins, the body's natural painkillers.

- ■ **Baths**: Aromatic oil extracts are added to warm water at a temperature of approximately 34°C for a relaxing effect. Flower petals are often added for an extra effect. An aroma bath treatment can be offered in normal bath water, but in many spas it is also given in a hydro or whirlpool bath, to have the effect of the water jet currents. Aroma baths are effective in that they combine the relaxing effects of heat and water with the additional benefits of the aromas and water currents. Baths are also offered with other ingredients such as milk and honey and mineral salts.

- ■ **Floatation tank**: Floatation baths contain water of approximately 25cm depth with a high concentration of salt, and the water is at a temperature of around 34°C. The salt, which is also a natural skin emollient and exfoliator, causes the body to float in the water. The feeling of weightlessness and the temperature of the water encourages the brain to go into a similar state to that prior to falling asleep, making it an ideal therapy for stress and high blood pressure. The therapy is often given in combination with lights and music to enhance the feeling of relaxation, or can be enjoyed in total silence and darkness for a sensory deprivation experience.

■ Massage

Whilst different massages use different techniques and have varying effects and health benefits, almost all massages will have a stress relieving effect. This can be attributed to the release of tension from the muscles, stimulation of the blood supply and the effect of physical contact on the body.

- ■ **Swedish massage**: The most widely used technique globally, which includes movements such as sliding/gliding, kneading, tapping, friction and shaking. Swedish massage has shown to be helpful in reducing pain, joint stiffness and helpful for persons with poor circulation. Although Swedish massage is accredited to Per Henrik Ling, the techniques were assembled by Johann Mezger who was Dutch.

- ■ **Foot massage**: An ordinary foot massage (not to be confused with reflexology) is a gentle general massage using Swedish techniques, concentrating on the feet, ankles, toes and calves. The massage is usually carried out on a normal massage bed with the feet slightly raised on a pad, but can also be performed whilst the guest is seated in a comfortable chair. The massage has the effect of improving the blood circulation, releasing tension, tiredness and stiffness in the feet and ankles, and is often preceded by a foot bath.

■ **Aroma massage**: Like aroma baths aromatherapy uses essential oils from plants to heal, alleviate pain and stress. These oils are highly concentrated botanical extracts, derived from leaves, bark, roots, seeds, resins and flowers. The oil is massaged into the body using different techniques depending on the result required. Aromatherapy massage is effective for the relief of stress and depression, poor circulation, high blood pressure, arthritis and some skin conditions.

■ **Hot stone therapy**: There are several types of hot stone treatments and/or massages. Hot stones, normally lava stones or basalt (a type of rock rich in iron that retains heat) are used. The stones are being heated whilst the body is massaged with oil. The warm stones are then pressed firmly into the muscles, gliding along the oil on the skin and may be placed in key Chakra points on the body for some minutes. As with most massages the hot stone massage is effective for back pain, poor circulation, stress relief and tension.

■ **Reflexology**: A form of massage using pressure on different areas of the body, mainly the feet, but also sometimes the hands and even the ears. Its approach is based on the belief that different points in the body are connected to different organs and bodily functions. By pressing these points, reflexology promotes itself as being able to relieve pain, improve overall health and speed up healing.

Popular non-western massage therapies

■ **Thai massage**: The massage is conducted on a floor mattress whilst the client wears light clothing. It is a full body treatment during which the practitioner uses steady and precisely directed pressing actions on the pressure points of the body. This is combined with passive stretching movements. Massaging these pressure points is believed to remove energy blockages and pain from the joints, spine and muscles. The massage increases muscle and joint mobility, flexibility and improves the blood and lymph circulation.

■ **Shiatsu**: Shiatsu comes from the Japanese words *shi* (meaning finger) and *atsu* (meaning pressure) and is a licensed medical therapy in Japan. The therapist uses palms, fingers, thumbs, knuckles elbows, knees and feet on the body's acupuncture points, along what are considered to be the body's meridians or energy channels. Shiatsu massages in addition to combating stress and pain, are believed to be effective in relieving headaches, respiratory and digestion problems.

Other massage techniques: include Lomi lomi from Hawaii, bamboo massages, Balinese and even massages with live snakes!

■ Other treatments

- **Wraps**: Spas will often offer a range of body wraps using ingredients which are applied onto the body and wrapped in foil or blankets, then left to be absorbed into the skin. Ingredients include various aroma oils, honey and cream, chocolate, muds and clay, algae, etc. Depending on the ingredients the packs may be effective for different skin conditions, detoxification, stimulating the metabolism, improving circulation and combating cellulite.

- **Scrubs**: the aim of scrubs are to clean and open up the pores and removed dead skin. Salts are normally used in this treatment, but sugars and other natural substances may also be employed. Scrubs can be followed by wraps and massages.

■ Beauty

A professional beauty treatment department in a spa will offer between five to eight facials and two to three different manicures or pedicures – some spas offer more, but having too many treatments can be detrimental as it can both overwhelm the clients and dilute the business. If the spa attracts a younger clientele, the spa should consider offering a range of express treatments (many younger clients are less willing to spend too much time on treatments – they want speed and result).

For resort, destination and hotel spas, given that many spas guests might only be visiting for a short time, the treatment menu should offer options that give visible results after one or two treatments.

A beauty treatment in a spa should be more than just a simple treatment. It should give the client a memorable and authentic experience by integrating massage, add-on touches, rituals, aromas, music and unique atmosphere.

The minimum a spa beauty department should offer is:

- **Skin facials**
  - ☐ Hydrating treatments for all skin types and for all ages combined with a manual based massage.
  - ☐ At least 1 treatment for oily and problematic skin.
  - ☐ Anti-aging (lifting, toning, revitalizing) 2-3 types.
  - ☐ Express treatments (hydrating, anti-aging, lifting, toning, brightening, mattifying, eye treatments).

- **Body treatments**
  - ☐ Body wraps for detoxification or toning (if there is a weight loss or detox package, body wraps can be included into the program).
  - ☐ Body scrubs to renew the skin surface.

- **Tinting**: Eyebrow, eyelash tinting.

- **Hands and feet**
  - ☐ Regular manicure / pedicure.
  - ☐ Shellac manicure.
  - ☐ Spa manicure / pedicure (including, massage and mask or paraffin).
- Grooming
  - ☐ Hair.
  - ☐ Make up.
  - ☐ Hair removal: soft/hard wax or sugaring (hair removal does not necessarily bring in much revenue so the treatments should be kept as short and simple as possible).

■ Beauty equipment

There are hundreds of different types of beauty equipment. Unfortunately, most require several treatments to show an effect. A good piece of equipment can be an excellent USP for day spas that have a regular clientele, but may not be necessarily suitable for destination, thermal or resort spas where guests might only be staying for a few days or at most a couple of weeks. For these short stays, guests most electro cosmetic treatments are not suitable, however LED light treatments and certain laser treatments (i.e. Mesol Laser) can act as an attractive add-on service.

Some popular beauty brands

8

Like equipment, there are literally thousands of beauty product lines. Here are some of the most popular found in spas:

- **Clarins**: French luxury spa brand, based exclusively on plants and plant extracts with manual treatments only (no equipment) using a unique Clarins technique.
- **Decleor**: French, based on essential oils and aromatherapy.
- **Babor**: German, precision formulas based on active ingredients with a tailor-made treatment approach.
- **Comfort Zone**: Italian luxury spa brand, a complete holistic spa brand, using both equipment and manual treatments to improve skin, body and mind.
- **Elemis:** A British luxury spa and skincare brand, which started on cruise ships, now popular worldwide, using organic extracts, pure oils and natural emollients.
- **Aromatherapy Associates**: A British brand offering skin, body and relaxational spa treatments, based on hand blended natural aroma oils for the mind, body and skin.
- **Thalgo**: Originally founded to supply thalassotherapy centers in France, this French brand's products are based on marine algae and sea.
- **Sothys**: French luxury skin and spa brand based on natural botanicals.

Spa and beauty product lines

Spas will also often use products from a professional spa brand line in their treatments as well as offering them for retail. The benefits of this are that normally the brand line will provide the products and rituals, training as well as the brand name and reputation. The downside is that the cost will be higher than using local products and doing inhouse training.

There are numerous spa and cosmetic brands, so choosing the right one(s) is an important strategic decision for the spa manager. When making this decision they should consider the following;

- How important is having a famous brand name to the spa?
- How relevant is the country where the brand originates from to the guests?
- How will it fit the spa concept, philosophy and other spa treatments – natural, organic, ritual, medical, etc?
- How will it fit the guest profile (nationality, age, class, purchasing power)
- Will it focus on facials or body treatments?
- Are there treatments for men?
- How simple is to use their products?
- What is the support given by the company?
- What training do they provide?
- How much money is needed to invest in the start-up?
- What minimum number of products (retail and treatment) do the brand insist you need to buy?
- What is the return on investment?

If inventory control is important, many companies offer boxed treatments with premeasured treatment doses with easy to follow step by step protocols.

Some spas will have their own inhouse line. Whilst this can emphasize the locality and uniqueness of the spa, an 'own brand' is not always easy to organise. Many manufacturers often will not be able to compete with the quality of the major brands, they will also expect a minimum quantity order to make the venture worthwhile, a quantity which might not be financially viable for the spas.

■ Spa treatment menus

A good spa treatment menu should fit:

- The spa concept (affordable, luxury, historical, modern etc).
- The type of spa facility (day spa, destination, hotel, medical etc).
- The clients' profile (older, younger, nationality, culture, class, men/women ratio etc) .
- The clients' goal (relaxation, beauty, slimming etc).

Ideally the menu should not be overlong or overcomplicated, as offering too much can be disorientating for clients. Styles of treatment information brochures vary, however the recent trends show that today's guests do not have time for long, flowing, flowery descriptions, they instead want to know the following information:

- What the treatment is – a clear name that indicates what the treatment is.
- How long the treatment is.
- The aim of the treatment.
- What happens during the treatment.
- Its immediate effects and long-term results.
- Possible contraindications.

The information should be clear, specific and concise.

Current trends

Today's spas are being influenced by the fact that wellness, fitness and spa services are now available everywhere – practically on every corner. Therefore, in order to be successful, spas need to offer wellness and spa experiences that are unique and in a unique setting. If spas are expecting their clients to travel to visit them, they have to be able to offer something more than what their guests can receive in their immediate locale or perform on themselves. People are becoming more educated, more travelled and therefore more demanding in what they expect.

With more focus on sustainability and with people becoming more discerning about what they put in and on their bodies, the 'natural' trend continues to gain momentum – consumers want to return to nature and natural products, and healing or the 'clean trend' as it is sometimes called, is now in vogue: clean air, clean food, clean therapies and clean thoughts.

The growing aging population demographic shift is affecting today's trends, resulting in an increased demand for anti and healthy aging programs (including rehabilitation and therapies for age related conditions). There is also a growing segment of older single women. As a result wellness programs influenced by the recent 'me too' movement are gaining in popularity, with spas offering female focused workshops and wellness experiences. Depression (a leading cause of disability in older women) is resulting in more demand for anti-stress, spiritual and mental wellness programs.

Because of this 'finding meaning' or 'transformational wellness' trend, more and more spas are offering lifestyle workshops and programs. New forms of popular exercise such as 'flying yoga' (suspended by bands) and 'intrinity yoga' (yoga on a slanted board) being just two examples, likewise new forms of meditation in unique environments – forest bathing (meditating in woodland) and meditating on surf boards are being offered. With CBD becoming legal in many

8

countries and states, meditation combined with small amounts of cannabis or psychedelic myco-mediations are finding their niche.

Silent retreats are also now well established, and at the other end of the spectrum, extreme wellness retreats are gaining popularity, which include exposing the body to extreme heat or cold (swimming in ice rivers, etc) sometimes combined with intensive physical activity in the form of boot camps.

The old model of hospitals and clinics delivering conventional medical treatments, and spas offering pampering and lifestyle products, is becoming more fluid; many spas have started to introduce rehabilitation and medical evidence based and/or aesthetic procedures treatments into their offers, whilst many clinics and hospitals (particularly in the USA) have introduced wellness services such as meditation, massage and aroma therapies, halotherapy and even hypnotherapy. In short, in many instances, spa and medical services are now being delivered under one roof – either in clinics or in spas.

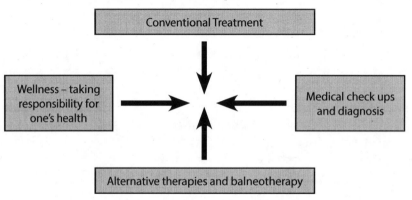

Figure8.3: Medical and wellness services in spas.

Feedback from the interviews – what the experts say

Spa managers were asked what they thought would be the main trends in spas in the future. Here is a summary of their responses.

■ Several interviewees refer to sustainability, green, energy efficient and eco-friendly spas. Emphasis is placed on natural locations, organic treatments (e.g. beauty, food) and more authentic traditional therapies using local, natural resources (e.g. mineral water, mud). Food should be healthy and veganism was noted as a current trend.

■ Healthy lifestyle is mentioned many times and the need for prevention. Ionana Marian, Secretary General of the Organization of Balneary and Spa Tourism in Romania suggests that "the spa therapist will become the client's mentors in all the wellness areas: food, sleep, daily movement, spa treatments, mental relaxation, spiritual evolution etc."

- An holistic approach is recommended, including the convergence of wellness and medical services. This can help to combat lifestyle diseases. Suggested services include evidence-based healing using local and natural resources, as well as high end technology medicine (e.g. immunotherapy, genetic therapy, rehabilitation robotics, DNA testing).

- It is suggested that treatment offers could be differentiated better according the customer's age, e.g., family spas, more spas for local guests, spas for aging guests, including those with dementia. Ideally, spas should be made more affordable for consumers in the way that fitness rooms have been.

- Mental wellness is noted as an important trend, including mindfulness and spirituality, as well as 'stress busting' which was described as 'the new detox'. The idea of 'brain optimisation' was suggested for integration into spas using non-invasive methods.

- The use of technology, especially artificial intelligence, was mentioned as an important tool for collecting data, personalizing service and creating customised products. However, the human touch is still considered to be essential in spas, even though robots could perform some tasks.

- Overall, it is considered that spas need to be multi-functional. As suggested by Stavros Mavridis, Wellness and Spa Director, "hybrid wellness facilities combining medical, wellness, ancient healing practices and spiritual services"; and by Andrew Gibson from SVP, Los Angeles "a more integrative approach between fitness, nutrition, relaxation, mindfulness and pampering".

8

Research and further reading

Even though it was published more than a decade ago, Cohen and Bodeker's (2008) book offers some useful insights into different aspects of the spa industry, including historical traditions as well as definitions. Tabbacchi's (2010) article about the growth of the spa industry and different types of spas is also still useful. Smith and Puczkó (2013) include a detailed history of health and wellness tourism which covers most regions of the world. Frost and Laing (2017) provide an interesting history of spa tourism including examples of spa towns. They build on the work of the historian John Walton, who has written several excellent works about the history of seasides as well as of spas (Walton, 2012). McCarthy (2017) writes about the psychology of spas and the therapeutic benefits of spa visits and treatments. The chapter by Diekmann, Smith and Ceron (2020) examines the changing structure of government support for spa services in both Western and Central Europe, in those countries where spa visits for health were traditionally state financed.

References

Cambridge Dictionaries Online (2019) https://dictionary.cambridge.org/dictionary/english/spa (accessed 26.08.2019)

Clapham, A. and Constable, R. (1982) *As Nature Intended*, Oxford: Heinemann.

Cohen, M. and Bodeker, G. (Eds) (2008) *Understanding the Global Spa Industry*. Oxford, England: Elsevier, p. 3.

Cooper, P. and Cooper, M. (2009) *Health and Wellness Tourism. Spas and Hot Springs*, Bristol: Channel View.

Crebbin-Bailey, J., Harcup, J. and Harrington, J. (2005) *The Spa Book*, Atlanta: Thomson.

Diekmann, A., Smith, M. and Ceron, J-P. (2020) 'From Welfare to Wellness: European Spas at the Crossroads', in A. Diekmann and S. McCabe (eds) *Handbook of Social Tourism*, Camberley: Edward Elgar Publishing, Chapter 9.

Frost, W. and Laing, J. (2017) 'History of spa tourism: spirituality, rejuvenation and socialisation', in Smith, M. K. and Puczkó, L. (eds) *The Routledge Handbook of Health Tourism*, London: Routledge, pp.9-19.

ISPA (International Spa Association) (2019) 'About ISPA', https://experienceispa.com/#about/ (accessed 26.08.2019).

McCarthy, J. (2017) 'The Psychology of Spa: The science of 'holistic' wellbeing', in Smith, M. K. and Puczkó, L. (eds) *The Routledge Handbook of Health Tourism*, London: Routledge, pp.127-137.

National Roman Museum (2014) 'Baths of Diocletician', http://archeoroma.beniculturali.it/en/museums/national-roman-museum-baths-diocletian (accessed 26.08.2014)

Smith, M. K. and Puczkó, L. (2013) *Health, Tourism and Hospitality: Spas, Wellness and Medical Travel*, London: Routledge.

Smith, V. (2007) *Clean – A History of Hygiene and Purity*, Oxford: Oxford University Press.

Tabacchi, M. (2010) 'Current research and events in the spa industry', *Cornell Hospitality Quarterly*, **51** (1), 102-117, Doi: 10.1177/1938965509356684

Walton, J. K. (2012) 'Health, sociability, politics and culture: Spas in history, spas and history: An overview', *Journal of Tourism History*, **4** (1), 1-14, Doi: 10.1080/1755182X.2012.671372

9 Health, wellness, mental and spiritual wellness

Ideally, staff working in the spa industry should have a clear understanding of the meanings of health and wellness and their related concepts.

Health

Promoting and providing opportunities to improve the health of its clients is the essence of what a spa facility should do, and this ideally should be actively driven by the spa manager – health being defined by the World Health Organization (WHO, 1948) as ...."as state of complete physical, mental and social well-being, not merely the absence of disease or infirmity". In other words, health is not just about being free of disease, it is about being well on all levels – physically, mentally and socially.

The World Health Organization's constitution also lists two other principles that are of particular relevance to spas:

1 The extension to all peoples of the benefits of medical, psychological and related knowledge is essential to the fullest attainment of health.

2 Informed opinion and active co-operation on the part of the public are of the utmost importance in the improvement of the health of the people.

   (WHO, 1946)

Taking these two principles into consideration, spa managers are in the ideal position of being able to promote the benefits of living a positive, healthy lifestyle and really help their clients to improve their well-being.

■ Health tourism

According to Smith and Puczkó (2018: 63) "health tourism covers those types of tourism which have as a primary motivation, the contribution to physical, mental and/or spiritual health through medical and wellness-based activities which increase the capacity of individuals to satisfy their own needs and function better as individuals in their environment and society".

Health tourism is seen as umbrella term for 'wellness tourism' and 'medical tourism':

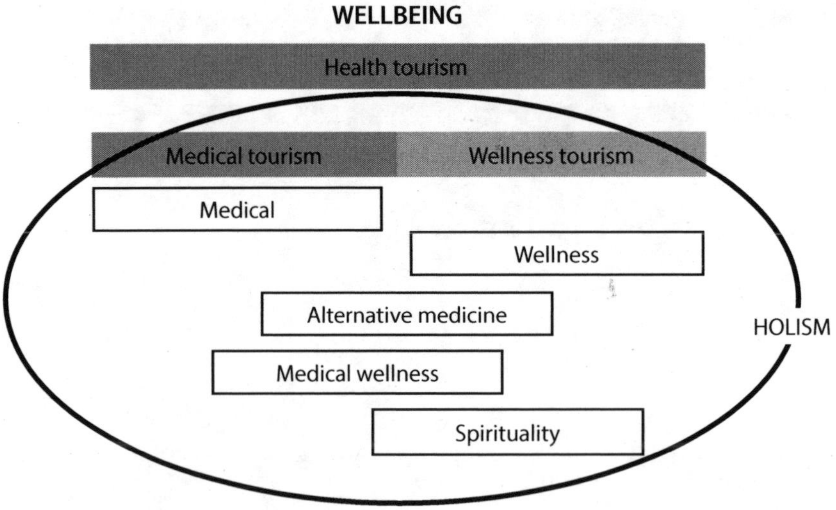

Figure 9.1: The scope of health tourism. Adapted from Smith and Puczkó (2018).

'Wellness tourism' refers to traveling to improve and balance one's overall health and wellbeing through preventative and proactive activities (such as fitness, diet, relaxation and healing treatments), whereas 'medical tourism' is where people travel from one country to another to receive medical treatment. 'Holism' or 'holistic' refers to either the mind/body/spirit connection or if referring to holistic medicine includes treating not just the illness but the root cause and inviting patient involvement (Smith and Puczkó, 2018)

■ Wellness

For anybody working in the spa industry, particularly internationally, it is important to be aware that like the word 'spa' the word 'wellness' also has different meanings to different cultures. In parts of Europe for example, it infers a sauna area or leisure facility offering pampering and relaxation services, whereas in America 'wellness' will encompass all areas of one's life from fitness, to diet, to relationships to even aging and finance. In the UK, wellness has similar connotations to the USA, but with the word 'wellbeing' being preferred.

With respect to definitions there are literally hundreds - Figure 9.2 gives just a few examples. In these examples, general themes that stand out are 'life-long quest', 'continual ongoing process', 'taking personal responsibility', 'optimum health', 'preventing illness' and 'holistic'. One particular theme worth emphasizing, is the need for an individual to take personal responsibility for their health and wellness, in other words wellness is not something that you can purchase or get once, but is a continual ongoing lifelong process.

"a conscious, self-directed and evolving process of achieving full potential."
— *The National Wellness Institute*

... **the active pursuit of activities, choices and lifestyles that lead to a state of holistic health.** *The Global Wellness Institute*

The quality or state of being healthy in body and mind, especially as the result of deliberate effort. An approach to healthcare that emphasizes preventing illness and prolonging life as opposed to treating diseases.
www.dictionary.com/browse/wellness

Wellness is an active process of becoming aware of and making choices towards a healthy and fulfilling life. It is more than being free from illness, it is a dynamic process of change and growth. A good or satisfactory condition of existence; a state characterized by health, happiness, and prosperity; welfare.
www.globalwellnessday.org/about/what-is-wellness/

Wellness is the act of practicing healthy habits on a daily basis to attain better physical and mental health outcomes, so that instead of just surviving, you're ***thriving***.
www.pfizer.com/health-wellness/wellness/what-is-wellness

Figure 9.2: Definitions of wellness.

Cohen and Bodeker (2008: 8) take the concept of wellness one step further by describing it as "a multidimensional state of being 'well' where the inner and outer worlds are in harmony."

In short, there is no one definition, however the Global Wellness Institute does offer a clean, concise description: "the active pursuit of activities, choices and lifestyles that lead to a state of holistic health" (Global Wellness Institute, 2020).

Where does wellness come from?

The pursuit of wellness and holistic health has been around in all parts of the globe for thousands of years, from Ayurveda in India and Chinese medicine from ancient China, to the ancient Greeks, where the physician Hippocrates focused on not just treating disease but on diet and lifestyle too.

The western concept of wellness has its roots not just from the ancient world, but also from the 18th and 19th centuries when the importance of clean, healthy living and diet fed its way into the mainstream.

The modern use of the word 'wellness' derives from the 1950s when J.I. Rodale launched *Prevention* magazine followed by the publication of Halbert L. Dunn's *High Level Wellness*, published in 1961. The concept of wellness as we know it today was first established in a university campus in the 1970s and then expanded with the fitness revolution of the 1980s and early 90s, followed by later integration into spa concepts.

Perhaps one of the most recent influences on the concept of modern wellness has been the study of blue zones which evolved out of a National Geographic expedition to discover the secrets of life longevity; its findings proving essential knowledge for anyone working in spas or health tourism:

9

Blue Zones

These are locations that have the highest percentages of centenarians (people who live to the age of 100 or more) – Loma Linda (California, USA); Nicoya, (Costa Rica); Sardinia, (Italy); Ikaria, (Greece) and Okinawa, (Japan). Each of these areas were discovered to have certain characteristics, for example in Loma Linda (California) they found a high number of Seventh Day Adventists who neither smoke nor drink and in Okinawa (Japan) the locals follow the 80% rule (eating until they feel 80% full) with a healthy diet of fish and fresh fruit and vegetables. However, it is the commonalities from these locations that proved to be the most interesting. In addition to being situated in beautiful surroundings (calm, relatively stress-free environments with pleasant climates) their inhabitants:

- Continually move naturally and moderately throughout the day (walking, gardening, working in the fields).
- Tend not to retire but remain active in older life too.
- Have a life where stress levels are low and managed (for example, in Greece and Sardinia afternoon naps are part of the culture).
- Eat a plant-based diet.
- Have a sense of purpose and spiritual faith.
- Belong to cultures with a sense of both community and strong family ties.

  (Buettner and Skemp, 2016)

These principles are the basis now for many spa programs and concepts, not only in terms of spa treatments, but as a founding basis for lifestyle change – principles which hopefully spa managers will demonstrate through leading by example!

The dimensions of wellness

The Global Wellness Institute lists six wellness dimensions:

Figure 9.3: The six dimensions of wellness. Source: Global Wellness Institute (2018).

- **Physical**: A healthy body through exercise, nutrition, sleep, etc.
- **Mental**: Engagement with the world through learning, problem solving, creativity, etc.
- **Emotional**: Being in touch with, aware of, accepting of, able to express one's feelings (and those of others).
- **Spiritual**: Our search for meaning and purpose in human existence.
- **Social**: Connecting with, interacting with, and contributing to other people and our communities.
- **Environmental**: A healthy environment free of hazards, awareness of the role we play in bettering rather than denigrating the natural environment.
  (Global Wellness Institute, 2018)

These components relate to, overlap and interact with each another and should not be viewed as separate identities. Spa managers should also be aware that new dimensions are continually being added to this wellness 'wheel', (financial and occupational being just two examples).

Emotional wellness

Emotions are a reaction to our thoughts, attitudes and the events and environment around us – in other words emotions can be compared to a barometer, reflecting our inner and outer worlds. Emotional wellness is described here as being aware of, in tune with, and listening to one's feelings. This sounds simple, but in today's fast paced competitive world, ignoring our emotions and ploughing on, regardless of the signals that they are sending is a common trait that can have a serious negative impact on our health. The role of a well conceptualized spa product should be to offer products that promote emotional self-awareness and services to educate and motivate guests to live a healthy lifestyle, presented in an environment conducive to bringing out positive emotions.

Physical wellness

Being physically fit, having good nutrition, time to relax and destress are essential to well-being. Cardio fitness, strength and flexibility are the essential components of physical wellness. Spas should offer fitness facilities and activities to improve all areas of fitness and diet, in an environment that supports relaxation and stress relief. In addition, an evidence-based healthy nutritional cuisine and dietary support should also be available.

Social wellness

Social wellness is dependent on having good communication and relationship skills. It does not matter how physically fit one is or how pleasant our environments are if our lives are being affected by conflicts and dysfunctional relationships. Who we choose to surround ourselves with has a considerable impact on the quality of our lives. Spas have the opportunity to offer programs and support for their clients on how to improve their communication and people skills (i.e. relationship workshops and other forms of counselling). Social wellness also has an impact on the design and layout of spas and should include spaces for both interaction (to bring people together) and solitude (for contemplation and relaxation). A recent study discovered that the more superficial interactions a person has, the more it increases their happiness level as it maintains a sense of belonging to a community – so spas have their role to play (Sandstrum and Dunn, 2014).

Environmental wellness

This does not only refer to living in harmony with our environment, but should include the spaces we live and work in, and how these can positively or negatively affect our wellness state. Buildings have the unique ability to uplift or depress our spirits. Zen gardens, meditative spaces, relaxation rooms and lounges are now part and parcel of most spa experiences. An uplifting spa environment is absolutely critical to the spa experience of the guest, not just in terms of being ecological, design, mood, space planning and lighting but even more importantly – how the energy of the team contributes to the spa atmosphere!

Occupational wellness

Often when workplace wellness is discussed (as we spend most of our working days in our work spaces), the emphasis is placed on building design and amenities, however, the atmosphere, energy and culture of a work environment will have the most impact on a person's wellbeing. A toxic work environment can destroy the benefits of any beautifully designed, ecologically friendly building. The commute to and from our workplace can also have a massive influence on the quality of our lives. Many spas now offer programs on managing careers, life and work-related skills.

■ Medical wellness and prevention

Another contentious terminology, connected particularly to spas in Central Europe, is that of 'medical wellness', sometimes referred to as 'prevention' (meaning 'disease prevention' or 'preventing health problems developing'). According to the Medical Wellness Association, medical wellness is defined as "an approach to delivering health care that considers multiple influences on a person's health and consequently multiple modalities for treating and preventing disease as well as promoting optimal well-being" (Breuleux, 2004: 1).

Essentially medical wellness combines evidence-based medical diagnosis and therapies with wellness elements in a clinical setting – practices which must be prescribed and coordinated by a doctor or health professional.

In the past, medical wellness and prevention programs in spas had a 'general' approach focusing on de-stressing, detoxing, weight loss and re-energizing. In recent times, these programs have evolved to specialize, so that a client will visit a medical wellness centre for a specific medical problem (e.g. lower back pain, early onset degenerative conditions, or high blood pressure), and in addition to tackling the specific disease or condition the program will be supported by general healthy lifestyle therapies adapted to the individual's goals and health needs.

As Figure 9.4 shows, the aim of medical wellness and prevention is to lengthen both the healthy part of one's life and at the same time improve the quality of one's life (and possibly lengthen the actual lifespan as well).

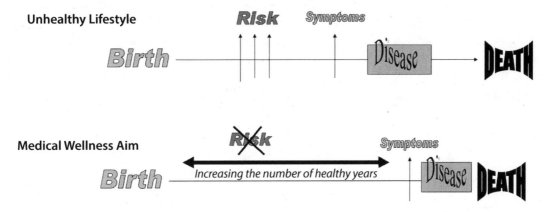

Figure9.4: The aim of medical wellness.

According to the World Health Organization, the main causes of death world-wide are heart disease, strokes and pulmonary diseases. Cancers and diabetes are also high up in the table (WHO, 2016). We know that most heart related diseases, type 2 diabetes and many cancers are mainly caused by lifestyle behaviours and choices. Spa managers have a role to play in promoting programs and services in their spas that promote and support healthy life choices to decrease the risk factors for these diseases in their clients.

With reference to cancer, according to Dr. Sanjay Gupta (the chief medical officer for CNN) it is possible for a person to reduce their risk by taking the fol-lowing 10 actions:

1, 2 and 3 NOT smoking. (Smoking is linked to at least three in ten cancer deaths according to the American Cancer Society).

4 Staying active. Inactivity and obesity are linked to cancer.

5 Eating plenty of fruits and vegetables.

6 Limiting the amount of red meat and processed meats in the diet, and meat that is consumed is lean.

7 Use low-fat cooking methods like roasting, baking, broiling, steaming or poaching. Also, choosing low-fat or non-fat milk and yogurt.

8 Limiting alcohol consumption or avoiding alcohol altogether.

9 Protecting oneself from the sun – wearing sunscreen to limit exposure to dam-aging ultraviolet rays.

10 Girls (and now boys) receiving the HPV vaccine before they are sexually active.

(Gupta, 2007)

It is possible to see the connections between modern evidence-based health advice from medical sources, the lifestyles of Blue Zone inhabitants and the dimensions of wellness. It is information from sources such as these that spa managers should use to form the bedrock of wellness and prevention programs in their spas.

Smoking and alcohol consumption

It is not enough for spas to simply provide guests with relaxation and services to get healthy, spa managers and team members have the potential to be much more proactive in combating the poor lifestyle habits of their clients. As emphasized in the CNN report, in addition to diet and sedentary lifestyles, smoking is identified as one of the main causes of cancer. Spas have a key role to play when it comes to providing guests with advice and programs to quit smoking. The objective of visiting a spa is to improve one's health, which if the client smokes, is in total contradiction to the aim of the visit. Spas, particularly medical and thermal spas which have doctors on the premises, are in the perfect position to really make an impact on the lifestyle of their guests. A doctor or fitness professional who is able to communicate effectively the importance of quitting smoking can essentially save a life.

There is more and more evidence that alcohol is far more damaging to our health than previously thought. A global study published in *The Lancet* has shown there is no safe level of alcohol consumption. Whilst moderate drinking may protect against heart diseases, the risk of cancer and other diseases outweighs these protections. The recommended limit is 14 units a week which is seven 175ml glasses of wine (Ives, 2018). Today's spas, even though income from alcohol sales might be an important revenue source, have a responsibility to highlight the dangers and help redirect consumer habits.

Mental and spiritual wellness

We continually are striving to seek out positive emotions and avoid negative ones. In order to be 'emotionally well' we have to be proactive in developing thought processes, healthy behaviours and habits that will have a positive effect on our emotional state. The problem is that healthy behaviours do not necessarily tend to produce an instant emotional change of state in the way that many unhealthy behaviours do. In other words, it is easier to have a glass of wine than go for a workout! It is for this reason that people turn to quick fixes such as alcohol, drugs, binge eating or diversions, such as shopping or planning the next holiday, as they result in instant pleasurable emotions.

Figure 9.5 shows clearly how the different wellness components and indeed poor lifestyle choices have their impact on emotions.

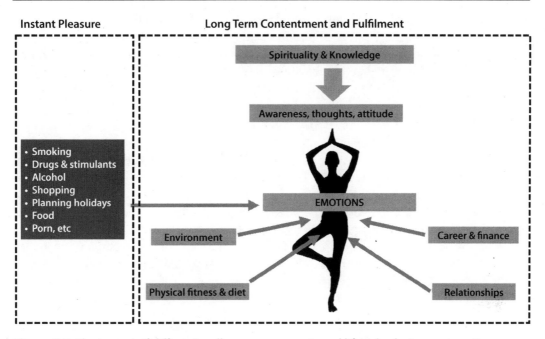

Figure 9.5: The impact of different wellness components and lifestyle choices on emotions.

As the picture shows, how we think, focus and direct our thoughts is critical to our overall wellness state. Having a positive (as opposed to a negative) spiritual belief also will strongly influence thought processes.

One of the most quoted facts regarding happiness is the '50, 10, 40% formula' (50% of happiness being determined by genes, 10% by circumstances and 40% by actions). Many psychologists and self-help personalities use this formula to prioritize the importance of positive thinking and attitude. Whilst our attitudes and our thought processes have a massive impact on our life, the importance of other factors (such as our relationships, physical health, and our work and social environments) should not be underestimated.

■ Happiness and mental wellness

There have been many studies examining the link between happiness, life satisfaction, mental health and success. According to these, it does appear that if somebody is happy, they tend to be kinder, less selfish, more cooperative, more successful, healthier and live longer. Here are two studies worth mentioning:

■ **The nuns study**: autobiographies from 180 Catholic nuns, written at the age of 22, were scored for happiness levels (positive, negative and neutral) then compared with their age of death. The difference in the median age at death between the negative and positive grades was 9.4 years. In short, the nuns who wrote positive autobiographies at a younger age lived the longest (Danner, Snowden, Wallace and Friesen, 2001).

■ **The college year book study**: the smiles of 100 college female students in a yearbook were categorized. Information about these women was followed up on at the ages of 21, 27, 43 and 52. Those who displayed positive emotional expressions had favourable outcomes in marriage (they were more likely to be married and to have stayed married) and in personal wellbeing (Smith, 2001).

■ Happiness and wealth

The connection between happiness and money is interesting to say the least. According to studies there is little difference between somebody who is 'just about' comfortable with their basic needs being met and multi-millionaires. What tends to be more important than the actual amount of money is how we perceive our wealth compared to those around us and the security that we feel about our future financial prospects. Financial wellbeing is necessary but it cannot replace physical, mental and spiritual wellbeing. There have also been studies into lottery winners, showing an immediate high on winning and then a descent back into a normal state after a period of time. This can be contrasted with the experience of amputees who experience extreme loss and despair at the time of the trauma, which later turns to acceptance.

Measuring happiness

More and more surveys are being produced showing the happiness and wellbeing level of countries' citizens. The World Happiness Report bases its measurements on GDP per capita, life expectancy, social support from friends and family, freedom to make life choices, generosity and donating to others, perceptions of corruption, happiness and laughter, worry, sadness or anger (World Happiness Report, 2019).

Nation states are beginning to realize that the happiness level of their citizens is an essential part of good governance. The United Arab Emirates has appointed a minister of state for positivity and happiness whose role is to develop benchmarks and tools to measure happiness, to include happiness into government policies and programs, and to promote happiness as a lifestyle in the community. (UAE government, 2019). Meanwhile the UK government has appointed a Minister of Loneliness to tackle health and social issues associated with living alone.

■ Influencers of the mental wellness trend

The pursuit of health and mental harmony has been around for millennia. The ancient Greeks recognised the importance of mental health and resilience, and this was reflected in *Stoicism*, practiced by Epictetus, Seneca and Marcus Aurelius, where the goal of life is to live in harmony and agreement with the nature of the universe and recognise that the only real possession one has is one's character (Robertson, 2013). It takes the view that we do not control and cannot rely on external events to bring happiness, only ourselves and our responses.

Religion has also played its part in the mental wellness trend, from Hinduism and its sacred texts 'the Vedas' (codes of conduct to live one's life), to Taoism from China, which like stoicism promotes living in harmony with nature, virtue, self-development and contemplation. The Abrahamic religions with their common themes of justice and compassion also have had their influence. However, it is Buddhism (which, because it does not include worshipping a creator god is not often seen as a religion in the Western sense of the word) and its emphasis on self-awareness, kindness, wisdom and meditation, that has had a major impact on mental health trends and on modern spa concepts, particularly in the West.

The self-help movement has also had a strong impact on the development of the modern spa mental wellness trend. The transcendentalist movement of the 19th century and the writings of Ralph Waldo Emerson promoting individual freedom and action were instrumental in opening the way for the self-help movement. By the first half of the 20th century, self-development started to gain popularity in the form of self-help books, most notably Dale Carnegie's *How to Win Friends and Influence People* and *How to Stop Worrying and Start Living* and Napoleon Hill's *Think Rich and Grow Rich* – (which is just as much about positive thinking and attitude as about financial gain). These books became the best-selling self-help books of all time. The themes of positive thinking and living a proactive life were further expanded on in a series of books written by Norman Vincent Peal with Christian faith as their foundation.

■ Recent leaders and influencers in the mental wellbeing and self-help movement

The list of personalities who have been instrumental in promoting positive thinking and mental wellbeing is continually increasing. People working in spas, particularly on the front line – should be aware of the most recognised self-help, mental wellness leaders:

- **Louise Hay**: often referred to as the queen of self-help became well known through her book, *Heal your Body,* published in the 1970s. Her message is that every thought we think will manifest itself in our life – therefore redirecting and controlling our thoughts should be the starting point for changing negative patterns and to living a life of wellbeing. Her message was later adapted and promoted in a book called *The Power* by Rhonda Byrne

- **Anthony Robbins**: an entrepreneur, author and perhaps the world's most famous life coach, took the step of positive thinking one step further, his message being that thinking positively is not enough. In order to achieve success and happiness, a strategy, plan and action is essential. He has become a world authority on leadership and organizational turnarounds and now offers his own training program for people to become life coaches.

- **Ekhart Tolle**: author of *The Power of Now.* Tolle's approach is based on Buddhist philosophy – self-awareness, observation of one's thoughts and feelings and realizing that unhappiness is caused not by outside situations but our internal reactions to them.

9

- **The Dalai Lama:** his views, similar to Ekhart Tolle's, promote the cultivation of values such as compassion, forgiveness, tolerance, contentment and self-awareness and discipline. Control of thoughts and mental discipline are key in achieving mental wellness and contentment.

- **Oprah Winfrey:** has used her platform as a chat show host and television producer as a force for good and also to give a voice to personalities like those listed above in promoting physical, spiritual and in particular mental health and wellbeing. She has now entered into a collaboration with Prince Harry and Apple in creating a new series on promoting mental health (or mental fitness as it is now being referred to) (Robinson and Respers, 2019).

The transformational wellness trend in spas

The transformational wellness trend, where clients seek to find meaning in their lives and develop their mental and spiritual wellbeing, is now a growing spa segment albeit more prevalent in the USA and western Europe. Related services and treatments can be categorized as follows:

- Mental wellbeing – mindfulness, psychology and counselling, life coaching, meditation.
- Social wellbeing – counselling and workshops, spaces and activities for interaction.
- Exercise (cardio, yoga, tai chi, qi gong).
- Diet – foods to promote mental health.
- Spiritual and metaphysical – treatments and therapies to promote spiritual health.
- Ayurveda.

Mental wellbeing

Self-awareness, being mindful and having the skills to guide our thought patterns, is the starting point for mental wellbeing. Spas which focus on mental and spiritual wellbeing will offer some of the following services:

- **Mindfulness:** the basic human ability to be fully present, aware of where we are and what we are doing, and not overly reactive or overwhelmed by what is going on around us (Mindful Org, 2014). A similar approach to Buddhism, Stoicism and the philosophies promoted by the Dalai Lama and Ekhart Tolle.

- **Counselling:** is where a therapist or expert gives advice to a client about a life issue, challenge or problem. Counselling, otherwise known as 'talking therapy', can be carried out individually (either in person, on the phone or online), in couples or in groups. Counsellors tend to focus on a particular issue or behavioural problem such as stress, weight problems, addiction and other life challenging issues.

- **Psychology**: on the other hand "is the study of the mind, how it works and how it affects behaviour" (Brazier, 2018). Although many spas do offer a psychologist, psychologists tend to deal with more serious mental issues and illnesses and addictions as opposed to a life coach or counsellor.

- **Life coaching**: in the same way that a coach will help to improve an athlete's sports performance, a life coach will help to improve areas of a person's life. This can be anything from setting health and fitness goals, to weight loss, to improving relationships, finance or career. Life coaching is different to counselling in that its starting point is not so much addressing a problem but improving existing performance and maximizing an individual's potential.

- **Cognitive Behavioural Therapy (CBT)**: a form of 'talking therapy', CBT a therapy commonly used for treating depression and anxiety. Its starting point is self-awareness and the ability to observe one's thoughts objectively, assess their relation to reality and then find solutions to overcome them. CBT is effective for eating disorders and, because its approach has similarities with stoicism and mindfulness, it is a preferred form of psychological therapy for spas.

- **Meditation**: is practiced by focusing on a single point. Examples include the breath, scanning the body, detached observation of one's thoughts or even focusing on a sound or chant. The aim of meditation is to improve self-awareness and the mental state and therefore the quality of life. It is effective in developing focus, attention span and concentration. Studies have shown meditation to lower stress, blood pressure and anxiety and improve mental and emotional health. Meditation is an important tool in any mental wellness program.

■ Social wellbeing

As mentioned previously, casual interactions play an important part in a person's quality of life and wellbeing. Spas are in the unique position of being able to promote social wellbeing through the following ways:

1. **Providing a layout and design conducive to both solitude and social interaction**: having spaces that encourage clients to interact, but also having spaces where clients can experience quiet and isolation, achieved through careful space planning and reinforced with interior design, lighting, smell and sounds.

2. **Offering programs that encourage social interaction**: lifestyle lectures on fitness, diet and relationships are common in many spas. In addition, activities that bring people together such as indoor and outdoor exercise classes, art and spa, learning different crafts, games and cooking lessons etc. In the 19th century, European spas were as much about social interaction as health – concerts, dancing and evening entertainment are still offered as part of the stay in most European traditional spa resorts. These types of spas tend to attract seniors, many of whom are single, therefore such social programs can help to combat loneliness and depression.

9

3 **Therapy and counselling on relationships**. These can include sessions on relationship skills, exploring intimacy for couples, dealing with life challenges such as bereavement or divorce.

■ Exercise

In relationship to mental wellness cardio exercise has an important role to play. Aerobic type exercise such as fast walking, jogging, stepping, swimming, dancing, cardio exercise classes (Zumba, step, aerobics) has been proved to reduce anxiety and depression. This is in part caused by increased blood circulation to the brain which influences the limbic system (which controls mood), the amygdala (which generates fear in response to stress) and the hippocampus (which plays an important part in memory and mood). Distraction from everyday routines and social interaction also will have a positive influence (Sharma, Madaan and Petty, 2006).

Exercises effective for mental wellbeing tend to be those that promote self-awareness, core strength, balance and flexibility such as:

- **Yoga**: with its origins in India, yoga (derived from the word *yuj* to bind) is a practice, philosophy and religion based on the eight yoga sutras. Modern yoga practiced in spas mainly focuses on '*asanas*' or poses and '*pranayama*' breathing and meditation. The aim of yoga is to balance, stretch and strengthen the body and mind through practicing asanas, breathing, stretching and meditating.

- **Tai Chi**: an ancient Chinese mind-body exercise that is commonly practiced in spas. It involves slow flowing, focused movements with deep breathing. Because Tai Chi is low impact and puts less stress on the joints, it is especially suitable for seniors and spas that cater for this segment. Tai Chi improves balance, posture, agility and coordination. It also has a good effect on mental concentration, focus and reduces anxiety and promotes a calm mind.

- **Qi Gong**: has many forms, from vigorous martial arts exercises to slower techniques. Many of the movements follow the pathways of the energy meridian lines. The aim of Qi Gong is to manage and master one's qi energy flow. Tai Chi is often referred to as a form of Qi Gong.

- **Autogen Training**: was developed by a German neurologist as a relaxation technique and is a form of self-hypnosis. Autogenic means 'self-induced'. In a relaxed state the exercise involves repetitions of a set of visualizations on each body part to induce deep relaxation. During the therapy the brain waves drop to a meditative state. It has been deemed helpful for stress, anxiety, sleep disorders and hypertension.

■ Diet

Diet can play an important part in attaining mental balance; a poor diet high in preservatives, caffeine and sugar will increase our mental stress levels. A spa which is offering cuisine options as part of a mental health program may consider the following types of food – though it should be emphasized concrete evidence regarding their effects on mental function is still debatable and that an all-round approach to good nutrition should be recommended as opposed to promoting specific foods in the form of 'magic' cures:

- Whole grains (that give a steady supply of energy throughout the day).
- Oily fish high in omega 3, pumpkin seeds, soya beans or walnuts (for healthy brain function).
- Berries and tomatoes high in anti-oxidants (which may help against memory loss).
- Blackcurrants high in vitamin C (which may help against stress).
- Broccoli high in vitamin K (to help the brain function).
- Sage (which may help boost concentration and memory)

(Lewin, 2018).

Stress and de-stress programs

Relaxation and stress relief is one of the main reasons why people visit spas. We all need a certain level of stress or excitement to propel us in our daily lives, but too much ongoing stress (chronic stress) can be seriously detrimental with symptoms of irritability, anxiety, depression, headaches and sleep problems. In the long-term, stress can contribute to cardiovascular diseases, increase the risk of type 2 diabetes, cause sexual and menstruation problems and a weakened immune system.

Perhaps some of the most popular mental-wellness related programs are those focusing on de-stress and reducing anxiety. In today's fast paced competitive world, stress is a major cause of depression and cardiovascular disfunction. A professionally compiled de-stress program should contain the following:

- A medical consultation and/or some form of counselling, life coaching or psychotherapy.
- Moderate dynamic cardio exercise, and exercises to relieve tension and improve flexibility such as yoga, tai chi, stretching, etc.
- Exercise to relax and focus the mind, such as meditation and autogen training.
- Treatments and experiences to help relax the body (heat focused experiences such as saunas, steam, thermal pools are particularly apt).
- A diet that removes all forms of stimulants such as caffeine, foods high in simple sugars, etc.

9

Anti-stress programs and trends

According to medical research carried out in recent decades, there is a direct link between mental health, chronic stress, disease and a low quality of life. Chronic stress (induced by physical, environmental, emotional etc. stressors) activates the sympathetic component of the autonomic nervous system producing a constant excess of the cortisol hormone. Excess cortisol damages the brain, immune system and accelerates the aging process.

A good anti-stress program should aim to activate the parasympathetic nervous system to have a fast and relaxing effect on the mind and body. It should also teach coping techniques for long term stress management. When delivering professional anti-stress programs, the spa should be able to provide a balance of relaxation treatments, a relaxing natural environment (calming scenery and climate) cardio-based fitness possibilities and meditation. These ideally should be coordinated by a trained medical professional or doctor. A healthy diet, omitting stimulants that can increase anxiety, and ensuring that the guest is able to really sleep comfortably during the stay is essential. For more complex anti-stress programs, stress management workshops and psychologist supported counselling sessions are necessary.

In the last 20 years, the main target markets for anti-stress programs have changed. In the early 2000s, anti-stress programs focused mainly on people prone to cardiovascular diseases (i.e. company managers, corporate leaders, etc.) and followed an 'illness-based medical model' – the typical western medicine approach. By 2010, the target market expanded to an 'anti-aging preventative care model' for middle aged and the aging population.

Recently, the trend is for anti-stress programs to focus on daily well-being, personal and group performance, creativity and life fulfillment, giving learning skills to enable clients to switch from anxiety to positive thought and behavioural patterns. These anti-stress programs are suitable for all target groups, the population in general, regardless of age, race or social position

Dr. Suzana Pretorian, consultant physician, Sovata & Braget Ensana Health Spa Hotels, Romania.

Ayurveda and spiritual spas

An Ayurveda spa is one in which all treatments and products are natural and follow Ayurvedic principles and traditions (ISPA, 2019). They will offer Ayurvedic treatments, diet, diagnosis and exercise which will involve yoga and meditation. Because many Ayurvedic programs offer weight loss, de-stress, detox, nutrition and preventative programs and sometimes spiritual services, there is an overlap with Ayurveda spas and destination/spiritual spas, meaning the challenges and spa management roles are similar. Ayurveda spas are not just to be found in India, there are Ayurveda spas world-wide, and Ayurvedic treatments are popular in Europe and America.

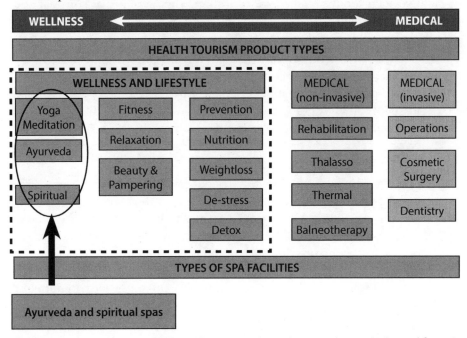

Figure 9.6: Products and services offered by Ayurveda and spiritual spas. (Adapted from Smith and Puczkó, 2009).

Ayurveda

Originating in ancient India, Ayurveda is a system of Hindu traditional therapy using plant-based healing medicines (derivatives of roots, leaves, barks and seeds), treatments and exercise (normally yoga) to restore health and balance the body. Because of its holistic approach, it is often categorized alongside spiritual spa products.

An Ayurveda practitioner analyses the body which is divided into five elements – space, earth, water, fire and air, then creates an individualized treatment plant based on diet (vegetarian, often detox) – exercise, herbal medications, yoga, meditation and treatments such as massage. A typical day in an Ayurveda spa will involve meditation, exercise (yoga), treatments with a personalized diet and medication plan.

- **Ayurveda massage**s: a relaxing oil is used to stimulate and increase circulation, examples include: Vishesh – a firm pressured massage with a squeezing action to help eliminate deeply rooted toxins; Shirodhara – massage combined with a hot oil poured over the forehead; Shira Basti where a container similar to a hat is placed over the head and filled with warm oil to absorb into the scalp (Crebbin-Bailey, Harcup and Harrington, 2005).

■   Spiritual spas

Buddhism, yoga, meditation and practices from the East have had a profound influence on today's global spa concepts. When looking at spiritual and metaphysical treatments and programs, there are two Eastern beliefs that spa managers should have an awareness of:

- **Chakras**: originating from the Sanskrit word for wheel or disc, these refer to the energy field throughout the body. There are seven main chakras starting from the bottom of the spine up to the crown of the head. Each chakra relates to specific body organs as well as the body's emotional, psychological and spiritual state. If the energy in a chakra is blocked, it is believed that there will be physical and emotional reactions. The aim is to keep each chakra in balance and the energy flowing freely through them.

- **Meridian lines**: according to ancient Chinese medicine the meridian lines and channels carry or hold energy (*qi*) around the body. Any blockages in the flow can result in health issues and a disruption in a person's wellbeing. Each meridian has its own flow and direction and connection to different bodily organs. Acupuncture (inserting thin needles at different points in the body) and acupressure (massaging or pressing different points in the body) are believed to release the qi energy and help return the body to normal thereby healing it.

Metaphysical therapies

There are certain geographical locations where spirituality and metaphysical therapies are extremely popular, California being a prime example. Culturally this area has an openness for esoteric approaches and has many examples of spiritual spa programs. People tend to turn to spiritual and metaphysical therapies when traditional medicine has failed or when they are facing a major life event, such as a serious illness or a bereavement.

Here are some examples of typical treatments found:

- **Reiki massage**: originating in Japan, reiki is an alternative therapy where hands are placed over the body (or area of pain) to transfer energy from the therapist to the client. With the aim of releasing blocked energy, reiki is similar in principle to acupuncture or pressure, but without touching the body. It is promoted as being effective in reducing pain and speeding up healing.

- **Hands on healing**: has been practiced for thousands of years and is prevalent in many religions particularly Christianity. By laying hands on the body – sometimes combining the action with a prayer or mantra on the afflicted area of the body, this energy therapy aims to induce self-healing physically, emotionally and/or mentally.

- **Crystal sound therapy**: uses the sound and vibration of crystal bowls to relax and heal the body. Its aim is to transform physical, emotional and mental wellbeing.

■ **Clairvoyance**: is claimed to be a psychic ability using the so-called 'sixth sense' as a form of extrasensory perception. A clairvoyant will claim to either see or feel events and people of a client's life, either past, present or future. People will visit a clairvoyant seeking information or advice or wishing to connect with deceased loved ones.

■ **Astrology**: is the belief that the position of the stars and planets at the time of one's birth predict personality and events, relationships and fortunes. People seek an astrologist when seeking information about the future or a current problem.

■ **Tarot cards**: tarot card readers claim that they can use the cards to see into the past, present or future. Normally a question will be asked – typically about a problem or live event – the cards are shuffled, laid down then read by the reader.

■ The placebo effect

Many people are sceptical about some of the services offered not just in spiritual spas, but in spas in general and there is good reason for this. Spas have used the placebo effect to sell their therapies or natural resources effectively for hundreds of years.

A placebo is a medicine or procedure that has no physiological effect often used in trials to test new medication or therapies. Data research from more than 5,000 patients have found that placebos worked just as well as anti-depressant drugs (such as Prozac) 81% of the time (Dispenza, 2014). The placebo effect is related to the extent of belief of the user.

Some therapies in spas have little or no medical evidence, but this is not to say that they do not have their value or place, however. As people become more educated and more sceptical, there is pressure to offer therapies that have concrete scientific evidence proving their effects, particularly when it concerns treatments using natural resources.

Surveys have shown that a proportion of the improvement of an illness or health is due to four factors, factors that spa managers should bear in mind in their spa operations:

1 The environment in which the treatment is received.

2 The relationship between patient and practitioner.

3 The way in which the illness is explained and approached by the therapist.

4 Healing as a result of belief in the treatment.

(Crebbin-Bailey, Harcup and Harrington, 2005)

9

Typical offerings of a spiritual spa

Esalen Spa in California, is a good example of a spa focusing on spiritual and mental wellness. Here are some of the workshops and programs that they offer:

- Arts and creativity: Creative expression, music and rhythm, visual arts, writing.

- Body and movement: nutrition, dance, healing arts, massage, yoga.

- Meditation and spirituality: contemplative spiritual studies, meditation and mindfulness, myths and rituals, personal reflection.

- Mind and psychology: neuropsychology, philosophical enquiry, transpersonal psychology.

- Relationship and self: family, gender, life purpose/visioning, relationship communication, sexuality.

- Leadership and society: business and entrepreneurship, leadership, social and political change.

Feedback from the interviews – what the experts say

Spa managers were asked what they thought are the most important lifestyle factors currently having an impact on the spa business. Here is a summary of their responses.

- Many of the respondents mention the problems of unhealthy lifestyles which eventually lead to chronic diseases. Spas are described by one respondent as spaces for educating guests about lifestyle improvement programmes including fitness and weight loss. The need for healthier nutrition comes up several times, but food scares and changing reports on healthy eating are also stated as factors that force people to change their diets constantly. Nataša Ranitović, CEO of Sunny Ltd. Wellness Consulting suggests that people want to change their lives: "Individual responsibility for health motivates people to take care of their physical, mental, emotional and spiritual state in search of balance, vitality, happiness and joy."

- Mental health is cited by many, who emphasise the need for mindfulness, psychological counselling, meditation and yoga, as well as relaxation. As suggested by Klaus Pilz, CEO of Bad Radkersburg, guests are looking for "time for myself – quiet relaxation with a touch of luxury". It is thought that people feel overworked, 'time poor', and constantly connected to technology, which leads to considerable stress. As stated by one respondent, people are more connected to the external world but are becoming more disconnected inside. Elena Bazzocchi, Global hospitality manager describes how "life has made going to the spa a need and not a privilege". However, one respondent also suggested that guests want quick fixes to their lifestyle problems because of time pressure – often in one weekend!

■ It was noted that people are living longer, which means active seniors but also an 'aging complex' and quest for 'eternal youth', 'smart aging' or 'reverse-aging' products. Examples are given of botox, fillers, oxygen/vitamin drip therapy and lipo-sculpture. As stated by Jane Wilson, Director and Editor of Thehealthcareholiday.com: "Anti-ageing attracts a lot of press – good and bad. This in turn is encouraging consumers to seek treatments to treat the effects of lifestyle habits – stress, excess weight, alcohol abuse, smoking, ageing".

■ Environmental issues and sustainability (e.g. energy saving, organic food, green products) were listed by several respondents, as well as the need to (re) connect to nature.

Research and further reading

There are always new reports emerging about wellness trends and healthy life-styles in the media. A few academic studies have also been undertaken that focus on the relationship between health, happiness and lifestyles, often within particu-lar segments of populations. Smith (2017) provides an overview of the lifestyle factors that influence health tourism demand, including spas, wellness hotels, retreats, medical facilities. These include physical, psychological, social and spir-itual motivations. Hudson, Thal, Cárdenas and Meng (2017) show that life stress plays a major role in behavioural intention to visit a wellness destination. Smith (2018) analyses the so-called 'U-bend' theory of life and why people tend to be unhappiest in mid-life (regardless of their culture or gender). She also examines why the main market for health tourism, wellness and spas tends to be middle aged and female. Kelly and Smith (2017) discuss the lifestyle factors that influ-ence peoples' desire to visit retreat centres. Again, they note the predominance of middle aged and female participants. Koskinen, Ylilahti and Wolska (2016) analyse the factors that influence senior spa and wellness travellers, including increasingly health conscious lifestyles.

9

References

Breuleux, (2004) 'Defining Medical Wellness', https://www.medicalwellnessassociation.com/wp-content/uploads/2017/08/Defining-Medical-Wellness-Definition-of-Terms-Breuleux-C.-2017-1.pdf (accessed 13/08/2019).

Beuttner, D. and Skemp, S. (2016) 'Blue zones, lessons from the world's longest lived', *American Journal of Lifestyle Medicine*, **10** (5), 318-321. Doi: 10.1177/1559827616637066

Brazier, Y. (2018) 'What is psychology and what does it involve?', Medical News Today, https://www.medicalnewstoday.com/articles/154874.php (accessed 17.08.2019).

Crebbin-Bailey, J., Harcup, J. and Harrington, J. (2005) *The Spa Book*, Atlanta: Thomson.

Danner, D. D., Snowden, D. A. and Friesen, W. V. (2001) 'Positive Emotions in Early Life and Longevity: Findings from the Nun Study', *Journal of Personality and Social Psychology*, **80** (5), 804-13, Doi: 10.1037//0022-3514.80.5.804

Cohen, M. and Bodeker, G. (2008) *Understanding the Global Spa Industry*, Oxford: Butterworth Heinemann.

Dispenza, J. (2014) *You are the Placebo: making your mind matter*, Carlsbad: Hay House.

Global Wellness Institute (2020) 'What is Wellness? Wellness Definitions', https://globalwellnessinstitute.org/what-is-wellness/wellness-economy-definitions/ (accessed 25/01/2020).

Gupta, S. (2007) 'Ten tips to cut cancer risk', 10 January, CNN, http://edition.cnn.com/2007/HEALTH/01/09/gupta.10tips/index.html (accessed 13/08/2019).

Hudson, S., Thal, K., Cárdenas, D. and Meng, F. (2017) 'Wellness tourism: stress alleviation or indulging healthful habits?' *International Journal of Culture, Tourism and Hospitality Research*, **11** (1), 35-52, Doi: 10.1108/IJCTHR-09-2015-0111

ISPA (International Spa Association) (2019) 'About ISPA', https://experienceispa.com/#about/ (accessed 26.08.2019).

Ives, L. (2018) 'No alcohol safe to drink global study finds', BBC News, 24 August, https://www.bbc.com/news/health-45283401 (accessed 16/08/2019).

Kelly, C. and Smith, M. K. (2017) 'Journeys of the self: the need to retreat', in M. K. and L. Puczkó (eds) The Routledge Handbook of Health Tourism, London: Routledge, pp. 138-151.

Koskinen, V., Ylilahti, M. and Wolska, T. (2016) '"Healthy to heaven" — Middle-agers looking ahead in the context of wellness consumption', *Journal of Aging Studies*, **40**, 36–43, Doi: 10.1016/j.jaging.2016.12.006

Lewin, J. (2018) '10 foods to boost brain power', BBC Good Food, https://www.bbcgoodfood.com/howto/guide/10-foods-boost-your-brainpower (accessed 18/08/2019).

Mindful Org (2014) 'What is mindfulness', https://www.mindful.org/what-is-mindfulness/ (accessed 17/08/2019).

Robertson, D. J. (2013) *Stoicism and the Art of Happiness (Teach Yourself)*, London: Hodder & Stoughton.

Robinson, M. and Respers, L. (2019) 'Prince Harry and Oprah are making a documentary series about mental health', CNN, 10 April, https://edition.cnn.com/2019/04/10/

entertainment/prince-harry-oprah-winfrey-mental-health-tv-series-intl-scli-gbr/index.
html (accessed 17/08/2019).

Sandstrum, G. and Dunn, E. (2014) 'Social interactions and wellbeing: the surprising
power of weak ties', *Personality and Social Psychology Bulletin*, **40** (7), 910-922.

Sharma, A., Madaan, V. and Petty, F. D. (2006) 'Exercise for mental health', *Primary Care
Companion to The Journal of Clinical Psychiatry*, **8** (2), 106, Doi:10.4088/pcc.v08n0208a

Smith, D. (2001) 'American psychological association. College photos indicate later
personality development and marital success', *American Psychological Association,* **32** (1),
14.

Smith, M. K. (2017) 'An overview of lifestyle trends and their impacts on health tourism',
in M. K. Smith and L. Puczkó (eds) *The Routledge Handbook of Health Tourism*, London:
Routledge, pp. 20-31.

Smith, M. K. (2018) 'Wellness in the 'U-bend' of Life: why the core market is middle-aged
and female', *International Journal of Spa and Wellness*, **1** (1), 4-19, Doi:10.1080/24721735.2
018.1438480

Smith, M. K. and Puczkó, L. (2018) *Exploring Health Tourism*, Madrid: UNWTO.

UAE government (2019) 'A guide to happiness and wellbeing at the workplace', https://
government.ae/en/about-the-uae/the-uae-government/government-of-future/happiness
(accessed 16/08/2019).

WHO (1946) 'WHO constitution', https://www.who.int/about/who-we-are/constitution
(accessed 13/08/2019).

WHO (2016) 'The top 10 causes of death', https://www.who.int/news-room/fact-sheets/
detail/the-top-10-causes-of-death (accessed 13/08/2019).

World Happiness Report (2019) https://worldhappiness.report (accessed 25/01/2019).

9

10 Physical fitness and nutrition, detox, weight loss and active programs

If one of the main roles of a spa is to promote health and wellbeing, the spa manager (and indeed their team) need to have a sound, basic understanding of the fundamentals of physical fitness and nutrition and their related products. This chapter aims to summarize essential fitness and diet information, however, it should be emphasized that this is just the basics, and that spa managers are advised to continually increase their knowledge of these topics. Treatments and programs related to fitness and diet are also included in this chapter.

Physical fitness

Being physically fit is essential to good health and wellbeing. If we are physically fit, we lower our risk of many diseases, we can carry out everyday tasks more comfortably/efficiently and we feel more confident in ourselves. Being fit also helps to reduce anxiety and increase a feeling of wellbeing. In good physical condition we also have better agility, coordination and balance as well as reaction time and speed.

According to the American College of Sports Medicine, all healthy adults aged between 18 and 65 years should have moderate intensity aerobic physical activity for a minimum of 30 minutes 5 days a week. In addition, they recommend for every adult to perform activities that maintain or increase muscular strength and endurance at least twice a week. Whilst on the surface this doesn't appear too extreme, taking into consideration how sedentary workplaces and lifestyles have become, actually fitting in this amount of exercise into a weekly routine can be quite a challenge.

Clinical studies have shown that regular exercise reduces the chances of cardiovascular diseases, hypertension, stroke, osteoporosis, type 2 diabetes, obesity, colon cancer, breast cancer, anxiety and depression (ACSM, 2010).

In order to understand clearly physical fitness, it helps to divide the different components into three key areas:

1 **Cardio** exercise, otherwise called **aerobic** training, that has an effect on our cardio (heart) vascular system (also called the circulatory system – the vessels that carry blood and oxygen around the body).

2 Exercises to develop **muscular strength.**

3 Exercise to develop **flexibility.**

The advice given in this chapter has been based on the American College of Sports Medicine guidelines for exercise prescription – the largest and most respected sports medicine and exercise science organization.

Cardio fitness

Whilst all of the above fitness components are necessary, cardio fitness is described first because it is the most important area of physical fitness. Not only does it play the major role in reducing the risk of the diseases listed above, but without a well-functioning heart and cardiovascular system we are putting our whole existence at risk. A strong bicep muscle can be useful and aesthetic, but it is not essential – a strong, fit heart is!

In order to exercise the heart and vascular system, large muscle groups (such as those in the legs and buttocks) need to be put under moderate to vigorous exertion over an extended period of time. During cardio training the heart and vascular system react to this exertion or load to pump the blood and oxygen to the muscles and take away waste products. Cardio exercise is defined as:

> …" the ability to perform large muscle, dynamic, moderate-to-high intensity exercise for prolonged periods" (ACSM, 2010).

Regular cardio training improves endurance, strengthens the heart and develops the body's ability to utilize oxygen.

- Examples of cardio exercise include running, fast walking, swimming, cycling, dancing, aerobic type activities.

- Examples of equipment that would be deemed 'cardio' are: standing and recline bikes, running machines, step machines, rowers and elliptical walkers.

- Examples of cardio or 'aerobic' type classes would include: aerobics, step, Zumba, dance and any class that involves dynamic movement using large muscles for an extended period of time.

Cardio level intensity and target heart rate

The intensity level at which a person trains when doing cardio exercise is extremely important. If the level is too high they will be working out anaerobically (building the strength of the muscles as opposed to training the cardiovascular system) and if the level is too low then they will not train the cardiovascular system enough to have an effect.

10

To understand how to perform cardio exercise at the right level, first it is necessary to know how to calculate the maximum heart rate:

Maximum heart rate = 220 – age.

So, if a client is 50 years old their maximum heart rate will be 170 beats per minute.

(A normal resting heart rate should be around 70 beats per minute).

Once we have calculated the maximum heart rate, we need to determine the target heart rate training zone. The Karvonen formula is a common way to calculate this. The Karvonen formula helps to determine the target heart rate (HR) training zone. It uses the maximum and resting heart rate with the desired training intensity to calculate the target heart rate.

Target heart rate = ((max HR – resting HR) x % intensity)) + resting heart rate

Calculating the target heart rate for a cardio training workout

First calculate the maximum heart rate (220 – age) minus resting heart rate (normally 70 beats per minute). Multiply this number by the percentage of desired intensity (for cardio exercise this is normally between 40% and 70%). Finally, add the resting heart rate.

Let us take a 50-year-old client with a resting heart rate of 70 beats per minute. Their maximum heart rate is 170 beats per minute (220 – age) minus the resting heart rate 70 = 100. We call this number the heart rate reserve (the difference between the predicted maximum heart rate and the resting heart rate).

To calculate the number of heart beats per minute required for a client to be training at an intensity of 60% of their heart rate reserve: 100 x 60% = 60. We add this number onto the resting heart rate: 60 (60% of heart rate reserve) + 70 (resting heart rate) = 130 (target heart rate).

In order to exercise the heart effectively it is recommended to perform moderate intensity exercise for at least 30 minutes 5 or more days a week (at 40% - 60% of the heart rate reserve (HRR)) or vigorous intensity exercise (at 60% - 85% of the HRR) for at least 20 – 25 minutes on 3 or more days a week.

Many cardio machines will automatically calculate a person's heart rate (although their accuracy is not always perfect). Alternatively, a person can take their own heart rate by placing two fingers between the bone and the tendon over the radial artery located on the thumb side of the wrist. They should count the number of beats in 15 seconds and then multiply by four.

A good spa fitness program will teach its guests how to exercise at the right level according to their heart rate reserve by calculating their heart rate. Exercising too lightly will have little benefit and performing cardio exercise too intensely (over 85% of the HRR) can cause the body to work anaerobically, therefore defeating the object of cardio training.

Blood pressure

Regular cardio exercise is the best prevention for coronary heart disease and hypertension (high blood pressure). Coronary heart disease is often caused by atherosclerosis where plaque builds up inside the arteries, over time narrowing them, limiting the flow of oxygen-rich blood to the organs and increasing the blood pressure which further exacerbates the problem. Atherosclerosis can lead to heart attacks, strokes and even death.

There are two numbers in the blood pressure reading:

- **Systolic** (the top number): this is when the heart beats and squeezes the blood through the arteries, this force is called systolic pressure.
- **Diastolic** (the bottom number): this is the pressure when the heart rests between beats and fills up with blood and gets oxygen.

According to the American Heart Association, normal blood pressure should be 120/80. Elevated is 120 -129/80 and first stage high blood pressure is over 130 – 139/80 – 89.

During exercise, whilst the systolic pressure will rise, the diastolic should stay around 80 in a healthy person.

The rate that a client on an aerobic exercise program progresses will depend on their health status and goals. One of the biggest mistakes made by most clients, and indeed instructors, is embarking on a program at too high an intensity and for too long a duration, beyond the body's capabilities. In such cases, the client often will exercise one or two times and then give up.

Strength training

Strength training has many benefits these include:

- Improved bodily strength.
- Increased bone and muscle mass (as we get older, we lose bone and muscle density, strength training helps combat this).
- Increased metabolism, both immediately and long after exercise, meaning that more calories are burnt, not just during exercise, but during daily life as well.
- It helps improve balance, coordination and posture.
- It can help support chronic disease management such as arthritis.
- Combined with aerobic exercise, muscle strengthening exercises help improve blood pressure.

According to the American College of Sports Medicine, it is recommended to train each of the main muscle groups 2 to 3 days per week with at least 48 hours separating the training sessions for the same muscle group.

Whilst performing the exercises, instructors should ensure that:

- The client is seated properly in the equipment, with good posture and their back supported.

10

- They perform a full range of movement without locking joints.
- The motion of the movement should be smooth and at an even tempo.
- Their breathing should be in harmony with the exercise (normally exhaling during the effort).

If a client would like to improve their muscle tone then the program should include lighter weights and more repetitions with a short relax between repetition sets.

If a client would like to increase strength and bulk (after a warm-up set with lighter weights), they should increase the heaviness of the weights, perform fewer repetitions and have longer rests between sets.

In teaching the exercises the instructor should:

1 First demonstrate the exercise.

2 Then place the guest into position correctly.

3 Using a light weight with low intensity, coach them during the exercise.

4 Emphasize correct breathing, posture maintenance and correct momentum.

5 Increase the weights whilst coaching, correcting and encouraging the client.

Flexibility

Flexibility can be defined as "the range of motion of muscle and connective tissues at a joint or at a group of joints". In contrast to the other fitness components, flexibility is highly specific to each of the joints of the body (Pate, Oria and Pillsbury, 2012). Stretching is one of the least practiced areas of exercise, but it highly necessary as:

- It helps prevent injuries (people who stretch regularly have 50% less injuries from overtraining muscles).
- It helps prevent stiffness.
- It helps speed the regeneration of the muscles.
- It increases flexibility and movement at the joints.
- It can help reduce tension and stress.

It is recommended to stretch before and after exercise, during training sessions after training a specific muscle or group of muscles, or anytime if the muscles are warm. The principles of stretching a muscle are as follows:

- Static stretching is the recommended mode.
- It should involve all the major muscle tendon groups of the body.
- The muscle should be stretched up until the point of the 'feel' of the stretch and then relaxed into it.
- The stretch should be held for 15 – 60 seconds.
- 4 repetitions per muscle group is recommended.
- Stretching should be performed at least 2 to 3 days per week.

In addition to individual stretching, flexibility classes are also an effective way to improve the overall suppleness.

Examples of classes that are excellent for improving flexibility include yoga, tai chi (described in the previous chapter) stretching class, spine classes, and Pilates.

- **Pilates**: Using body weight, springs, pulleys and ropes. Pilates is a form of flexibility training that also improves strength and core muscle effectivity. In addition to improving muscular strength and flexibility, it is good for posture and rehabilitation from injury. It is a popular form of exercise for athletes, dancers and also seniors and people with back problems.

Functional training

In the past decade, functional training has become a major trend. In our daily life we move at different angles with varying degrees of weight, not on fixed planes like on most strength equipment. Functional training (like Pilates) is a dynamic, multi-planar method of exercise mirroring real life movement using body weight, TRX cables, bars, medicine balls and other weights. These are utilized through compound movements (movements using several muscle groups), improving your body's ability to work as one unit. Because it involves working in free range, it is an excellent way to improve strength, balance and coordination.

■ Summary of fitness advice for healthy adults

The American College of Sports Medicine recommends that exercise should be prescribed on the FITT principal;

F = frequency of exercising (how often)

I = intensity (level)

T = time (length of time)

T = type of exercise

Cardio exercise is recommended on most days of the week or at least between 3 to 5 days a week, at a moderate intensity for a total of at least 150 minutes, either intermittently or in bouts of 30 minutes. The more vigorous the exercise, the higher the chances of injuries occurring. A variety of exercises are therefore advised to avoid stress of the body. In the initial phase of exercise increasing duration/time should be the focus (+ 5 – 10 minutes every 1 to 2 weeks for the first 4 – 6 weeks of the program). After one month, the frequency, intensity and/or time of exercise can be adjusted upward.

Strength exercise is recommended to train every major muscle group using multi-joint exercises and targeting both the agonist and antagonist muscle groups 2 to 3 days a week with a 48-hour rest between the different muscle groups. Each muscle group should be trained for a total of 2 to 4 sets with a reasonable rest between sets of between 2 to 3 minutes – the heavier the weight, the longer the rest. The greater the resistance, the fewer number of repetitions need to be completed. To improve strength, 8 to 12 repetitions are advised. To improve endurance rather

10

than strength and mass, 15 – 20 repetitions should be performed with shorter rests and fewer sets. Each set should be performed to muscle fatigue.

Flexibility in a stretching session should last 10 minutes in duration involving all the major muscle tendon groups of the body with 4 or more repetitions per muscle group, 2 to 3 days per week. Stretches should be performed statistically to the point of mild discomfort but no more.

■ Fitness consultations in spas

The goal of giving fitness consultations in spas should be to create a fitness program that not only is appropriate to the health condition and goals of the client but one that will also motivate the client. This is dependent on a good relationship between the client and the instructor. A client who sticks to working out regularly for six months is likely to carry on working out thereafter. Maintaining the motivation in those first few months therefore is critical.

The fitness consultation has three parts:

1   Greeting and getting to know the client – this is important as the sooner they feel comfortable with the trainer, the more likely they are to respond to instruction and advice.

2   The consultation itself.

3   Designing the training plan.

Before the consultation most clients should fill out a physical activity readiness questionnaire (PAR-Q). There are a number of different versions of the PAR-Q questionnaires, however, these are the most common questions:

■   Has your doctor ever said that you have a heart condition and that you should only do physical activity recommended by a doctor?

■   Do you feel pain in your chest when you do physical activity?

■   In the past month, have you had chest pain when you were not doing physical activity?

■   Do you lose your balance because of dizziness or do you ever lose consciousness?

■   Do you have a bone or joint problem that could be made worse by a change in your physical activity?

■   Is your doctor currently prescribing drugs (for example, water pills) for your blood pressure or heart condition?

■   Do you know of any other reason why you should not do physical activity?

(VeryWellFit, 2020)

The purpose of the questionnaire is to screen guests in case they have a contradictory health problem. Most of the questions relate to possible cardiovascular risks and/or joint or bone problems that could be made worse through physical activity. Most well run spas and fitness facilities will have a form like this which will be signed by the client before any exercise participation. The questionnaire was designed to identify those for whom such exercise might be not suitable. Generally, if a client has answered yes to any of the questions and is over the age of 40 they should consult a doctor before embarking on an exercise program. Likewise, if the client has a cold or flu, they should wait until they are better before starting.

In the fitness consultation, the instructor should take (at the minimum) the following measurements:

- A body mass index (weight divided by height squared – in kilograms/metres). A BMI of over 25 is considered overweight, over 30 obese or under 18.5 underweight. These increase the risk of cardiovascular disease.

- The waist/hip ratio (WHR) – the circumference of the waist, divided by the circumference of the hips. (There is a health risk for younger men if the measurement is more than 0.95 and for younger women at 0.86. For clients older than 60 the limits are slightly higher; 1.03 for men and 0.90 for women).

- The resting heart rate, should be between 70 and 90 beats per minute (over 90 would be cause for concern).

- The resting blood pressure should be around 120/80 (120 – 139 systolic and above and 80 – 90 diastolic and above would be cause for concern).

Different countries and guidelines have varying instructions for when to send the client to see a doctor before embarking on a fitness program. Generally, if the heart rate is over 90 at the time of the test (and the client is in a relaxed state) and/or the blood pressure is elevated (over 130 – 139/80 – 89) the instructor, after repeating the measurements, should refer the client to the doctor for a check-up before prescribing exercise. If the waist hip ratios and/or BMI are over the limit in addition to the blood pressure and/or heart rate is elevated, the instructor should also refer the client to a doctor. If the client insists on exercise, the spa should ensure they sign a responsibility of risk form stating that they have been advised not to exercise and take full personal responsibility for any consequences that arise because of their decision.

■ Designing the training plan

All training plans should take the following into consideration:

- The goals should be realistic and motivating for the client (i.e. exercise that they enjoy and are interested in).
- It should include a cardio warm up, mobilization and stretch at the beginning.
- It should contain a cardio exercise part.
- It should involve some strength development exercises.
- It should include a cool down on cardio exercise and development stretching.

10

■   Exercise advice for special groups

Pregnancy

Healthy pregnant women are advised to exercise throughout their pregnancy. If a woman has had a sedentary lifestyle or medical condition, they should consult a doctor before embarking on a fitness program. Cardio exercise is recommended for a minimum 3 days a week at a level of moderate intensity using large muscle groups. Exercise that can cause loss of balance, in the supine position or has a trauma risk should be avoided. Strength exercises with 12 – 15 repetitions are also recommended. Hydration is important to avoid heat stress.

Children

Children below 13 years old should exercise daily 3 – 4 days a week, moderate to vigorous intensity doing activities that they enjoy and that are appropriate for a child. Strength exercises of 8 – 15 repetitions are permitted but only if they are properly supervised – these should use body weight rather than equipment. Because of their immature thermoregulatory system, children need to be checked for overheating and should drink water regularly.

Seniors

For those over the age of 65 physical activity helps slow down the aging process and changes in body composition, it also helps to manage chronic diseases and reduces the risks of physical disabilities. Exercise for seniors should include all 3 components – cardio, strength and flexibility. Cardio exercise should be carried out 5 days a week at a moderate level or 3 days a week at a more vigorous level. Exercise that does not carry orthopaedic stress, such as swimming, cycling is recommended. Strength exercises are recommended 2 days a week involving major muscle groups with 10 – 15 repetitions. Stretching should be carried out at least 2 days per week at a moderate intensity combined with balance exercises. Nordic walking, tai chi, stretching and spine improvement classes are excellent form of exercises for seniors.

Arthritis

Clients with arthritis should avoid rigorous exercise when there is acute inflammation. Longer warm up and cool down times are advised 5 – 10 minutes minimum. Aerobic exercise is recommended 3 to 5 days a week in short amounts of 5 – 10 minutes, then progressing in duration. Strength exercises 2 to 3 days a week (if someone is in pain they should start with static contractions around the joint before progressing to dynamic movement), the intensity being dependent on the pain level. Stretching and mobility should be performed daily. Exercises like swimming that put low stress on joints are preferred. Longer duration of activity is preferred over increased intensity. They should exercise when pain levels are at their lowest. Functional exercises to improve balance and coordination are recommended.

Hypertension

All clients with high blood pressure should have a medical examination before exercising. Regular exercise can help reduce blood pressure and the emphasis should be placed on cardio exercise supported by moderate level resistance training. Aerobic exercise is preferred on most days of the week, either continuous or intermittent (in bouts of 10 – 15 minutes for at least 30 minutes per day) and resistance training 2 to 3 days with the minimum of one set of 8 – 12 repetitions and 8 to 10 exercises targeting different muscle groups. Many individuals with hypertension are obese or overweight, therefore reducing calorie intake should also be looked at.

Overweight and obesity

If someone has a body mass index (BMI) of over 25 they are classified as being overweight and over 30 obese. Overweight and obesity are linked to many chronic diseases, diabetes mellitus, cancers and musculoskeletal complications. Reducing caloric intake and increasing physical activity is recommended for such clients. They are advised to exercise primarily aerobically using large muscle groups for 5 days a week at a moderate to vigorous intensity – 30 to 60 minutes a day to total 150 minutes a week progressing to 300 minutes. If someone is not fit enough to exercise at these levels, they can accumulate the exercise needed in bouts of 10 minutes supported by an increase in daily activity. Strength training is also advised. Eating and behavioural habits should be targeted in such an exercise program.

■ Fitness spa stays and programs

Re-energizing and active fitness programs are popular in many spas and normally follow a structure such as:

Guest arrives

↓

Fills out lifestyle questionnaire / PAR- Q forms

↓

FITNESS CONSULTATION
Weight/height measurements, heart rate, blood pressure, BMI, Waist / hip ratio, fat %
respiratory function, chlorestrol level, lifestyle counselling

↓

PROGRAM
Daily physical exercise (cardio/strength/flexibility) – classes, personal training, outdoor
activities (e.g. Nordic walking, hiking) treatments, high energy diet

↓

FINAL CONSULTATION
Evaluation of program, follow up advice

↓

Guest leaves

Figure 10.1: Typical fitness / active spa program.

10

The components of an effective fitness stay

The Sha wellness clinic in Alicante, Spain provides an excellent example of a well put together fitness stay which has the aim of achieving optimum fitness, increasing tone and strength and improving joint function, as well as acquiring knowledge and skills to change personal habits to be able to maintain physical condition back home. The program includes:

- Personal physical exercise, posture training, outdoor functional training and classic training

- A personalized nutrition plan

- A strict control of weight and physical state to achieve fitness goals

- A range of natural therapies including osteopathy and physiotherapy

- Recommendations and workshops to make lifestyle changes.

For high performing clients, boot camps are also proving popular. Such programs normally run over 2 or 3 days with intense workouts, jogging, hiking, competitive games, stretching, yoga and treatments combined with a high energy diet.

Diet and nutrition

The human body can thrive on many types of diet (i.e. Asian, Indian, Mediterranean etc). Unfortunately, the so-called Western diet (sometimes referred to as WPD – Western Pattern Diet) concentrated on high intakes of red and processed meat, fried foods, high fat dairy products, refined grains and sugar, is not one of them.

Obesity, heart disease, high blood pressure, diabetes and certain cancers are not age-related diseases but lifestyle-related. People who eat the Western diet suffer substantially higher rates of these diseases than people eating any number of traditional diets. In the early decades of the 20th Century, medical professionals working with a wide variety of native populations around the world began noticing an almost complete absence of chronic diseases that had recently become commonplace in the West (Pollan, 2008).

The human body is able to ingest thousands of different substances. To be healthy, we need between 50 and 100 different chemical compounds and elements. However, in the Western diet, just four crops account for two thirds of the calories we eat – refined soy, corn, rice and wheat (Pollan, 2008). These are foods that have been stripped of nutrients, vitamins and minerals – in other words empty calories. These refined foods can cause overeating, obesity, an increased risk of heart problems and type 2 diabetes.

- # Foods to be avoided in a healthy spa diet or menu

    - **Refined carbohydrates**: there are two types of carbohydrates – refined sugars and refined grains (which have had their fibrous and nutritious parts removed, in particular white flour) (Bjarnadottir, 2017). Refined grains (white bread, white pasta, white rice) should be avoided in a healthy spa cuisine.

    - **Simple sugars:** we now eat vast quantities of simple sugars compared to what humans ate in previous centuries. Simple sugars are added to many pre-packaged and canned foods to enhance their taste. The trend of drinking sugary drinks has added to this obsession with sugar. According to the American Heart Association, the maximum amount of added sugars that should be consumed daily are: men 150 calories (37.5 grams) and women 100 calories (25 grams), or 10% of the daily calorie intake (Gunners, 2018). Simple sugars and foods containing simple sugars (except certain fruits which contain other nutrients) should be excluded in a healthy spa menu.

    - **Salt**: like sugar, salt is added to many processed and pre-packaged foods to exaggerate their taste. Too much salt contributes to high blood pressure leading to strokes and heart disease. Salt intake should be no more than 5 grams a day (equivalent of 2 grams of sodium) by limiting salt in cooking and sauces and choosing products with a low sodium intake (WHO, 2018). Spa menus should have low sodium content.

    - **Trans fats**: are natural oils like palm oil which have been pumped with hydrogen to make them solid at room temperature. They are found in baked and fried foods, pre-packaged snack and foods such as frozen pizza, biscuits, cooking oils and spreads. Industrial trans fats are not part of a healthy diet and should be avoided both in daily life and in spa eating experiences. Some countries have now reduced the legal limit of amount of trans fats permitted in foods. Spa menus should avoid offering any products containing trans fats.

    - **Saturated fats**: are generally found in animal foods – meat, butter, dairy and foods that have animal fats in them like pastries, cakes etc. They are also found in coconut oil and palm oil. Saturated fat raises the level of low-density cholesterol in the blood which in turn increases the risk of heart diseases and stroke. The American Heart Association recommends eating 5% of calories from saturated fat, whereas the other guidelines say 10% (Heart Organisation, 2015). In a spa diet or cuisines, saturated fatty foods should be kept to a minimum.

    - **Processed and smoked meats**: such as hot dogs, salami, bacon and ham are connected to many diseases such as high blood pressure, heart disease, bowel and stomach cancer. Nitrates are in processed meats to preserve colour, improve flavour and prevent bacteria growth. Nitrate in processed meat can turn into a cancer compound. Processed meats are also high in saturated fat. These all should be excluded from a spa menu.

    - **Red meat**: according to Cancer Research UK (2019), consuming too much red meat which is high in saturated fat (such as minced and frozen beef, pork and

10

lamb) increases the risk of cancer, whereas fresh white meat, such as chicken and fish pose less of a risk. Whilst red meat can be offered in spas, it should be as lean as possible, not fried and offered in smaller quantities.

- **Alcohol**: there is strong evidence that alcohol drinking can cause several types of cancer. The more someone drinks regularly over time, the higher their risk, and this also includes light drinkers who consume no more than one drink a day (National Cancer Institute, 2018). According to new UK guidelines, men and women are advised not to drink more than 14 units a week, spread over 3 or more days, with drink-free days – this is because alcohol is far more dangerous to our bodies than previously thought.

  A single shot of spirits = 1 unit.

  A small glass of red wine 125ml = 1.5 units.

  Half a litre (one pint) of beer = 2.5 units.

  Spas should actively promote other beverages (green and herbal teas, juices, healthy smoothies) as an alternative to alcohol.

- **Caffeine**: is the world's most powerful stimulant. Whilst it boosts alertness and energy, it can also cause headaches, heart palpitations, sleep problems and anxiety. It also reduces the amount of iron we absorb from the body and increases the amount of calcium lost (Norris, 2007). Caffeine is present in energy drinks, chocolate, some painkillers and cold cures. Spas should try to promote herbal and green teas instead of caffeine drinks.

How spas should approach healthy eating

The amount of daily calorie intake is important in a spa menu. Guidelines stipulate that on average women should consume 2,000 calories per day and men 2,500.

The foods we eat should have variety in order to receive the right amount of nutrients, 80 – 90% being whole foods – in other words foods that are not processed. Natural, whole foods high in nutrients should be preferred over foods that are high in fat and low in nutrients.

The U.S. dietary guidelines say 45 to 65% of calories should come from carbohydrates, 20 – 35% from total fat (not saturated) and 10 to 35% from protein.

- **Protein**: is important to build new cells and replace those that are damaged. There is animal protein (e.g. meat, fish, eggs, dairy) and vegetable protein (e.g. beans, lentils, nuts, seeds, wholegrains and soya products).

- **Carbohydrate**: is necessary for energy, simple sugars (which are quick and easy for the body to break into glucose for energy) and complex carbohydrates (which are broken down more slowly).

- **Fats**: are also for energy, to protect organs, to absorb certain minerals, to make essential hormones, to build cell membranes and for healthy brain function. Fats can be divided into monounsaturated (e.g. olive oil, canola oil peanut oil) and polyunsaturated (e.g. sunflower, corn oil, fish oil).

- **Fruits and vegetables**: a healthy spa diet should be plant based, focused on fruit, vegetables, legumes (beans / lentils) and whole grains such as corn, oats, wheat and brown rice. Vegetables can be raw or cooked, however cooking will remove some of the nutritional value. We should consume about 400 grams of fruit and vegetables per day which is about five portions. Potatoes and starchy foods are not included (WHO, 2018).

- **Complex carbohydrates**: fibre (e.g. fruits, vegetables, nuts, beans, whole grains) and starch (e.g. whole wheat bread, cereal, corn, rice, peas) are the two main types of complex carbohydrate. Fibre, otherwise called roughage, cannot be broken down, therefore passes through the intestinal tract relatively unscathed. It is necessary for good digestion, blood sugar regulation and cholesterol maintenance.

- **Nutrient dense protein**: such as lean meat, chicken, fish, beans, peas and legumes.

- **Dairy products**: dairy and fortified soy products are a vital source of calcium. Low fat dairy products such as low-fat milk / yoghurt, cottage cheese and soy milk are recommended.

- **Water**: is needed for every process in the body especially digestion, cooling the body and removing waste products. Our body is 2/3 water, and losing just one or two percent can affect energy levels. 1.5 to 2 litres of water are recommended every day, in small amounts and not just drunk when feeling thirsty, as thirst indicates dehydration.

- **Vitamins and minerals**: vitamin molecules are tiny chemical enablers, regulating reactions that digest food and release its energy. They are also needed for immunity, healing wounds and to prevent disease (Norris, 2007). They are only needed in tiny quantities. Minerals on the other hand have a range of functions from the health of our bones and teeth and maintaining the blood's fluid composition to the effectivity of our nerves to transmit signals:

  - ☐ **Magnesium**: muscle and nervous system function and healthy bones (nuts, seeds, green vegetables, pulses, wholegrains – meat and dairy products).

  - ☐ **Potassium**: Blood pressure control, fluid balance and nerve muscle function (nuts, sesame seeds, lentils, green leafy vegetables).

  - ☐ **Iron**: to carry oxygen in the blood, immunity and brain function (liver, kidney, red meat, eggs, beans and lentils, green vegetables, dried fruit).

  - ☐ **Calcium**: for bones, teeth, nerve and muscle function (dairy products, some fish, Tofu, figs, kale, leafy green vegetables).

  - ☐ **Zinc**: for immunity, and preventing infection and sperm production in men (meat, shell fish, fish, chicken, eggs, dairy, seeds, nuts, wholegrains, leafy green vegetables).

It is interesting to note how many minerals are contained in green leafy vegetables and plant-based foods – another reason why spas should be focusing on plant based menus.

10

■   Specific healthy foods that spas should include

- ■ **Garlic**: lowers cholesterol, blood fats and reduces the clotting tendency of the blood, therefore appearing to offer protection from cardiovascular disease. It is also antiseptic and antibiotic counteracting many kinds of bacteria and fungi (Weil, 2008).

- ■ **Ginger**: helps the digestion of proteins, tones the circulatory system and is said to have anti-cancer effects (Weil, 2008).

- ■ **Green tea**: because of its content of catechins that lower cholesterol and have antibacterial and anticancer effects (Weil, 2008). Population studies in Asia suggest that 5 or more cups a day could reduce heart disease and cancer (Norris, 2007).

- ■ **Yoghurt**: the health impact of bifidobacterial (the good bacteria) produces substances that kill off some of the bad bacteria in our system. These good bacteria feed off a component in dietary fibre present in foods like onions, leaks, asparagus, artichokes, wheat, oats, bananas and pulses. So, whilst yoghurt is especially healthy, so is eating a plant-based diet (Eyton, 2006).

- ■ **Blueberries**: full of antioxidants, vitamin C and E.

- ■ **Tomatoes**: high in lycopene that can help protect against prostrate and lung cancer.

- ■ **Broccoli**: filled with all sorts of vitamins, antioxidants and fibre.

What makes 'spa cuisine'?

Good nutrition and moderation are essential to maintaining a healthy lifestyle. Red Mountain Resort's restaurant, Canyon Breeze offers a food philosophy of choice, not limited by one single dietary style. We believe, that delicious and whole healthy foods are one and the same. While many consider "spa cuisine" synonymous with diet food, it is really about offering clients dishes made from the healthiest of ingredients. This cuisine is ecologically thoughtful, as we consciously choose foods that are regionally and locally sourced, and at their highest seasonal quality. We choose pasture raised meats and sustainably harvested seafood. Spa cuisine should delight the senses with fragrant spices, the use of colourful vegetables, presented in a simple and elegant fashion. This style of cuisine provides you with a sense of comfort knowing that you are nourishing your body well with the highest quality whole food products.

Tracey Welsh, General Manager

■   General advice for healthy spa diets and menus

- ■ They should not include packaged and processed food.

- ■ They should take into consideration that guests are eating what the animal ate too – the sources of the meat and dairy products are important!

■ They should reflect the eating patterns of omnivores (plant based with small amounts of meat).

■ They should be based on wild, natural foods, greens and leaves – the soil and how the food has been grown is also a factor and should be taken into consideration.

■ Meat should be used for the flavour rather than the main meal.

■ Portions should encourage a client to eat until they are 80% full.

(Pollan, 2008)

■ Diets and trends

It seems to be in human nature to look for the magic bullet to make us healthy or alternatively, avoid ill health. Nutrition, however, is not so simple. Whilst there will always be trends in foods and diets, which are in and out of fashion, from a spa perspective, rather than yield to the temptation to jump on the current bandwagon, sound evidence-based diets and menus should be the priority. Here are some current dietary trends:

■ **The Mediterranean Diet**: is widely supported as being one of the healthiest traditional diets and is based on natural plant foods, fish, olive oil, poultry, beans and grains and small amounts of wine. It is also low in trans fats and processed meats and foods. Studies have proved that it promotes cardiovascular health and it is a recommended diet for diabetics. It has a relatively high fat content, but it is low in saturated fat and high in monounsaturated fat. It is a recommended diet for spas.

■ **Acid-alkaline diets**: if the PH levels in the body fall out of normal range it can be fatal. Acidic foods (meat, fish, eggs, grains, alcohol) are said to make the body more acidic and therefore vulnerable to disease, whereas alkaline foods (fruits, nuts, legumes, vegetables) are said to improve your health (Leech, 2018). The principle of the acid-alkaline diet is to focus on the foods that are alkaline, to prevent the body being put under acidic stress. Despite the fact that there is debate over the science of the acid-alkaline diet, it many respects it mirrors the Mediterranean diet and therefore can be recommended for spas.

■ **The Palaeolith diet**: The Paleo diet is based on foods thought to be consumed in the Palaeolithic era (pre-farming 10,000 years ago). It includes lean meats, fish, fruits, vegetables nuts and seeds – foods that would have been eaten by hunter gatherers. Refined foods and foods consumed as a result of farming such as grains, beans, dairy products, sweets and processed foods are excluded. Providing the meat offered in the diet is lean and not fried, the diet can be recommended for spas, particularly because of its avoidance of processed manufactured ingredients. Because grains and dairy products are excluded, it is popular with lactose and gluten intolerant clients.

■ **Low Carb diets** (Atkins, Dukan, South Beach, Ketogenic): not all carbs are the same, and as discussed, we should reduce sugary carbs and focus on starchy

10

carbs particularly those with a high fibre content. The body needs carbs for energy and fibre for good intestinal and all-round health. Whilst cutting down on simple sugars is recommended, we need complex carbohydrates for energy. Any food can cause weight gain if overeaten, but in fact carbohydrates, gram for gram, contain fewer than half the calories of fat. Carbohydrates are necessary for energy for exercise, and omitting them will cause earlier onset of fatigue (NHS UK, 2018). Low carb diets normally have quick results, but because they are high in saturated fat can raise cholesterol levels. These diets are not generally supported by mainstream dieticians.

- **Gluten and lactose**: have become the current buzzwords. Gluten, a protein composite found in wheat, is excluded in a gluten free diet as a treatment for celiac disease (which causes fatigue, depression diarrhoea and bloating) affecting 1% of the population – although more people claim to have a reaction. Lactose intolerance is an inability to digest lactose, a sugar found in milk, (which causes bloating, diarrhoea and inflammatory bowel disease) affecting 5% of people in the West. Food allergies are on the rise but this is different to food intolerance. A 2008 study published in the journal *Allergy* revealed that although 34% of parents reported food allergies in their children, only 5% were found to have a genuine allergy (Geddes, 2015). If clients suspect they are intolerant then they should be tested professionally by a doctor – statistically the number of people who are averse to lactose and gluten is relatively small, however, gluten and lactose free diets are a popular trend which spas may need to take into consideration.

Detox and weight loss

Detox and weight loss programs do not and should not have the same aims. Whilst the client may lose weight on a detox program, the goal should be to cleanse and detox the body from the inside out, not not lose weight. Because rapid weight loss is not supported by health professionals, short weight loss programs in spas are also not advised. In their place, weight loss programs should focus less on crash weight reduction and more on changing lifestyle habits, with only a small amount of weight loss acheived during the program.

Detox cures

These are based on the premise that our bodies accumulate toxins (which can be the cause of feeling run down or ill) which need to be flushed out through diet, lifestyle changes and treatments. Detox cures have been popular in Europe for the last hundred or so years, promoted by figures such as Dr. Franz Xavier Mayr with his intestinal detoxification to improve digestion, metabolism, energy and well-being (Crebbin-Bailey, Harcup and Harrington, 2005) and Dr. Max Bircher-Benner a pioneer in natural healing, who promoted healthy lifestyels and diets and gave us the world famous swiss Birchermuesli. Spa detoxing will involve diets (such as juice/soup/tea diets and diets of healthy fruits and vegetables), meditation and yoga to help improve mental wellness, combined with treatments such as:

- *Colon hydrotherapy:* where a health professional flushes out the colon with a pipe inserted into the rectum with water.

- *Herbal enemas:* given with different herbal substances such as coffee, wormwood, pepperment, wild yam, red clover and yellow dock in various combinations for different effects, such as detoxification, laxative, muscle cramps and treatment for IBS.

- *Body wraps:* seaweed, mud, clay and even honey are spread over the body and wrapped in plastic in the belief that they will draw toxins out of the system.

- *Heat treatments:* such as saunas and infrasaunas, as sweating is believed to emit toxins.

All of these treatments have conflicting evidence and medical opinions as to their effectivity with regards to actual toxin discharge.

- *Lymphatic drainage massage:* the lymphatic system is responsible for removing waste products from the body. Health conditions such as infections and cancer treatments, can interupt its flow causing lymph fluid to build up. Lymphatic drainage massage is a light stroking massage on areas of the lymphatic system to improve the lymphatic circulation. A doctor's prescription is normally required and the treatment should be carried out by a qualified physiotherapist. Lymphatic drainage massages are evidence based.

A professional spa detox cure should follow a format such as:

1 A medical and dietry consultation (BMI, waist hip measurements, full medical examintion and possibly laboratory tests).
2 Two days to slowly reduce the food.
3 Four to five days juice and/or soup and/or tea every 2 hours.
4 Treatments / exercise (meditation yoga).
5 Then back on light foods slowly for one to two days.
6 A final consultation (possibly with comparative laboratory tests).

Weight loss programs

Crash weight loss programs are not advised for spas even though they do have a market demand. Programs instead should focus on motivating their clients to make lifestyle changes. According to the American College of sports medicine guidelines, a weight loss program should target a 5% to 10% reduction in body weight over a 3 to 6-month period, by reducing calorie intake by 500 – 1000 calories per day. General guidelines include:

- Exercise and diet combined (cardio and strength).
- Optimal hydration at least 2 litres of water per day.
- Eating less than 1,200 calories a day in small frequent meals, with only very low-calorie food after 6pm.
- A negative caloric balance of 500 calories per day
- Losing no more than 1kg a week.

10

As important as diet and exercise is the support, advice and counselling required to make lifestyle changes. Weight issues are normally accompanied with other mental, emotional and behavioural challenges, so a psychologist or specialist specialized in weight loss and food addiction is advised. Many spas offering weight loss programs run into challenges purely because they underestimate the mental and emotional issues that often accompany being overweight. Spas should only offer such programs if they can also provide the mental and behavioural experts to lead the program.

VivaMayr Detox Cure C

The Mayr detox cure was developed almost 100 years ago by an Austrian doctor who believed that we poison ourselves by eating the wrong things. The diet is a combination of holistic and modern medicine to promote inside out healing. In addition to an individual diet plan, it includes herbal teas, no sugar and daily abdominal massages and other treatments like colonic hydrotherapy. It is famous for making their clients chew their food 40 – 60 times before swallowing. Other rules include:

- Drinking 2 litres of water a day, but not during meals.

- No raw food after 4pm.

- Four- or five-hours in-between meals.

- A larger breakfast, a normal lunch and light dinner.

- Not eating when stressed.

- Alkaline brightly coloured foods.

Sleep

Getting good quality sleep at regular times is as important as diet and exercise in maintaining health. Sleep not only is important to the function of the brain but affects almost every organ and system in the body. Not getting enough sleep or having poor quality sleep increases the risk of high blood pressure, cardio vascular diseases and mental disorders. Adults need between 7 and 9 hours sleep but after the age of 60 night-time sleep is lighter and more interrupted. In order to maintain good physical fitness, a healthy adult should ensure that they are getting the right amount of sleep in a regular routine. Spa hotels should ensure that their rooms are suitably designed (from blackout curtains, to comfortable mattresses, to noise control) and that in the spas themselves there are quiet relaxation spaces for guests to nap in.

Feedback from the interviews – what the experts say

The subjects of nutrition, fitness, detox and sleep were mentioned by the interviewees as important dimensions of healthy lifestyle and spa experiences. Here is a brief summary of their comments:

- Food is usually listed by respondents in conjunction with exercise as one of the main pillars of a healthy lifestyle, along with rest and stress management. As suggested by Andrew Gibson from SVP, Los Angeles "The main trend will be a more integrative approach between fitness, nutrition, relaxation, mindfulness and pampering". Similarly, Claire Way, Managing Director of Spa Strategy states that "Consumer awareness of lifestyle factors is impacting the wellness business as a whole. This ranges from a desire to improve their health through exercise and food choices to awarenesses of how workplace and home stress affects the body physically and emotionally".

- It is suggested that spa guests will turn more towards personal nutritionists as well as fitness trainers for advice and guidance.

- Interviewees emphasise some of the newer trends in healthy eating such as organic foods and vegan diets.

- The quality of spa cuisine is considered important and ideally, should be sourced locally using natural ingredients. Avoiding food waste is also an essential part of sustainability.

- Some respondents mention the increasing number of reports and media coverage of food scares, sugar intake and superfoods which are encouraging people to change their diets constantly.

- Weight loss and slimming are not mentioned as often as the need for healthier diets. However, obesity is cited as one of the main lifestyle problems of contemporary living.

- Detox is still popular, however, more than one respondent suggested that stress management was taking over from detox as the most saught after service.

- Sleep disorders are mentioned as being one of the common symptoms of modern life.

10

Research and further reading

There are countless research reports and studies about healthy nutrition, fitness and active lifestyles. It is worth referring to the studies listed by Harvard Health Publishing (2020a, 2020b) as these are updated frequently and tend to be based on sound medical evidence. Two interesting studies were published in *The Lancet* in 2019. The first by GBD (2019) summarises a risk assessment study across 195 countries and found that a suboptimal diet is responsible for more deaths than any other risks globally (including smoking). They quote that the leading dietary risk factors for mortality are diets high in sodium, low in whole grains, low in fruit, low in nuts and seeds, low in vegetables, and low in omega-3 fatty acids. The second study by Forouhi and Unwin (2019) emphasises the importance of sustainable and plant-based diets. It is important to note that recent global research studies on health and nutrition tend to emphasise more strongly the foods that are missing from peoples' everyday diets than those that are present. An interesting but perhaps controversial study by Klein and Kiat (2015) provided quite compelling evidence to suggest that detox diets and treatments *do not* support weight management or toxin elimination, may present health risks and should be discouraged by health professionals. An interesting research paper emerged which proved the connection between spa therapy (balneotherapy) and the relief of sleep disorders and mental stress (Yang et al., 2018). Ohuruogu (2016) summarises the important contribution that physical activity and fitness make to overall health, wellness, longevity and quality of life. This includes better and more restful sleep, weight management, increased self-esteem and self-confidence esteem. Thompson (2018) analyses global fitness trends for 2019 and some of the top trends are wearable devices, group training, high-intensity interval training, fiteness programmes for older adults and bodyweight training.

References

American College of Sports Medicine (2010) *ACSM's Guidelines for Exercise Testing and Prescription*, 8th edn, Alphen aan der Rijn: Wolters Kluwer Health.

Bjarnadottir, A. (2017) 'Why refined carbs are bad for you', 4 June, Healthline https://www.healthline.com/nutrition/why-refined-carbs-are-bad (accessed 22/08/2019).

Cancer Research UK (2019) 'Does eating processed and red meat cause cancer?', https://www.cancerresearchuk.org/about-cancer/causes-of-cancer/diet-and-cancer/does-eating-processed-and-red-meat-cause-cancer (accessed 22/08/2019).

Crebbin-Bailey, J., Harcup, J. and Harrington, J. (2005) *The Spa Book*, Atlanta: Thomson.

Eyton, A. (2006) *The F2 Diet*, London: Bantam Press.

Forouhi, N. G. and Unwin, N. (2019) 'Global diet and health: old questions, fresh evidence, and new horizons', *The Lancet*, **393** (10184), 1916-1918, Doi. 10.1016/S0140-6736(19)30500-8

GBD (2019) 'Health effects of dietary risks in 195 countries, 1990–2017: a systematic analysis for the Global Burden of Disease Study 2017', *The Lancet*, **393**, (10184), 1958–72, Doi. 10.1016/ S0140-6736(19)30041-8.

Geddes, L. (2015) 'Are food intolerances fact or fad?', 16 August, *The Guardian*, https://www.theguardian.com/society/2015/aug/16/leave-it-out-are-food-intolerances-fact-or-fad-gluten-dairy-free-from-coeliac (accessed 23/08/2019).

Gunners, K. (2018) 'Daily intake of sugar', 28 June, Healthline, https://www.healthline.com/nutrition/how-much-sugar-per-day (accessed 22/08/2019).

Harvard Health Publishing (2020a) 'Healthy Eating', https://www.health.harvard.edu/topics/healthy-eating (accessed 05/02/2020).

Harvard Health Publishing (2020b) 'Exercise and Fitness', https://www.health.harvard.edu/topics/exercise-and-fitness (accessed 05/02/2020).

Heart Organisation (2015) 'Saturated fat', https://www.heart.org/en/healthy-living/healthy-eating/eat-smart/fats/saturated-fats (accessed 22/08/2019).

Klein, A. V. and Kiat, H. (2015) 'Detox diets for toxin elimination and weight management: a critical review of the evidence', *Journal of Human Nutrition and Dietics*, **28**, 675–686 Doi: 10.1111/jhn.12286

Leech, J. (2018) 'The alkaline diet', 25 September, Healthline, https://www.healthline.com/nutrition/the-alkaline-diet-myth (accessed 23/08/2019).

National Cancer Institute (2018) 'Alcohol and cancer risk', https://www.cancer.gov/about-cancer/causes-prevention/risk/alcohol/alcohol-fact-sheet (accessed 22/08/2019).

NHS UK (2018) 'The truth about carbs', https://www.nhs.uk/live-well/healthy-weight/why-we-need-to-eat-carbs/ (accessed 23/08/2019).

Norris, C. (2007) *You Are What You Eat: Live Well, Live Longer*, London: Virgin Books.

Ohuruogu, B. (2016) 'The contributions of physical activity and fitness to optimal health and wellness', *Journal of Education and Practice*, **7** (20), 123-128.

Pate, R., Oria, M. and Pillsbury L. (2012) *Health Related Fitness Measures for Youth*, Washington: National Academies Press.

Pollan, M. (2008) *In Defense of Food*, London: Penguin.

Thompson, W. R. (2018) 'Worldwide Survey of Fitness Trends for 2019', *ACSM Health and Fitness Journal*, **22** (6), 10-17, Doi: 10.1249/FIT.0000000000000438

VeryWellFit (2020) 'The physical activity readiness questionnaire', https://www.verywellfit.com/physical-activity-readiness-questionnaire-3120277 (accessed. 03/02/2020).

Weil, M.D. (2008) *Spontaneous Healing: How to Discover and Enhance Your Body's Natural Ability to Maintain and Heal Itself*, London: Sphere.

WHO (2018) 'Healthy diet', https://www.who.int/news-room/fact-sheets/detail/healthy-diet (accessed 22/08/2019).

Yang, B., Qin, Q-Z., Han, L-L., Lin, J. and Chen, Y. (2018) 'Spa therapy (balneotherapy) relieves mental stress, sleep disorder, and general health problems in sub-healthy people', *International Journal of Biometeorology*, **62**, 261–27, Doi:10.1007/s00484-017-1447-5

10

11 Mineral/thermal springs, spa hotels and balneotherapy

Mineral spring spas are to be found situated over natural spring sources or wells and are located in all continents across the world.

China and Japan together account for 54% of global revenues and 73% of all establishments. Japan alone, with its estimated 20,972 *onsen* (thermal baths), is home to nearly two-thirds of all thermal/mineral springs establishments in the world. The remainder of the top markets include a large number of European countries with a long history of using thermal/mineral waters for curative and therapeutic purposes. (Global Wellness Institute, 2018). European thermal/mineral spas, in terms of revenue generated and their influence on the spa product as a whole, play an important role internationally in the spa industry, therefore anyone working in this field should have an understanding of what they are and how they work.

Thermal/mineral springs, thalasso and spa hotels

A mineral springs spa is defined as: "A spa offering an on-site source of natural mineral, thermal or seawater used in hydrotherapy treatments". (ISPA, 2019).

Sea water spas can also be incorporated into this definition, as similarly to mineral springs, they use seawater instead of thermal/mineral water in their treatments. Historically, Brittany in France is seen as the most famous, traditional Thalassotherapy resort destination.

Thalassotherapy is "the use of seawater in cosmetic and health treatment" (Oxford English Dictionary 2009). The word comes from the Greek '*thalasso*' (meaning the 'sea'). Normally in a thalasso facility there will be a heated seawater pool and a number of related treatments, such as hydrotherapy also using seawater and sea mud or algae packs. Similar in concept to thermal spas, thalasso spas, whilst they may offer beauty and relaxation services, are more focused on longer term stays for the treatment of muscular skeletal/mobility conditions and so can also come under the 'balneotherapy' umbrella. Certain treatments will be administered by qualified physiotherapists (i.e. massage and physiotherapy both in and out of the pool, hydrotherapy treatments such as baths, showers and wraps).

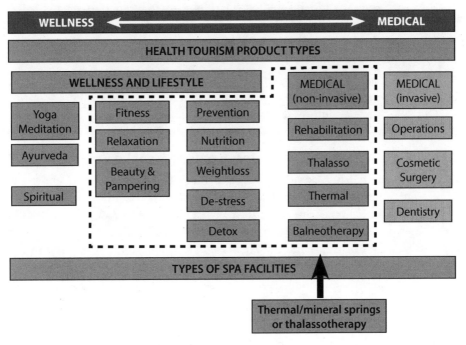

Figure 11.1: Products and services offered by thermal/mineral springs or thalassotherapy spas. Services will vary depending on whether the spa is leisure or medical. (Adapted from Smith and Puczkó, 2009).

■ Types of thermal/mineral and thalasso spas

Thermal/mineral leisure day spas

Thermal/mineral day spas can be found across the world in places where there is geothermal activity, particularly in Central Europe. These are either operated privately or by local municipalities. Many historical baths like the onsens in Japan or the thermal Ottoman baths in Turkey and Central Europe still run today in much the same way as they did in the past. Newer, extensive thermal day complexes, such as the Blue Lagoon in Iceland, or the large outdoor thermal aqua parks prevalent in Central Europe (most notably in Austria, Slovakia and Hungary), are growing in number. In these a single spa can boast over 40 pools, aqua and spa experiences and many hectares of spa gardens! They are predominantly leisure and relaxation facilities for the mass market, although many have day clinics specializing in rheumatology for patients on subsidized local insurance schemes.

- **Challenges**: because these types of spas can be high in volume, attracting sometimes several thousand visitors a day, they can be demanding to operate. There is also in parts of the world, particularly in Central Europe, an oversupply of these types of spas. The challenge for many may just be to break even

11

financially, many are subsidized and run at a loss. These types of spas also tend to offer a similar product for a similar target market (i.e. leisure/families), resulting in little differentiation. If they are to be sustainable in the future, they will need to diversity and to offer unique experiences to be competitive. They are also highly reliant on the image and attractions of the destination they are situated in.

- **Management**: to operate one of these spas, several years of management experience in the leisure, spa or hospitality sectors would be a pre-requisite. Such spas require strong leadership skills, strategic planning and detailed knowledge of both the financial and technical aspects of large leisure facilities.

Thermal/mineral spa medical centers (sometimes called medical spas)

Incorporated into some of these types of public day spas are clinics or medical centers operated normally as part of the national health service. Patients on state insurance schemes are prescribed rehabilitation-based treatments and bathing in thermal water, alongside physiotherapy-based and balneotherapy treatment. In historical European spa towns, these clinics will often be housed in the original spa treatment buildings.

- **Challenges**: with state insurance being cut, many of these spa medical centers often show signs of a lack of investment and are in a run-down state. Hydrotherapy treatments in the UK were phased out decades ago (due to a lack of evidence regarding their effectiveness). Whilst many countries in Europe still support balneotherapy and hydrotherapy (either in day spa medical centers or in private thermal spa hotels), with more pressure on government health spending budgets, gradually support for these types of spas is being cut.

- **Management**: these thermal facilities are run in the same way as clinics, normally with a head doctor responsible for the day to day management. A medical qualification (such as a degree in medicine and specialization in rheumatology) would be required to manage this type of facility. The day to day operations are supervised by a head nurse who reports to the doctor.

■ Traditional European 'spa hotel'

A spa hotel or resort is a hotel where the key purpose for guests visiting is the healing effects of a natural resource (such as thermal water, seawater, natural carbon dioxide gas, salt water, radon gas or healthy climate). The spa and spa treatments offered are based on this natural resource and will normally offer physical rehabilitation therapies as its core product. Spa hotels/resorts differ from a resort/hotel spa where guests might or might not choose to visit the spa. In a spa hotel all the guests will be receiving treatment and using the spa. Up to 70% of the guests in these types of spas are repeat guests, coming on stays for between two and three weeks.

Historically spa hotels were built next to the thermal/mineral spa medical centers or thalassotherapy centers. Guests would stay in the hotel and visit the spa medical center daily for treatment. Over the last decades the trend has been for spa hotels to introduce their own natural resources, treatments and spa clinics in the hotel itself or connect themselves to the spa clinic via corridors so that their guests can access all services under one roof.

In Central and Eastern Europe, huge spa hotel complexes were constructed in the 1970s and 80s, many of them are still operating today with a mix of guests on government subsidized insurance packages and private guests. In recent years, traditional spa hotels have introduced fitness, beauty, relaxation and pampering services as well as prevention, de-stress, detox, weight loss programs and nutrition. Some spa hotels even offer dentists, cosmetic surgery and Ayurveda departments.

In recent years, many state of the art, new spa hotel developments, complete with clinics, treatments and wellness leisure facilities have been constructed to a high standard all over Central Europe.

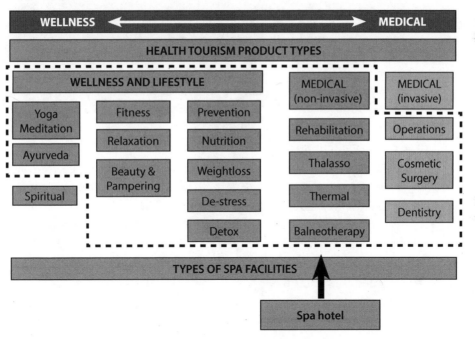

Figure 11.2: Products and services offered by spa hotels. (Adapted from Smith and Puczkó, 2009).

- **Challenges**: many of the older European spa hotels, particularly those in Eastern Europe have suffered from a lack of investment. Because these spas focused almost entirely on physical rehabilitation centers for predominantly musculo-skeletal diseases, they attracted and many still do, a senior market who return each year. Unfortunately, the downside of appealing to this guest segment, is that the clients pass on and have to be replaced. Given that these clients tend to visit the spas in groups of the same age, large groups of clients stop visiting abruptly, meaning that the fluctuations in business can be quite dramatic. With the wellness trend growing and the demands of the new senior generation changing, many traditional thermal and thalasso spas have moved towards wellness and leisure. Whilst this may have had been beneficial in the short term, challenges have arisen due to leisure guests purchasing shorter stays and conflicts of interest between the difference of expectations between the leisure and medical guests.

- **Management**: a spa in a spa hotel will either be run by the doctor or a manager or head nurse. The organizational structure can vary depending on the company's approach. Sometimes a manager will be in charge or in other cases a head doctor; in some instances the doctor will be responsible for the medical operations, with the manager responsible for the business and day to day operations, and both reporting to the resort director. This set up can sometimes blur the lines of responsibility and be the cause of conflicts. Given the large number of different departments and products, ranging from medical, to fitness, to therapy, to wellness and beauty, not to mention pools and saunas, these are highly complex operations to manage. A spa manager in a spa hotel would be expected to have a health qualification (such as nursing or physiotherapy) as well as hospitality and supervisory experience. Because this is in part a medical operation with strict medical and legal stipulations, the position ideally suits a health professional with extensive experience in medical or leisure spa operations.

The traditional European spa normally will have:

- A natural resource (not always just thermal mineral water but other natural resources including salt, natural CO_2 gas, radon gas, mud, peat, seawater etc).
- A tradition of healing (spas in 19th century were places where people went to receive treatment or to be 'cured', hence the German term 'kur').
- Medical and rehabilitation services – full-time doctors, nurses, physiotherapists and other medical staff on site to deliver the treatments.
- Healthy surroundings – places of scenic beauty, in natural healthy surroundings.
- Leisure pools and sauna complexes.
- Fitness possibilities.
- Relaxation and beauty treatments.

In order to understand the concept of a traditional European spa, it is necessary to be familiar with these terms:

Balneotherapy

This is a contentious term and therefore is often not listed in many dictionaries. The word comes from the Latin for 'bath' and refers to treatment of disease through bathing. It is generally linked to spas that use thermal and/or mineral water, or thalasso centers, however it is also sometimes used to include therapies that use other natural resources such as salt water, natural CO_2 gas or even radon gas. Balneotherapy primarily caters for the treatment of mobility dysfunctions.

English language descriptions of balneotherapy will often refer to it as "not evidence based", which is not entirely accurate. Many notable clinical trials and studies have not yet been translated into English or if they have been translated, the quality of the translation has been poor and therefore discrediting the whole study. Another important point to mention is that balneotherapy is a general term to encompass a wide range of different treatments and (combinations of treatments), individually prescribed for several types of diseases and medical conditions, therefore conducting specific clinical double-blind trials is almost impossible.

There are however many scientific studies showing that a comprehensive stay of a personally-tailored spa and balneotherapy treatments demonstrate improvement in patients' mobility and speed and a decrease in the pain according to the visual analogue scale for pain (VAS).

Traditional European health resorts, like many holiday destinations in Europe, are facing the challenge that their target groups are changing. Medical spas and thermal destination resorts, (those that have climate and other natural remedies as their main attraction) generally will have historical, sometimes outdated facilities adjacent to luxury design hotels and leisure aqua parks. This has somewhat blurred the lines of what makes a spa destination, particularly as the target groups are not so clearly defined as in the past. However, this new mix of different generations of guests, each with their unique motivations, has also its advantages and as a result many traditional 'cure' resorts and spa towns are no longer considered senior hubs. Nowadays such resorts also cater to a more cash-rich clientele, and in the summer large numbers of families with children. The destinations that are proving to be successful focus on quality of infrastructure and service. Spa hotels in these spa towns and surrounding areas, which traditionally offered high class medical check ups and balneotherapy treatment, now combine such stays with healthy aging programs and mental wellness, but at the same time retain their natural healing resources as their main attraction/USP. It should not be underestimated how such facilites have the potential to both promote and protect the most important asset we all have – 'health'. The future will mean protecting the enviroment of these unique historical spa destinations through sustainability and truly valuing them as a jewel of nature – an integral part of European culture and life.

Csilla Mezösi, Secretary General of ESPA

Rehabilitation

In this context, rehabilitation means "restoring to a former condition" (Oxford English Dictionary, 2009) and is the provision of services to help people regain functions they have lost due to illness or injury. Primarily, in a spa setting, this refers to therapies that help restore movement and mobility (e.g. the treatment of diseases such as arthritis, rheumatism and injury resulting from accidents or surgery), but it can also include, bowel and bladder problems, chewing and swallowing, and speech. Physiotherapy is normally a central focus of the rehabilitation product which will include active and passive exercises, mobilization, medical massage in combination with electrical and heat treatments.

Introduction to mineral and thermal water

Please note definitions of what waters are considered 'mineral', 'high/low mineralized', or what temperature waters are considered 'thermal' are dependent on the source country's legislation.

Mineral water and thermal water are not the same. *Mineral water* is defined according to the quantity of minerals and *thermal water* according to the temperature. Many thermal waters are also mineral waters (therefore called *thermal mineral water*) and many waters are cold mineral water.

Mineral water in most of the Central European countries is defined as water obtained from a spring, lake or well, with at least one of the next properties:

- its temperature at source is higher than 20°C.
- it has at least 1000 mg/litre (L) of minerals.
- has one or several proven therapeutic effects.

According to its temperature at source, mineral waters are classified as the following:

- **Cold springs:** (under 20°C) which are prescribed in health spas as an internal drinking treatment for digestive, hepatic and biliary, metabolic and urinary diseases.
- **Warm or thermal springs** (normally originating from greater depths). Thermal waters can be divided into the following categories:
  - ☐ *Hypothermal* water: between 20°C and 31°C.
  - ☐ *Thermal* water: between 32-38°C (including homeo-thermal values between 34-38°C).
  - ☐ *Hyperthermal* water: above 38°C (waters above 80°C are normally but not always of volcanic origin, heated from the magmatic interior of the earth – like the geysers of Iceland or thermal waters in Japan).

Thermal water may or may not be highly mineralized. In either case, thermal water has been traditionally used and is currently used for external (bathing) treatment for musculoskeletal diseases, neurological, skin, peripheral circulation diseases and some gynaecological conditions.

Since 1980, Europe Union legislation, based on Directive 777/80/EEC, makes a clear difference between drinking mineral waters for 'daily' use, and mineral waters for medicinal usage, namely 'medicinal mineral waters':

Mineral waters for 'daily' drinking (are considered 'dietary products' and not needing medical supervision) are classified as follows:

■ Natural mineral water – for drinking, normally sold in bottled form.

■ Spring water.

■ Drinking water.

Medicinal mineral waters destined for medical purposes are considered 'medical products' and are prescribed only under medical supervision for drinking, inhalation, bathing, etc. – usually in health spas. Medicinal waters focus on certain well-defined and/or evidence based curative properties, due to temperature, combinations of dissolved substances, or both.

Medicinal mineral waters are defined as:

■ Waters containing more than 1000 mg total dissolved substances (TDS) per litre (group A).

■ Water containing less than 1000 mg/L TDS, but containing certain compounds at curative concentration (group B). Sometimes there is an overlap in terms of temperature, mineralization, composition between examples A and B.

■ Waters verified by clinical tests demonstrating that the water contributes to the prevention, alleviation or treatment of certain complaints. An exception is made for water that has been known for its healing effects for a long time.

Medicinal mineral waters are prescribed for a short period (days/year) or periodical use (for example once or twice a year).

Medicinal waters can be drunk if they adhere to all of the potability (safe to drink) criteria.

Mineralization

Mineralization refers to total dissolved substances (TDS), and also to the concentration of certain molecules.

For all *drinking* waters (bottled, respectively medicinal) the scale moves around 1000 mg/L (i.e. 1 gm/L), between 50 and 15,000 mg/L (the upper limit for drinking).

Mineralization scale for *bathing* waters (and also for inhalation and gynaecological treatments) is as follows:

■ low concentration waters: below 1000 mg/L

■ medium concentration waters: between 1000 – 15,000 mg/L

■ concentrated mineral waters between 15,000 – 35,000 mg/L (e.g. sea water)

■ high concentration waters: between 35,000 – 150,000 mg/L

■ very high concentration waters: above 150,000 mg/L (i.e. above 150 grams/L).

Physiological considerations

The heat of the thermal water has undisputedly a physiological effect on the body. After an initial increase of heart rate and blood pressure as the body temperature increases, the blood vessels dilate, lessening the resistance to the blood flow resulting in a slowing down of the heart and lowering of the blood pressure. A thermal water bath mineralized or not mineralized therefore will have these effects on the body:

- A lowering of blood pressure.
- Increased buoyancy and relaxation of muscles.
- Relief on muscles and joints.
- An increase of O_2 to organs, removal of CO_2, lactic acid and waste.

The absorption of minerals through the skin

The skin is the largest organ of the body. The primary function of the skin is to provide a barrier between the body and the external environment. This barrier protects against the permeation of ultraviolet (UV) radiation, chemicals, allergens and micro-organisms, in addition to the loss of moisture and body nutrients. This means that the absorptive capacity of healthy skin for substances from the outside is very limited. To get through the skin, a substance must penetrate the epidermis or has to be absorbed by sweat glands or hair follicles.

There are many studies proving and disproving the effectiveness of mineral water when absorbed through the skin through bathing. Whilst certain minerals are indeed absorbed through the skin membrane, there is conflicting evidence in proving that they reach the targeted area to have an effect once absorbed externally through the skin membrane. This is with the exception of hydrogen sulphide (H2S) and carbon dioxide (CO_2) whose effects are evidence based.

■ Mineral benefits and effects

Six chemical elements — oxygen, carbon, hydrogen, nitrogen, calcium and phosphorus — make up 99% of your body mass. The next five — potassium, sulphur, sodium, chlorine, and magnesium — provide that last 1% in slightly varying degrees. The main elements found in natural thermal or mineral springs are calcium, carbonates, chlorides, fluorides, iron, magnesium, sodium, sulphates, sulphides. The main gasses are carbon dioxide, hydrogen sulphide, nitrogen, oxygen and sometimes radon. (Cooper and Cooper, 2009).

Sodium (Na)

The water has an appropriate salt content for drinking, inhalations and bathing. Salt has an antibacterial effect and dependent on the levels can be suitable for drinking, inhalations and bathing. From a bathing point of view, salt water can have a positive effect on dermatological conditions such as psoriasis and eczema.

Sulphur

Sulphur is the third most abundant mineral in the human body. The skin, hair, muscles and bones contain about half the sulphur in the body. Wrinkles, sore muscles and joint pain can be an indication of a sulphur deficiency.

Sulphurous mineral waters have been used for the following treatments:

- **Drinking**: (for waters with less concentration of salt) for digestive, hepatic, biliary, urinary, metabolic diseases and allergies.

- **Inhalation treatments**: for chronic respiratory diseases, infections, allergies.

- **Bath treatments**: for chronic rheumatism and musculoskeletal degenerative conditions, post traumatic disorders, neurological, dermatological, gynaecological diseases.

Sulphate (SO4)

Whilst it is thought, and often promoted in spas, that sulphate penetrates through the skin during bathing to have a beneficial effect on the cartilages and connective tissues, there is a lack of hard evidence to support this. Naturally if drunk and digested, however the sulphate would be absorbed into the body.

Calcium (Ca)

Calcium is the most abundant mineral in the body and is vital to the health of the muscular, circulatory and digestive systems. It is also important for the building of bone in addition to supporting the function of blood cells. If consumed orally calcium would be absorbed into the system, however, there is not enough evidence to support the effectivity or absorption of calcium through the skin membrane.

Magnesium (Mg) and chloride (Cl)

Chlorine compounds play an essential role in the electrical and pressure of extracellular fluids and in the acid-base balance of the body. It is absorbed during digestion. Magnesium is required for DNA and RNA synthesis, reproduction, and protein synthesis. Moreover, magnesium is essential for the regulation of muscular contraction, blood pressure, insulin metabolism, cardiac function, vasomotor tone, nerve transmission and neuromuscular conduction. There have been several studies concerning transdermal magnesium effects, and whilst it is not scientifically yet proven, there are studies that have shown an increase in magnesium in the body after bath treatments.

Hydrogen sulphide (H2S)

Hydrogen sulphide is a gas often present in wells and is what will give the water its sulphurous smell. Hydrogen sulphide is intensely lipophilic meaning it passes through the skin membrane rapidly both in and out. It is eliminated both through the urinary and respiratory system. Studies have shown hydrogen sulphide (H2S) is absorbed through the skin where it has a biological effect on the body. This is evidence based. Effects of hydrogen sulphide (H2S) as a bathing treatment:

- **General**: induces sleep, activates memory and cognition, protects the neurons, has an anti-oxidant and anti-inflammatory effect.

- **Circulation**: vasodilatation in the kidneys, lungs, digestive system, nervous system, blood pressure regulation, protects against ischemia.

- Most notably its effect is **pain modulation** and **reducing acute/chronic inflammation** in the skin, respiratory system, nervous system, muscles and joints.

11

■ Indications and contra-indications

Indications

There are a wide range of medical conditions that the traditional European spa will treat. These include chronic degenerative muscular skeletal (bone and joint) diseases, rheumatoid arthritis and soft tissue rheumatism, osteoarthritis of the spine and joints, neurological diseases, lower back pain, frozen shoulder, disc problems, certain diseases of the respiratory system. In short, diseases normally connected to the onset of aging.

Certain spas will specialize according to their unique natural resource or tradition. There are spas specializing in diseases of the kidney and urinary tract, diabetes, oncology, chronic inflammatory gynaecological conditions and infertility and skin diseases particularly psoriasis (which is also often linked to severe arthritis), dermatitis, eczema and acne.

Contraindications

This refers to the diseases and conditions that the spas will not be able to treat and which could even be aggravated by a spa stay. These include: any infectious diseases, malignant tumours, serious cases of anaemia and haemophilia, acute thrombosis, fever, pregnancy and people who are seriously ill who require nursing. Spas will differ as to what level of disease progression they are willing to undertake.

The medical stay

■ The doctor's visit

The spa stay will begin with an initial doctor's consultation where the doctor will conduct a basic examination (heart rate, blood pressure and physical examination), check the past medical history and past and present medications and then prescribe the treatments. There will normally be a weekly check-up to monitor how the therapies are progressing.

■ Traditional European spa therapies and stays

The therapies will take place in the various spa departments. In most traditional European spas, you will find the following therapy areas: balneotherapy, physiotherapy, heat packing, hydrotherapy, electrotherapy and inhalation. The number of treatments per day will be between 2 – 4 and the stay in the spa resort between 2 – 3 weeks.

A consultation in a health spa

My typical medical spa consultation is as follows: first, greeting the patient, shaking hands, observing the body language of the guest, their posture, their tone of voice and even their hand's temperature! Then I ask the guest to take a seat. I will have checked their length of stay, if it is just a short stay of a number of days or a longer 1-2 or 3 week stay as this will determine which treatment regime will be effective. Then I proceed with asking health and lifestyle related questions, such as what are their main complaints, what health conditions they have (malignant tumours, pacemakers, metallic implants), what medications are they on etc, to ascertain if there are any contraindications related to the natural healing resources and treatments offered in the spa. If they have brought them, I will also check their documentation such as lab tests, imaging - X-rays, CT, MRI, ultrasound, previous reports) while listening to them talk about their medical history.

The second part of the consultation is the medical examination. Whilst they are undressing, I will ask questions regarding their medical history related to the main complaints and also try to gather further information about their lifestyle (activities, movement, nutrition, stress etc).

The examination involves:

- Examining the joints/muscles/soft tissues: standing position, walking, laying down – specific testing force, range of motion, blood pressure, heart rate, lungs, abdomen; peripheral arteries and veins, skin, specific neurological and balance testing where needed.

- Establishing a diagnosis and explaining to the patient their health risks in short and long-term.

- Giving written recommendations: lifestyle, lab analysis, imaging, other medical examinations.

- Prescribing the treatment regime including local natural healing factors (e.g. mud, CO_2, drinking mineral water, inhalations, etc.), as well as other procedures (medical massage, electrotherapy, hydrotherapy, etc.).

- Explaining the correct use of the free facilities (salt water pool, Aquafitness, saunas, Kneipp, etc.) the advised time and sequence they should use these facilities whilst recommending other wellness activities such as the fitness, local walks etc.

- I finish off the consultation by asking them if they have any more questions or information they would like for the follow up consultation and show them where to go should they have any questions on the treatments or if the treatments cause any undue effects.

Dr. Suzana Pretorian, Consultant physician, Sovata & Braget Ensana Health Spa Hotel, Romania

11

Balneotherapy therapies

- **Thermal mineral (or hot spring) bath**: carried out in pools or individual bath tubs from between 10 to 20 minutes at temperatures ranging from 36°C to 40°C, the heat of the water dilates the blood vessels, in turn the blood pressure decreases and lowers inflammation and pain levels. The body is also able to relax by being buoyant in the water. Spas promote the water by proclaiming that the minerals are absorbed through the skin where they inhibit the degradation of collagen in the cartilages. The treatment improves mobility and lowers pain and inflammation making it a key therapy in the treatment of mobility diseases.

- **Mineral drinking water**: originates from a natural spring and/or underground source where the dissolved mineral content is minimally 1000 mg/l. Depending on the type of spring, the water will have particular benefits for different organs of the body such as the digestive system, liver, kidneys and urinary tract. In spas where there is a variety of spring types and where the spring water is a signature treatment, doctors will prescribe the dosage and water type to be consumed. The steam from heated spring water can also be prescribed as an inhalation treatment for allergies and respiratory conditions. Mineral water when heated is also used for individual bath therapies, much like the thermal mineral bath.

Other natural resources

Other natural resources are used in European spas which sometimes also come under the 'balneotherapy' umbrella:

- **Carbon dioxide bath**: is administered in an individual bath tub for approximately 20 minutes at a temperature of between 28°C and 34°C. The carbon dioxide gas will normally be naturally present in the water, or if it is not, commercial CO_2 gas can be artificially pumped through a tube. The CO_2 bubbles coat the skin like fizzing mineral water inhibiting the body's uptake of oxygen. This results in a lowering of the heart rate and blood pressure and after a course of treatments the blood circulation, kidney function and sexual performance (vasodilatation). Because of this effect on sexual performance, it is promoted as a natural Viagra, without the side effects of Viagra. The effect of CO_2 is evidence based.

- **Dry CO_2 bath and injections**: CO_2 natural gas emitting from the earth in the form of volcanic "mofettas' is also used as a popular spa therapy. CO_2 gas is applied in the form of dry gas bags or filled into dry sunken basins where clients can sit or added to mineral water where it has a blood pressure reducing effect. This treatment works on the same principle as the carbon dioxide bath and has the same effects. CO_2 gas is also used in the form of injections to reduce pain, inflammation and speed up the healing process.

- **Mud or peat packs**: mud or peat cool down approximately four times more slowly than water. Mud is extracted from the bottom of thermal springs (or alternatively the mud is soaked in thermal spring water); peat is a mixture of decomposed plant material. All contain a high content of minerals, which are promoted by spas as contributing to the health of the cartilages and sinews when absorbed through the skin. The substance will be applied either partially or all over the body, at a temperature of between 40°C and 45°C. The body is then wrapped up in blankets. After 20 minutes, the mud or peat is hosed off and a dry wrap for another 20 minutes may follow. The heat packing helps reduce local swelling around the joints and muscle tension. For swelling caused by acute inflammation heat packs are contra-indicatory.

In several thermal spas mud therapy is also offered in the form of 'mud pools', which are thermal water pools with a mud base and high mud content. The effect is similar to a thermal bath combined with a mud pack.

- **Salt**: either from heated sea water or natural salt water from some other source (such as a Salt Lake). It is administered either in pools or individual bath tubs at a temperature of between 32°C and 36°C. Like the thermal bath, the treatment will last for around 20 minutes. Because of the effect of the salt, the buoyancy of the body is greater than in normal water. It is used to treat rheumatic, skin and also gynaecological complaints in the form of irrigation treatments. Salt is also used for inhalation purposes and saline vapours are inhaled in saline chambers or through a pipe/tube. More recently salt caves have come into fashion. These are nothing new – real salt caves have been used for treating respiratory conditions for hundreds of years.

- **Radon bath**: Radon is an odourless, colourless gas which in high doses is dangerous and thought to cause cancer, however in prescribed doses it has been used as a treatment for people seeking relief from arthritis, pain and mobility diseases in the form of dry treatment and inhalation. There are spas in Austria, Poland and Germany that have had a tradition of using radon as a natural therapy.

  It is normally offered in two forms, either where radon is present in a thermal bath (20 minutes approximately at 36°C– 39°C), or in prescribed time doses in caves or old mines, which have a high radon content. Persons undergoing treatment will be allocated a number of visits to caves, generally between eight to 12 admissions.

Physiotherapy techniques

'Physiotherapy' refers to therapies and techniques applied to help restore movement and function to anyone affected by an injury, disability or health condition.

- **Individual physiotherapy:** There are many different physiotherapy methods designed to restore physical mobility. They will include active and passive movements as well as mobilization and manipulation. Other methods include visualization, active muscle contraction, active assisted movements, free active movements and breathing exercises. There are also exercises to improve balance, strength and flexibility.

11

- **Group physiotherapy**: Group classes were very popular in the 1970s and 1980s. Persons suffering from similar medical conditions on state insurance paid stays received physiotherapy exercises in groups according to their common complaints (e.g. a group for lower back treatment, hip problems, cardio rehabilitation etc). Group classes are still popular but more focus is now placed on individual physiotherapy.

- **Medical/rehabilitation massage**: This is sometimes referred to as the 'classical' massage and involves a variety of techniques mainly based on Swedish massage. The aim is to target areas where secondary changes have occurred as a result of injury somewhere in the body and to speed up the recovery process by improving circulation to the problematic area. In addition to improving blood flow to the targeted region, the massage will also relax or stimulate the muscles and help relieve pain. This massage is either carried out as a full-body massage or a partial massage.

- **Segment and/or connective tissue massage**: These are very specialized techniques targeting the nerve connections and endings. The massage is carried out in one of four areas: the head and neck, the back, the chest or the pelvis. One technique involves the masseur pressing the thumb and forefinger along short or long curved lines. This action is very particular and not only promotes healing in the area being massaged, but also has a 'reflex' effect promoting healing in the entire body. It has been found to be very effective in relieving stress, fatigue, sleep and digestive disorders as well as high blood pressure.

- **Manual lymph drainage**: This is a specialized massage to assist the performance of the lymphatic system, particularly where there has been a problem. The massage involves light rhythmical movements of the hand to the lymph nodes and lymphatic system. It stimulates the lymph node activity to cleanse the body and assist the flow of lymphatic fluid to remove toxins, debris, cell waste and dead particles. The massage can focus on different parts of the body.

- **Manipulation and mobilization**: This is a manual technique used to treat blockages in the joints that are causing pain and restricting movement. These are mainly located in the spine. The purpose of the treatment is to release the segment and restore the joint to free movement. First, the problematic area is placed under pressure, then it is released though a small quick forceful movement. There are other techniques such as a slower pulling and releasing of the muscles as well as passive stretching.

- **Traction**: This is a passive treatment that uses weights to induce stretching of the soft tissues in the spine. Traction in spas is either carried out in a dry form using a bed in which the angle can be adjusted or in water/thermal water where the person is suspended either from the neck or shoulders and weights are placed on the feet to stretch the spine.

- **Ultrasound**: Ultrasound treatment is normally carried out in an electrotherapy department, however it is classified as a physiotherapy treatment. It is based on a high frequency sound delivered as a micro massage which is converted into heat and mechanical energy in the tissues. In addition, it improves the blood circulation, the nutrition of the tissues as well as relieving pain.

Heat packing

- **Paraffin**: Paraffin hardens at a temperature of approximately 55°C and is prescribed as a more extreme heat treatment than peat or mud. For this reason, it cannot be applied all over the body, but just on certain parts, most commonly the hands. There are several types of application, such as soaking, brushing or applying the paraffin in a thin layer onto the necessary area of the skin. The heat relaxes the muscles, eases chronic pain and promotes healing.

- **Parafango**: This is a mixture combining dry mud and paraffin. As with paraffin, it is only applied to certain parts of the body, but in a layer of one centimetre. The parafango piece is heated in a special unit to a temperature of 38°C–45°C and then placed onto the prescribed area. The intensity is slightly lower than paraffin which means that it can be applied to a larger surface area of the body. It has the advantage also that it is not necessary to shower after the pack, making it an easier treatment to administer. The effects, however, are more or less the same.

- **Other packs**: Spas use a variety of other cream packs for inflammation and pain. These will include rheumatic creams such as antiphlogistic and sulphur, which have a cooling effect when applied onto the skin. The mixture will be applied to the affected body part, wrapped in plastic foil and then covered with a blanket.

Hydrotherapy

These treatments have their roots in Kneipp and Priessnitz and the hydrotherapy revolution of the 19th century, when water was believed to hold the secret cure for most illnesses. Hydrotherapy treatments usually involve massaging problematic areas of the body with warm water and currents.

- **Hydromassage**: This is a treatment similar to a jacuzzi and carried out in a bath of 35°C–37°C for 10 to 20 minutes that has currents of whirling water. Aroma oils and essences are sometimes added to enhance the experience. The effects include relaxation, improved circulation and a loosening of muscle and joint stiffness.

- **Underwater jet massage**: This is also administered at a temperature of 35°C–37°C. A powerful jet of water is released through a hose which is then directed by a therapist on the main muscle groups of the body, targeting specific problematic areas. By varying the distance and angle it is possible to adjust the intensity of the water pressure coming from the jet. This treatment is a deep massage and releases stiffness in the muscles and connective tissue.

- **Stepping bath**: Two different footbaths are filled with water, the first at a temperature of between 40°C–42°C and the second at between 10°C–16°C. Both feet are placed into the hot footbath, then the person steps on the spot for one

11

to two minutes, after this the person then steps into the cold water footbath and continues stepping for 15 to 30 seconds. This whole cycle is repeated between six and 10 times. The treatment has a positive effect on circulatory disorders (cold feet) and early stage varicose veins. It also helps improve the condition of the ankle ligaments and is an effective rehabilitation treatment for feet and lower limb injuries.

- **Scottish spray**: This consists of a pressurized jet of water which is directed at the body from a distance of three to four metres, during which time the temperature is alternated by a therapist. There are several variations that can be applied for this treatment, one being 30 seconds with a warm jet 38°C–42°C, follow by a cold jet of 16°C–18°C for five seconds. During the alternating temperature sequences, the water jet is directed at different parts of the body – for example the upper and lower extremities, the torso and belly from the front and back. This treatment improves the circulation system, metabolism and immune system.

Electrotherapy

There is a wide variety of electrotherapy treatments available in spas these including: nerve stimulation by electric current., micro massage via electrical pads with a small vacuum, stimulation via electrical current and electric currents used to help the absorption of medicine into the body. Electrical treatments can also be combined with water such as the galvanic bath. Electrotherapy treatments have a number of effects such as muscle and nerve stimulation, pain relief and micro-massage. Magnetic therapy is also widely practiced whereby the body is exposed to a weak, artificial, pulsating magnetic field, which supposedly has the effect of recharging the magnetic stimulation of the cells, thereby supporting the healing process.

■ Inhalation

Inhalation therapies have their roots in 19th century spa treatments, when respiratory conditions were more prevalent. Some spas today offer steam inhalation therapies using mineral or spring water to cleanse the respiratory tracts and dissolve mucus. (Medicaments are also prescribed for this purpose). The vapor is normally inhaled through a mouth-nose mask or pipe/tube for mouth/nose for between 10 – 20 minutes.

- **Salt inhalation**: Salt has a natural anti-bacterial effect. During the inhalation process, salt particles are inhaled into the respiratory system and lungs, where they break down mucous and have a cleansing effect. Salt inhalation is either prescribed through an inhalation mask/tube which is inhaled into the mouth/nose, or a salt chamber where salt vapor is pumped into a small room. The person receiving the treatment normally inhales from between 10 – 20 minutes.

- **Salt caves**: Salt caves are constructed from natural salt creating an environment of salt particles. During the treatment, which is conducted on a relaxing bed in the cave, the salt particles in the air are inhaled – and have the same effect as a salt inhalation therapy. Because the salt particle content is not as high as in a salt inhalation chamber or by inhaling through a tube, the treatment normally lasts for a longer time, from 45 minutes to one hour, making it an excellent relaxation experience as well.

- **Oxygen inhalation**: An increased supply of oxygen to the body enhances the immune system, improves the function of the heart, elasticity of the lungs and mental health as well as being helpful for all-round health. The oxygen is normally inhaled through a tube into the nose whilst the person receiving the treatment relaxes in a comfortable chair. The treatment lasts for about one hour and sometimes spas will offer a vitamin drink at the end.

The traditional European medical (or balneotherapy) stay

The traditional European 1, 2 or 3 week stay has not changed much in 100 years. Here is an example of a traditional balneotherapy spa stay:

1 Arrival and check in.

2 Doctors consultation (full medical examination and review of patient's documentation x-rays, previous reports etc).

3 Laboratory tests.

4 2 – 4 treatments a day from the treatments listed above (Balneotherapy, physiotherapy, heat packs, hydrotherapy, electrotherapy, massage, inhalation).

5 Weekly check up with doctor.

6 Final consultation and medical report.

7 Sometimes a dietary consultation and diet plan.

The stay will normally include full or half board, full use of the spa and fitness facilities, exercise classes.

■ Traditional European spa hotel trends

Spa hotels recently have been influenced by two main factors:

1 **The senior market:** and the changing characteristics of senior clients. They are becoming more educated, more travelled and more discerning. From a marketing perspective, seniors are no longer just one segment:

☐ OPALs (old people with active lifestyle) – seniors who may have some health issues, but are generally active, enjoy being active and are willing to try new experiences.

☐ WHOPs (wealthy, healthy older people) – similar to the above but with plenty of disposable income, ready to spend their money on health and wellness experiences.

☐ Older people with special needs – similar to the traditional medical spa guests, seeking medical treatment for age related conditions (i.e. musculo-skeletal diseases, etc.)

11

☐ A growing number of older single women – who can be any of the above, looking for social interaction and experiences in which they feel safe.

This has been the motor and force for traditional balneotherapy spas to diversify and specialize.

2 **Wellness:** has also had its impact on the traditional spa. Many have incorporated lifestyle programs alongside or integrated them into the traditional balneotherapy stay, such as detox, weight loss, anti-aging, beauty, relaxation, prevention and active fitness programs. Here are two examples:

Example spa packages

Les Thermes Marines De Saint Malo in France offers in their 6 day 'Sea and Harmony package': 3 aqua relax session, 3 yoga, 10 hydrotherapy treatments (affusion and underwater showers, marine draining, jet baths) and 1 Ayurvedic Indian massage, 1 Chinese Energy massage, and 1 foot reflexology.

Hotel Carbona Héviz in Hungary offers in their spine strengthening cure: a 7 night stay: spine examination, 6 spinliner treatments, 2 pilates sessions, 2 individual physiotherapy, underwater traction, 5 Bemer treatments, 3 massages and 1 body peeling.

Feedback from the interviews – what the experts say

Some of the respondents, especially those from Central and Eastern Europe (e.g. Croatia, Czech Republic, Hungary, Romania, Serbia, Slovakia) are working in thermal mineral or medical spas. Below is a summary of their comments about balneology and the use of healing waters:

■ The most important elements in a thermal mineral spa include the specific natural healing resources (thermal waters, mud) as well as evidence-based medicine (supported by clinical trials and research).

■ Quality is mentioned as an important aspect, including national monitoring schemes for state-supported balneology spas. This can refer to the quality and safety of the waters and muds themselves, the treatments or therapies, as well as the surrounding natural environment. Therapies should be organic, traditional and authentic where possible.

■ Special training and education are needed to administer thermal medical therapies (balneotherapy).

■ More than one respondent suggests that medical thermal treatments need to be conducted separately from leisure and wellness activities.

■ It is suggested that one of the main trends for the spas of the future will include evidence based and scientifically supported treatments using natural and local resources and ingredients (e.g. mineral water, mud). More hydrothermal therapies may be introduced in countries where they are not so widely used currently (e.g. USA). One respondent from Romania refers to "high standard, accredited classic balneology treatments, as well as integrative medical treatments". Nataša Ranitović, CEO of Sunny Ltd Wellness Consulting suggested a growth in "Authentic spa experiences based on spa tradition and natural healing factors (thermal waters and mud) in thermal spa destinations. Rediscovering health benefits of saunas, thermal bathing and mud applications".

Further reading

Numerous publications have emerged in recent years which examine the importance of thermal waters, hot springs and balneology. Yang et al. (2018) provide an overview of the general health benefits of balneotherapy, including relieving stress and sleep disorders. Smith, Puczkó and Sziva (2015) and Smith and Puczkó (2017) discuss the role of balneology in health tourism, including numerous examples from around the world and a case study of Hungary. Bender et al. (2014) focus on the medical and research evidence for balneology especially in Hungary. Several studies have been undertaken about changes in the financing and funding systems for thermal baths, e.g. Derco (2017) and Derco and Pavlisinova (2017) in Slovakia and Szromek, Romaniuk and Hadzik (2016) in Poland.

Profile, motivation and segmentation research of thermal spa guests was undertaken by Priszinger and Formádi (2013) in Hungary, Dimitrovski and Todorović (2015) in Serbia and Dryglas and Różycki (2017) and Dryglas and Salamaga (2017, 2018) in Poland. Several authors have also researched the changes in spa functionality from the original healing and rehabilitation function to a recreational, leisure or wellness one, e.g. Speier (2011) and Kiralova (2014) in the Czech Republic, Kasagranda and Gurňák, (2017) in Slovakia and Hadzik, Ujma and Gammon (2014) in Poland. Some authors have written about the changing nature of thermal spa resorts and spa towns, e.g. Jónás-Berki et al. (2014) in Hungary and Kraftova et al. (2013) in the Czech Republic. Research has also been undertaken on hot springs in Asia, especially in Japan. Romão, Machino and Nijkamp (2018) describe the high number of onsen in Japan located mainly in rural areas, which may have potential for wellness tourism. Ryu, Han and Lee (2016) show that for Koreans visiting Japan, 'spa' was the most preferred experience. Chang and Beise-Zee (2013) refer to 18 hot spring regions in Taiwan and Lin (2013) notes how hot spring destinations in Taiwan have built resorts, hotels and facilities to accommodate growing numbers of tourists.

11

References

Bender, T., Bálint, G., Prohászka, Z., Géher, P. and Tefner, I.K. (2014) 'Evidence-based hydro- and balneotherapy in Hungary—a systematic review and meta-analysis', Int J Biometeorol, 58, 311–323, Doi: 10.1007/s00484-013-0667-6

Chang, L. and Beise-Zee, R. (2013) 'Consumer perception of healthfulness and appraisal of health-promoting tourist destinations', Tourism Review 68 (1), 34-47, Doi: 10.1108/16605371311310066

Cooper, P. and Cooper, M. (2009) Health and Wellness Tourism. Spas and Hot Springs, Bristol: Channel View.

Derco, J. (2017) 'Impact of health care funding on financial position of Slovak medical spas', Tourism, 65 (3), 376-380, Doi: 10.1080/13683500.2019.1685472

Derco, J. and Pavlisinova, D. (2017) 'Financial position of medical spas – The case of Slovakia', Tourism Economics, 23 (4), 867–873, Doi: 10.5367/te.2016.0553

Dimitrovski, D. and Todorović, A. (2015) 'Clustering wellness tourists in spa environment', Tourism Management Perspectives 16, 259–265, Doi: 10.1016/j.tmp.2015.09.004

Dryglas, D. and Różycki, P. (2017) 'Profile of tourists visiting European spa resorts: a case study of Poland', Journal of Policy Research in Tourism, Leisure and Events, 9 (3), 298-317, Doi: 10.1080/19407963.2017.1297311

Dryglas, D. and Salamaga, M. (2017) 'Applying destination attribute segmentation to health tourists: A case study of Polish spa resorts', Journal of Travel and Tourism

Marketing, 34 (4), 503-514, Doi: 10.1080/10548408.2016.1193102

Dryglas, D. and Salamaga, M. (2018) 'Segmentation by push motives in health tourism destinations: A case study of Polish spa resorts', Journal of Destination Marketing and Management 9, 234–246, Doi: 10.1016/j.jdmm.2018.01.008

Hadzik, A., Ujma, D. and Gammon, S. (2014) 'Wellness and spa provision in the Silesian health resorts of Poland', in M. K. Smith and L. Puczkó (eds) Health, tourism and hospitality: Spas, wellness and medical travel, London: Routledge, pp. 321–328.

Jonas-Berki, M., Csapo, J., Palfi, A. and Aubert, A. (2015) 'A Market and Spatial Perspective of Health Tourism Destinations: The Hungarian Experience', International Journal of Tourism Research 17, 602–612, Doi: 10.1002/jtr.2027

Kasagranda, A. and Gurňák, D. (2017) 'Spa and Wellness Tourism in Slovakia (A Geographical Analysis)', Czech Journal of Tourism, 6 (1), 27–53, Doi:10.1515/cjot-2017-0002

Kiralova, A. (2014) 'Medical Spa and Wellness Spa – Where Are They Heading? The Case of the Czech Republic', in K. S. Soliman (ed.) *Crafting Global Competitive Economies: 2020 Vision Strategic Planning & Smart Implementation*, IBIMA conference, pp. 516-527.

Kraftova, I., Mandysova, I., and Matěja, Z. (2013) 'Specifics of the Czech Spa Industry and categorization model of spa towns', Scientific Papers of the University of Pardubice, 28, 43-54

Lin, C. (2013) 'Determinants of Revisit Intention to a Hot Springs Destination: Evidence from Taiwan', Asia Pacific Journal of Tourism Research, 18 (3), 183-204, Doi: 10.1080/10941665.2011.640698

Priszinger, K. and Formádi, K. (2013) 'Comparative analysis of health tourism products and online communication of selected Hungarian spas and hotels', in M. K. Smith and L. Puczkó (2013) Health, Tourism and Hospitality: Spas, Wellness and Medical Travel, London: Routledge, pp.285-290.

Romão, J., Machino, K. and Nijkamp, P. (2018) 'Integrative diversification of wellness tourism services in rural areas – an operational framework model applied to east Hokkaido (Japan)', Asia Pacific Journal of Tourism Research, 23 (7), 734-746, Doi: 10.1080/10941665.2018.1488752

Ryu, K., Han, J. and Lee, T. J. (2016) 'Selection Attributes of Travel Products: A Case of Korean Tourists to Japan', Journal of Travel & Tourism Marketing, 33 (5), 671-686, Doi: 10.1080/10548408.2016.1167360

Smith, M. K., Puczkó, L. and Sziva, I. (2015) 'Putting the thermal back into medical tourism', in N. Lunt, D. Horsfall and J. Hanefeld (eds) Handbook on Medical Tourism and Patient Mobility, Cheltenham: Edward Elgar Publishing Ltd, pp.393-402.

Smith, M. K. and Puczkó, L. (2017) 'Balneology and health tourism', in M. K. Smith and L. Puczkó (eds) The Routledge Handbook of Health Tourism, London: Routledge, pp. 271-281.

Speier, A. R. (2011) 'Health tourism in a Czech health spa', Anthropology & Medicine, 18 (1), April, 55–66, Doi: 10.1080/13648470.2010.525879

Szromek, A. R., Romaniuk, P. and Hadzik, A. (2016) 'The privatization of spa companies in Poland – An evaluation of policy assumptions and implementation', Health Policy, 120, 362–368, Doi: 10.1016/j.healthpol.2016.02.011

Yang, B., Qin, Q-Z., Han, L-L., Lin, J. and Chen, Y. (2018) 'Spa therapy (balneotherapy) relieves mental stress, sleep disorder, and general health problems in sub-healthy people', Int J Biometeorol, 62, 261–27, Doi: 10.1007/s00484-017-1447-5

11

12 Experience design and developing spa concepts

Experience creation

Successful spas focus on delivering quality, authentic, memorable experiences for their clients. An experience can be defined as something notable or important that happens to a client, something that has a beginning and an end. Creating amazing experiences for their guests should be a key aim for a spa manager.

It is necessary not only to take into consideration the actual experience but also how the experience fits into the entire spa journey as well. Each part of the journey should flow seamlessly, one into the other, whilst at the same time each part is distinctive.(Dewy, 1934).

Experience 'value creation' is about taking the spa experience onto the next level, not just making it memorable and satisfying but also profitable – "customer experience value creation is the performance of actions that increase the worth of goods, services or even a business" (Businessdictionary, 2019). 'Increase' here being the operative word!

Experiences in spas are driven by moments of engagement, or touchpoints, between people and brands, and the ideas, emotions, and memories that these moments create (Aarts and Marzano, 2003). When designing experiences in the spa environment, the following components should be considered:

- **Sensory** (how the experience affects the five senses).
- **Affective** (how the experience affects emotions and feelings).
- **Creative cognitive** (the thought processes of the client before, during and after the experience).
- **Physical behaviour and lifestyle** (of the clients having the experience).
- **Social group or cultural related influences** (and what impact they have on the client's expectations).

Sensory

The best spa experiences are interactive, lifting the client's spirits by igniting their senses: touch, smells, sounds, tastes and visuals. The more activated the senses, the more memorable the experience will be and the greater potential for the client to seek to repeat the experience. In creating experiences, the spa manager should ask themselves the following questions:

- How can I make this experience **visually appealing**? What will the clients see as they move around the spa? How can the interior design, lighting and decoration contribute to the experience?

- What are the **sounds in each zone** of the spa? How can different types of sounds improve the mood of the spaces? Would music or noise effects be preferred? More importantly, where is it necessary just to have total silence?

- What about **smells and aromas** – good and bad? What does the client smell as they step in through the door? (That first smell makes an impressionable impact). How do the changing rooms smell? The pool areas? Are they damp and musty or fresh and clean smelling? What aromas could enhance the treatments and spa waiting areas?

- What will the guest **touch** during their visit (towels, robes, slippers)? More importantly how will the guest be touched by the therapists? Spas are tactile but they must also respect personal space. When and how is it appropriate and in what way to touch the guests?

- What **tastes** can be incorporated into the spa journey? Will there be fresh fruit at the reception, healthy nibbles and herbal teas in the relaxation areas? What will be the concept of the spa menu? How can the tastes be linked to the treatments in the spas or the local culture?

- What about the **sixth sense**, those intangible feelings that the guest picks ups from the atmosphere and vibe of the spa? How do the staff contribute to the energy they create in the spa? How is the manager setting the example?

Affective

This refers to the arousal and activation emotions, their intensity and the impulse of the client to either move toward having an experience or away from it. Obviously in a spa the manager wants the guest to move toward experiences, so much so that they want to come back and repeat their visit again and again. Therefore, the spa manager needs to know the stimulus points in the spa journey, not just those that bring out positive emotions, but also those that hinder it as well.

Cognitive

Experiences are influenced by both the expectation prior to the experience as well as the event itself. Once the experience has happened it will remain in the client's memory forming a basis for new preferences and expectations (Larsen, 2007). Spa managers need to produce experiences that both live up to the guests' expectations and that lodge themselves positively in the client's memory, so much so that they will want to retain the experience and repeat it again and again.

12

Physical behaviours and lifestyle of the clients

These will have a direct impact on the experiences offered and the levels at which the clients will want to experience them. This is influenced by factors like health status (sedentary/active, fit/unfit, etc) and interests and hobbies.

Social group or culture

These will also affect their choices and preferences – class, level of education, age, nationality, culture, religion, sex, income level, sexual orientation, etc.

When creating an experience, all of these five components should be taken into consideration. In addition, there are also different stages of an experience. Aho (2001) lists seven:

1 **Orientation** (awakening interest in the clients).

2 **Attachment** (strengthening their interest).

3 **Visiting** (the actual experience).

4 **Evaluating** (when the client critically compares the experience with other experiences).

5 **Storing** (when the client stores the experience through photos, films, souvenirs or just memories).

6 **Reflection** (when the client remembers and reflects on the experience).

7 **Enrichment** (when the client cherishes the memories of the experience and plans to repeat it).

What is interesting to learn from this is that the spa experience begins before the actual visit and ends long after. Depending on the type of experience, it might or might not cover all the stages. The degree of intensity of each different stage will vary – the stronger the intensity level of each stage the more likely it is to carry on to the next one.

Experiences in spas do not just influence the guests or clients. they also affect areas of the business (Boswijk, Thijssen and Peelen, 2007: 145–146), for example:

1 Internal business perspective, core competences and technology.

2 The organisation's people and culture.

3 Innovation and creativity capacity.

(Zátori, 2013)

■   Types of experiences

Spa managers will normally be involved in creating three types of experiences:

1 **A micro experience:** "... is a **small, subtle, affordable** and **memorable** touch that resonates with customers for years. Not difficult to achieve, but challenging to design into the behaviour of a whole team or organisation. When it comes to these experiences, what we're most often talking about with micro experiences is those that are designed and executed at ground level" (Hill, 2017).

I was staying in the Ritz Carlton Abama hotel in Tenerife on a conference. I was feeling tired and stiff so I asked at the front desk for some bath salts to be sent to my room. Later after the conference finished, I went back up to my room and there was a beautiful bed display with a flower and a card from the housekeeper saying that she hoped I enjoyed my bath. When I went into the bathroom it was decorated with petals, there was a candle on the side and a little pack of beautiful bath salts. I was impressed with the effort that they had put into making a whole micro experience out of a simple request for bath salts.

Elena Bazzocchi, Global Hospitality Manager at Lemi Group

This example not just shows how the customer's expectations were exceeded but also how hospitality is clearly at the core of the resort's culture. It shows a real understanding of a detailed approach to minor customer interactions and how such experiences can have a major positive effect on the overall stay.

2   **Medium level experiences**: this might include introducing a new treatment or service into the spa or spa package.

3   **A complete experience**: a complete experience is the end to end customer journey, right from clicking on the website to returning home. It does not just include the time in the spa, it also includes the journey to and from the facility, the expectations before the journey and the memory afterwards.

Developing spa concepts, spa design and branding

Part of the role of the spa manager is to come up with ways to utilize their spa space more efficiently by generating more profit directly (i.e. through the implantation of a new product or service to sell) or indirectly (through improving the customer experience). The most common areas a spa manager will come across include:

- Making use of unused space.
- Making a used space even more profitable.
- Changing treatments or product lines to improve profitability and/or customer satisfaction.
- Renovating an entire spa or part of a spa.
- Building a new spa concept from scratch.

Figure 12.1 shows how project proposals are put together.

Initially an outline of the project is written up and the proposal submitted (the items within the dotted line). If the idea, concept outline, sketch plan and numbers are approved, then a more detailed concept plan can be put together.

12

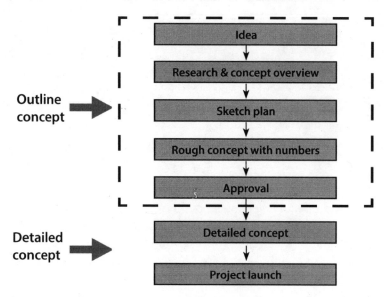

Figure 12.1: The process of putting a project proposal together.

One common fault that many spa managers and operators make is proposing an idea based on their preferences and likes, however, what the spa manager likes and what the market demands may be are two different things. In order to really understand what services are needed or missing the spa manager should:

- Ask the customers' opinion (through surveys and talking to them directly).

- Ask the opinions of the staff – after all they are the ones in direct day to day contact with the clients.

- Examine the trends (through reading industry magazines, lifestyle articles and visiting trade exhibitions and conferences).

- Go out and look at the competition, competitors offering a similar product (existing peers), superior competitors and award winners (stretch peers) and competitors developing new ground breaking facilities (future competition) (Connor and Cohen, 2008).

- Asking the owners or the bosses for their opinion. (The more enthusiastic the decision makers the more likely the chance of approval!).

In order to create a successful spa product, spa managers should base their decisions on concrete data and statistical information. First look at the key data – the number, revenue and trends of the different treatments, feedback from partners and the number and types of guests and their feedback.

Within reasonable limits the decision on what to do with the space, should be based on such research and data rather than the apparent constraints of the space. Fitting the concept into the space is the responsibility of the designer or architect, but it is the spa manager's job to come up with the concept. Of course, a spa manager with a good eye for interior design and space planning can contribute their ideas and suggestions.

A spa manager is more likely to get their idea or project approved if they have conducted thorough research and if the proposal is logical and fits the philosophy and vision of the spa. How the spa manager presents the proposal is also important – it needs be put together succinctly in a well thought out presentation with attractive pictures, graphics and credible figures. The spa manager will then need to pitch their idea convincingly, selling their proposal to the decision makers, pointing out why it is necessary for the business and why it is sustainable in the long term. Ultimately the project proposal will only be accepted if the numbers behind the idea are convincing. This means putting together a feasibility study.

■ What is a feasibility study?

A feasibility study (also referred to as a feasibility analysis) is an evaluation and analysis of a project or system. Its aim is to evaluate whether or not the project is technically and financially feasible. Financially feasible, means whether the project is achievable within the estimated cost and whether it makes good business sense (i.e., will it be profitable?) Put simply: a feasibility is an analysis of how easily or successfully a project can be completed (Market Business News, 2019).

In order to see if a project is feasible a 'return on investment' (ROI) calculation is required. A ROI evaluates the gain (or the loss) made on an invested amount compared to the amount of money invested. It is measured through a percentage. A simple ROI is calculated by the formula:

(Gains from the investment – Investment Costs) / Investment Costs.

Imagine a new sauna complex is built and the investment is costed at €100,000. The revenue projection is €900,000 Euros, profit projection is €125,000 Euros

(125,000 - 100,000) / 100,000 = 0.25 or 25% (Return on Investment)

Most investors in the spa industry will want a return of at least 18 – 20% (Barnes, 2016).

Return on investment is also depicted in terms of payback years.

If we imagine that a massage room for couples has been built onto the spa as an extension. The investment is €28,000 and the profits projected for the years after construction are:

Year One	Year Two	Year Three	Year Four	Year Five	Total
8,835	9,718	10,690	11,759	12,935	53,937

A quick way of working out when the investment will be paid back is €53,937 / 5 = €10,787 (average profit per year). €28,000 / €10,787 = 2.5 years. Of course, this is not entirely accurate as the profit is not the same each year. To calculate a more specific return the following is needed:

By looking at the profit results we can estimate that sometime in Year 3 we will pay back the €28,000.

Add Years 1 and 2 together. This should equal €18,553

Minus the investment by Years 1 and 2. €28,000 – €18,553 = €9,447

12

Divide the result by Year 3 profit. €9,447 / €10,690 = 0.88 (0.9)

Add on the first 2 years. The investment will be returned in 2.9 years.

There are no fixed rules, however generally speaking, you would expect a new spa service such as a salt cave or an infra sauna to pay back in under five years maximum; services like a new piece of beauty equipment can even pay themselves back in a year. A fitness club should pay back its investment between 5 and 10 years and a hotel, which should break even at about 7 years, should repay itself in between 10 and 15 years.

Often the spa manager will be asked to put together different versions of a feasibility based on a best- and worst-case scenario. They should not forget to take into consideration the full operational costs into account when working on the feasibility – maintenance, labour etc. The borrowing costs should also be accounted for whether it's coming direct from an investor or loan.

■ Making use of unused space

If we imagine that there is an empty room in the spa or a unused space (i.e. under the stairs, the end of a corridor, an empty storage space, etc) the spa manager should ask themselves:

- What can I do with this space to make more revenue/profit?

  And/or

- How can I transform this space to give more added value to the customer's experience?

If the above two examples are not possible, the spa manager should think of other alternatives. These can range from space to add to the customer's experience or even an extra room for staff, or more office or storage space, if needed.

It should be emphasized that sometimes empty unused space can have an undefined aesthetic value. A large, spacious reception area, with several square metres not utilized may actually add to the atmosphere of the booking and the guest journey. Not every space needs to have a function, sometimes a space's only function is for purely for visual delight and a 'feeling' of space.

■ Making a used space more profitable

It might be that a used space can be utilized more effectively to have the potential to generate more profit than at present. If the demand for a certain treatment is decreasing (sunbeds are a prime example) by changing the function to something else (e.g. a massage hydro bed) revenue can be drastically improved. In such cases, the feasibility should be based on the projected forecasted profit of the new service minus the performance of the existing profit – as it is the difference in the profit that will determine whether or not the idea is feasible.

The spa manager should look at each space and treatment, the revenue they bring in and how these can be improved. This is why having a report based on revenue per treatment room and service is useful.

■ Changing product lines to improve profitability and/or customer satisfaction

One issue that is fairly common in a spa facility is the need to change spa or beauty product lines. Spa retail and treatment lines fall in and out of fashion; what might have worked for the spa for the last ten years, might be no longer suitable for the new client base. Maybe the clients have changed, maybe they have got bored of the existing brand, maybe the facility is re-evaluating its concept or maybe it is just simply time for a change.

The aim of changing a spa and/or beauty product line must be to increase profitability and at the same time satisfy the expectations and needs of the guests, not just because it's a line that the owner or spa manger likes. When deciding on which line(s) to choose, the spa manager should consider the following:

- Should it be a 'professional' brand (i.e. the products are only available for sale and use through the spa outlet and not purchasable in retail shops or airports)?
- Whether or not it is necessary to have an international product line with a recognisable name or will a local brand suffice, or a mixture of the two?
- How the line will fit the level of the spa (3, 4 or 5 star).
- How the line will meet the needs of the profile of the guests (age, nationality, sex, culture, etc).
- How the ingredients of the products and delivery of the treatments fit in with the concept of the spa (e.g. natural, aromatic, bio, medical etc).
- How organised and strong is the local representation. It does not matter how good the products are or how strong the brand name is if the local support is weak. This point is absolutely critical. Brand representation can be excellent in one country and dreadful in another.
- What quality of marketing, PR and training support is offered by the product company? Normally this should come at no cost to the spa.
- The quality of the brand's standardized treatment methods.
- Does the company offer quality, regular training *in the local language*?
- Is it possible to negotiate a contract where only the retail products are bought once they have been sold in the spa?

To select their brand line, the spa manager should evaluate as many suitable professional spa and beauty brands as possible as there are always new and exciting concepts being introduced into the market. Attending trade exhibitions and conferences or B2B hosted buyers' events is an excellent way to source out suppliers.

Once a selection has been shortlisted, the spa manager should visit the product line's headquarters to see for themselves how the company is run and to get a feel for what it will be like to work with the organisation – after all this is going to be a long-term partnership. Next it is necessary to get the staff on board which will mean organising treatment trials and demonstrations with the therapists to gauge their reaction.

12

Once the decision has been finalized the spa manager should put their proposal together, it should include:

■ A summary comparison of three shortlisted companies.

■ A price comparison of the shortlisted companies (operational and start-up) and the existing brand.

■ The strengths and weaknesses of the shortlisted companies.

■ A feasibility study for the proposed finalist including the *difference in performance* between the *current product line's* performance and forecasted performance the proposed *new line*.

■ Renovating an entire spa or part of a spa

The starting point for an entire spa renovation (or partial renovation) is the same as for any other project. In order to make the right strategic decisions, particularly when considering an investment for a large project it is not just enough to consider the current needs, but to ask the question: what will be the needs and trends in five- and ten-years' time?

Before getting excited and jumping in to plan something that might not work, the spa manager should also have some idea as to what restrictions there could be. Whilst their job is to submit the concept and leave the space planning to the architect or designer, they should also be realistic (for example 20 square metres will be too small for a fitness room, a 300 square metre pool is perhaps unnecessary for a small club spa of 50 members etc.).

When examining competitor spas to get ideas, it is not enough just to look, the spa manager should visit the competition as a guest, experience the guest journey and see what works and what does not – everything from the front door, to the treatment rooms, to the toilets and showers.

Who is the market?

The market whom the spa will want to attract, both in the near and distant future, is critical to the concept. Before embarking on a large renovation project, spa manager should ask themselves:

■ Who are my guests?

■ Who will they be in the future?

■ Why are they coming now?

■ Why will we want them to come in the future?

■ What treatments and services do they want now?

■ What will they want in the future?

■ What is our destination's USP and reputation? (How can the spa link into this?)

■ What is our country's USP and reputation? (How can we capitalize on this?)

Figure 12.2: Assessing the market for a new service or facility. Adapted from Dvorak et al. (2014).

Why guests come and what they want when they arrive are two different things. It might be that they are motivated to come for their health, the scenery, the reputation of the destination etc, but actually what they want when they get there may be something different such as relaxation, passive treatments and some outdoor activities. Through research it is imperative to distinguish the gap between these two needs. The motivational needs (the reason they want to visit) is what should be focused on in the marketing, however their actual needs (what they really want when they get there) this is what needs to be created in the services and facility.

Location is a major factor. Different locations will have their impact on the concept (e.g. a spa in a residential area might aim to offer more pampering services aimed at women, a spa in a business district maybe more fitness orientated). Generally, day and club spas will be either where people live, work or on route between the two and hopefully on a convenient traffic route. If it is a destination or resort spa the question will be – what does the spa need to offer in order to attract people to make the effort to travel to it? Spa services are available now in every town globally. To get guests to travel distances, particularly long distances, resorts, destination and hotel spas need to offer something different that clients cannot get elsewhere, something magnetic. How the guests get there is also a factor – if it is public transport, how convenient is it? If it is by car, what about parking? The guest journey begins at the point of enquiry – the journey to the spa is also a key part of the experience.

12

■ SWOT analysis

In order to investigate the viability of a spa concept a SWOT analysis is an excellent way to examine the strengths, weaknesses, opportunities and the possible threats of the project. Figure 12.3 is an example of a SWOT analysis for a club spa in an inner-city area.

STRENGTHS	WEAKNESSES
Spa reputation, products, services, customer service, facility etc	Location – off the beaten track, parking, wrong side of town
OPPORTUNITIES	THREATS
Potential to offer new services, space to expand, expanding nearby residential area, growing economy	Reputation of surrounding area, rising rents in the complex, changing demands of customers

Figure 12.3: Example SWOT analysis.

The initial project proposal

The first proposal will be a general submission of the idea to see if it is worth proceeding with the project concept planning. As it will be submitted to the directors or owners, it needs to be punchy and to grab their attention – too much information and they might lose interest, too woolly and they will start to pick holes. A good guideline is:

1   A short summary of the project and its aim.

2   A short explanation of why the project is necessary.

3   A description of the market and its needs.

4   A summary of how the project will be marketed.

5   A description of the facility (with a sketch layout, images and pictures).

6   A brief summary feasibility with the main figures for the first five- or ten-year's performance and the return of investment.

7   A SWOT analysis.

8   A summary of the benefits of doing the project and the consequences of not.

We are often asked, "What is the concept?" and when approaching a spa and wellness development project the answer to this question has to drive the design and the user experience; and it has to be driven by understanding the consumer. Hand in hand with the concept, the development has to align with the financial potential of the space to prevent over or under building. Define who your consumer is; what is the story and innovation that appeals to them. At the same time really understand the financial projections and build to support that growth; incorporating flexibility in to the nuances of the design will provide more opportunities for change as the business develops.

Claire Way, Managing Director, Spa Strategy

■   Planning the layout

Whilst a spa manager is not expected to be an architect or designer, they need to have an awareness of the critical points to be aware of in the layout and traffic flows of a spa. Key points in planning a spa facility include:

- ■ Correct sizes and spaces of treatment areas and rooms (each should have revenue calculation based on forecast usage, best- and worst-case scenarios).
- ■ Space utilization to maximize profit opportunities.
- ■ Logical access and traffic routes.
- ■ Wet and dry area separation and traffic.
- ■ Layouts that take into consideration operational costs, in particular manning costs (e.g. not building two receptions when one will do).
- ■ Correct ventilation, temperature control.
- ■ Effective water drainage in wet areas.
- ■ Correct floor finishes for the different spa areas.
- ■ Enough storage, cleaning and staff areas.
- ■ Interior design to last (spas are not normally renovated every 5 years, what is built now should still look 'appealing' in 10, 15 or even 20 years' time).

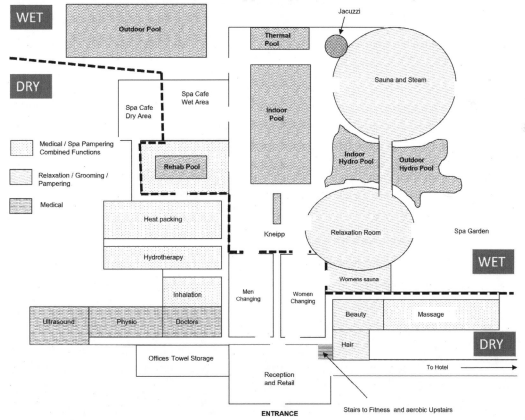

Figure 12.4: A good example of a thermal medical spa.

In the layout in Figure 12.4 certain areas are allocated for medical services (doctors, physio, ultrasound), but some treatments (heat packs, hydrotherapy, inhalation and massage) can also be offered to both guests coming on relaxation and/or medical visits. Dry areas and wet areas are also clearly separated, which is a must for any type of spa. Traffic routes are logical, for guests coming from the hotel, from outside and even those guests just coming for treatments and not using the pool areas. Manning points have also been strategically placed with the café able to serve both guests just for treatments and guests using the pool areas.

Whilst the aim of this chapter is not to give a detailed spec for each treatment room, here are some considerations and important points in the planning that the spa manger should take note of:

- **The entrance**: is a key touchpoint in the client's journey, it should not just be functional, it should set the scene for the whole spa experience with lighting, decoration, design signage, etc.

- **The reception**: is the welcome space, it must create a positive first impression for the start of the spa experience. The size and number of reception workplace stations should be taken into consideration, as well as the anticipated traffic at peak times – no guest wants to be standing in a long queue. A decision needs to be made whether the desk should cater for standing customers (if there is a high traffic and quick interactions) or sitting customers (for spa hotels where the package scheduling can take some time) or alternatively a mix of both. The reception is the ideal place for selling and displaying merchandise and this should be planned thoroughly with the advice of a retail professional. Safe deposits are another consideration, as is a cloak room for spas in cold climates. It is advised not to have the office linked to or behind the reception as this can become a 'hang out' for staff. Thought should be given to how the spa treatment and service information will be communicated – either through interactive tablets, screens or pamphlets. Each of these options should be well thought through and their placement designed into the overall concept. If towels are to be handed out (and deposited) this should also be planned into the design. Receptions are places to meet and greet, areas to wait and relax in before or after treatments, a clear vision and concept for these activities should be created.

- **Waiting areas and corridors**: should be planned into the concept to avoid having chairs in lines outside treatment areas. Alcoves, with sofas, pictures, soft lighting can enhance the client's visit. Likewise, the corridors connecting the different spa services can become a micro experience or touchpoint in the journey. One spa in the Czech Republic designed their spa corridors into an exhibition with historical pictures of the spa and old original baths and piping displayed with explanations. Another spa created different themes in different corridors (for example one corridor had a forest theme and when the guest walked through it, forest sounds played, the next a water theme, where running water could be heard etc).

■ **Treatment rooms:** the minimum size of a massage or treatment room should be 12 square metres (3 x 4 metres). This leaves enough space for the treatment bed and the therapist to work in. Whilst a shower can also fit into this space, it can be a bit tight, so for treatments requiring a shower, more space should be added. For flooring, tile, wood or PVC type finish is advised, never carpet. A wash basin, a small unit for storage, a shelf, hook for the guest's clothes and mirror are all essential. Lighting should have direct (for cleaning) and indirect options (for treatments) with a dimmer to adjust the tone. Different music options should be available with sound level control. In addition to the treatment bed, there should be a stool for the therapist, a chair for the guest and a container for the dirty linen. Temperature is a key issue – 22°C would be recommended – no client wants to freeze, but any warmer and it can be too hot for the therapist.

■ **Changing rooms:** there are several options for changing rooms. In smaller and more upmarket operations, separated men and women are the norm, with some cubicles for guests who desire more privacy. However, in large high-volume spas, co-ed changing rooms with private changing cubicles can be an option. Temperature is important (around 24°C is comfortable). Spas should consider underfloor heating, and smooth surfaces are advised (anti-slip PVC or tile) never carpeting. Lighting should have direct (for cleaning) and indirect (for mood) options. Music and televisions can add to the experience. Vanity stations are essential, with mirror, shelf, hairdryer etc. A built-in spin drier for wet swimwear is also necessary. Toilets and showers should be positioned between the changing room and entrance to the spa wet areas, the layout ensuring that traffic does not cross over pooling water. Locker sizes are dependent on spa type, but each locker should have at a minimum, space for two hangers, a shelf for personal items and a place for shoes. Benches underneath the locker themselves are more practical and comfortable than placed in the centre of the changing room. Whatever key system is chosen, it should be one where clients can choose their own locker rather than be automatically assigned.

■ **Showers:** no mosaic, particularly on the floor – mosaic involves grouting which is difficult to clean, and mosaic can break off, causing sharp edges. Taps and shower heads should be simple to use and hardy – if the taps are too complicated to operate the clients will break them. There should a built-in shelf for personal items – not screwed into the tiles as these tend to break off. Showers should have doors rather than curtains for privacy. Adequate sloping for drainage is critical and the showers should be placed to ensure that any water pooling outside the shower is not on a traffic route. Hooks for towels and dressing gowns should be at hand, next to the shower itself.

■ **Pools:** as with the changing rooms, an air temperature of around 24°C is preferred, and ventilation should be sufficient to prevent steaming. There should be no sharp corners anywhere. Tiles should be slip proof and curved at the joins to the walls for easy cleaning. There should be suitable sloping and a

12

sufficient number of drains to avoid water pooling. No swimming pool should be smaller than 10 metres long, and depths can range from 1 metre upwards (in certain locations if the depth is under 1 metre it may not be necessary to employ a lifeguard). Mosaic is not also advised for pools, as in time, pieces break off creating a hazard with sharp edges. Repairing mosaic will also mean having to drain the pool. Lighting should be both direct (for cleaning) and indirect (for mood).

- **Saunas**: the trend now is for as much glass as the space will allow, making it easier for guests to see out and in, and the larger the sauna the better. Eight square metres is a recommended minimum size – any smaller and the space becomes uncomfortable for the guests, with an increased risk for accidents. Coals should be covered with a guard. It should be possible to access under the wooden seating to clean sweat from the floor underneath. Music and sound in the sauna can enhance the experience.

- **Steam rooms**: larger tiles are preferred not mosaic – the grooves between tiles collect sweat. Steam rooms can be smaller than a sauna as people tend to sit rather than lie down. Care should be taken that the pipe emitting the steam is not directed where it can cause burns to guests.

- **Plunge pools**: showers should be placed immediately before the entrance to the plunge pool to ensure that guests actually shower before using it. The placement of the plunge pool should take traffic routes into consideration so that guests do not have to walk through pooling water.

- **Jacuzzis and hydro pools**: jacuzzis and jets make noise. Having them in a spa area can destroy any peaceful atmosphere, therefore thought should be given to their placement. For hydro pools, the experience should be carefully thought through (i.e. types of jets – geysers, foot jets, wall jets for the back at different levels, shoulder showers, bubble baths etc, and the suitable positioning in the pool).

- **Relaxation rooms**: silence and tranquillity should be enhanced through design, lighting and ensuring that the room is not disturbed by noise (e.g. from pool area/jacuzzi/children's areas etc). Relaxation bed choices will depend on guest types. High volume spas need practical easy to clean loungers, luxury spas should offer mattresses, cushions (waterbeds are also worth considering) etc. Waterproofing the mattress is an important point as no guest wants to relax on a damp mattress. Sound and music will depend on the category of spa, with options ranging from central systems to personalized music headphones. Guests will expect amenities and food and beverage options (herbal teas, healthy snacks).

■ The detailed concept proposal

If the initial proposal has been accepted then the spa manager will be expected to coordinate a detailed plan of the project. This will include:

- A summary.
- A more detailed plan layout.
- A description of each area(s), the key services in each area and what the guest will experience.
- The different profile types of guest profile and target groups (hotel guest, day spa guest, VIP, single women, business people etc).
- A complete end to end guest journey description for each type of guest profile (i.e. hotel guest visiting spa only, hotel guest on package, day spa guest, treatment only guest, VIP guest, a guest just wanting to look around… etc).
- A list of proposed treatments and packages.
- Pricing.
- A spa marketing and sales strategy and plan.
- Staff organisation chart, job descriptions, shifts and costs.
- A budget based on the feasibility study.
- A preopening plan.

■ Preopening plan

Preopening plans vary but will include;

- Sales office set up. Normally in a day or club spa, the sales office will be set up at least 6 months before opening so that memberships can be presold and site tours can be offered. This will have its own budget and plan.
- FF&E (fixtures, fittings, equipment) list. A list will be collected of all the equipment and fittings needed in each room.
- Operational systems – standard operational procedures, treatment protocols, brand standards all have to be written, based on the guest journeys.
- Cleaning standards and systems – all have to be put together. This is normally completed in conjunction with the company that will be supplying the products.
- Health and safety systems and procedures.
- Inventory of all start up materials.
- Security – systems and lock inventories.
- Training and recruitment, staggered according to employment start dates. Normally the manager will be recruited first (who will put together the job descriptions, contracts and training plan), followed by the sales team, then the department heads, then the therapists for training, then reception, and finally the cleaning staff.

12

■   Managing the spa brand image

The spa concept and the brand image should go hand in hand. Reviewing the brand, its vision, mission, values and goals is a continuous process. Every year or two years the spa image and brand should be assessed – its brand identity, how the brand is communicated, its reputation and planned developments.

Two exercises that can help in this reviewing process are a competitor placement and personality slider. First the spa is placed in a chart according to the competition (hopefully it will be offering something different or better than the competition), the criteria in this example are: exclusive, mainstream, leisure, medical – but these can be altered of course. From that a personality slider (more detailed qualities) can be put together to define the key characteristics of the brand.

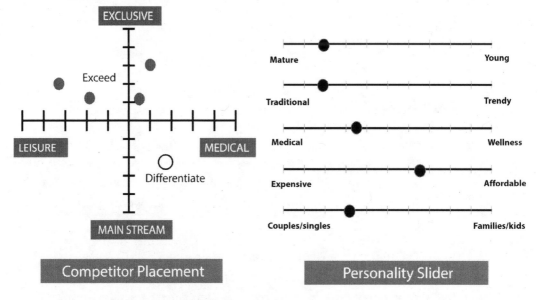

Figure 12.5: Competitor placement and personality slider charts.

From these two exercises, a 5, 10 and even 15 years strategy and project plan with medium- and long-term goals can be put together.

The word *authenticity* has been mentioned many times in this book, as more and more people seek original unique experiences. To stand out from the competition and to compete with the many health spa destinations, spas have to offer something different. They can do this by connecting the experiences to the uniqueness of the location and by looking to locality for inspiration by:

■ Using locally sourced natural products.

■ Integrating the local natural resources into the products offered in the spa.

■ Basing treatments and experiences on local authentic traditions.

■ Incorporating the local culture into the spa rituals and experiences.

Sustainability and spas

Sustainability (the ability to sustain or uphold), means to be in coexistence with the world, not using resources to the detriment of the planet or of future generations. In the spa environment, sustainability concerns four key areas:

1 **Environmental** – the impact that the spa operations have on the environment.

2 **Social** – the impact the spa has on the people working and using the spa and the people that the spa may have an effect on (e.g. the local community).

3 **Economic** – the long-term impact that the spa business will have on the local economy.

4 **Personal** – how the spa can promote the wellbeing of the individual.

Spas cannot ignore the sustainability revolution. There is a serious demand for spas to play their part in protecting the environment, and to contribute positively economically to it. People, particularly the younger generations, are becoming far more astute. Businesses that are seen to be putting profits before their environment, staff and local communities place themselves at a serious risk.

According to Bonnie Baker, the founder of Green Spa Network, consumers are showing increased interest not only in business operations but in company values as well. They want to buy from businesses they trust (Spa Executive, 2019). 'Thinking before purchasing' is in its early stages, but the future will be one where customers will ask questions like; "What effect does this spa have on the environment?", "What is the spa doing with its profits, are they investing back into the business and community or not?", "How are the staff being treated? Are they working for fair wages and professional conditions or not?", "Is this spa situated in a country which protects human rights and the environment?" etc.

A spa which is sustainable may require more time to return on its investments, as being sustainable means valuing profitability not in the short-term (i.e. from financial quarter to financial quarter), but rather in years or even decades. Since being sustainable includes cost saving and making an effective use of resources, it will lead to increased profitability in the long term! It is not enough just to have a green logo and a vision; sustainability needs to be incorporated and put into action, in the daily operation. Sustainability can only become part of the culture if the staff are on board, which means getting them actively involved. Sustainability therefore needs to be a core module in the training system and built into the work processes. Getting the staff motivated and building sustainability into the daily operation of the spa is a first key step in making a spa more sustainable.

The art of being successful in this field is to find the right balance between being sustainable and meeting the needs of the customer – this is not always easy. Here are some key areas that spa managers should think about:

■ There should be policies and practices to focus on waste prevention, reduction and recycling. Rubbish separation (clearly labelled and managed) is a minimum standard that all spas should now have in operation.

12

■ The spa should be designed or have at least have long term plans to implement a sustainable water management system. There should be an efficient waste water management policy both for the present and in the long term.

■ There should be an increased awareness and actions to reduce energy consumption through more efficient usage, technology, insulation and space utilization.

■ Spas do not require strong lighting; energy efficient solutions should be implemented wherever possible. As much natural lighting as possible should planned and utilized in spa concepts.

■ Laundry has a huge impact on the environment. Spas should look at ways to reduce the amount and weight of laundry, use eco-friendly laundry detergents and energy efficient washer/driers.

■ Purchasing – spas should be choosing minimal packaged goods, bulk options and local products that require less transport.

■ Cleaning materials are a major source affecting air quality, therefore, spas need to purchase more environmentally friendly products which are less harmful to health at reasonable cost.

■ Using recycling containers or, better still, using durable containers (instead of disposables).

■ Plastic should be avoided wherever possible (plastic water bottles are a huge polluter) and reusable containers should be used instead.

■ The spa product line reflects the spa's commitment to sustainability. No spas should be using products known to contain health risks, such as parabens, petrochemicals, etc. Organic and natural are the buzzwords of today, but standards surrounding these terms are undefined. The guests of the future will demand products that are 'clean' products and as natural as possible, but also products that have a minimal impact on the environment as well.

■ Soaps, shampoos should not contain ingredients harmful to the environment (i.e. phosphates).

■ Spas should be contributing to their cultural heritage and the local economy by promoting the local culture, incorporating its traditions and ethics into the spa.

(Bali International Spa Academy, 2015)

As the list shows, being sustainable is good for business economically as in the long term it reduces costs, influences efficiency and increases productivity, but more importantly, at their core, spas do much more – they support health, wellbeing and happiness for their customers and they provide (or should provide) healthy positive work environments for the local population.

Up until now, countries have been judged on their success by GDP (Gross domestic product), the measure of the economic performance of a country (the value of the goods and services produced within a country). Each year the GDP percentage has to grow. However, the earth's resources are not infinite and with a growing population, the world cannot support unending material consumption and waste. Other measurements are now defining a country's success such the health, life satisfaction and the happiness of its populations. Spas and spa managers have a key role to play, not just in terms of producing profits, but more importantly playing their part in contributing to the sustainable wellbeing of individuals and communities. This can only have a positive effect on society as a whole and the world we live in.

> Every existing operation, new development and renovation needs to consider their position on sustainability and how that fits with their wellness concept. Ultimately it is the guest who will measure your authenticity; decide how the business want to be measured and live and breathe this position. Consumers, our industry and governments will continue to measure your sustainability message versus your actions and will hold up those that do and do not walk the talk.
>
> Claire Way, Managing Director, Spa Strategy

Feedback from the interviews – what the experts say

The interviewees were asked about their views of changing customer demands as well as measures that should be taken to make spas more sustainable. Here is a summary of their responses:

- Nataša Ranitović, CEO of Sunny Ltd. Wellness Consulting, provides a good summary of spa customers' needs and expectations "Spa customers are in search of unique experiences. They are taking a more proactive and holistic approach towards their health and prefer to combine more different experiences while exploring spa destinations e.g. combining spa services, hiking, forest bathing, spiritual practices, local cuisine, culture,history etc. They are more demanding in terms of spa concepts,offers and quality of services".

- Several respondents state that customers are looking for quality experiences, good service, personalisation, fast results, as well as greener spas.

- For economic sustainability, it is suggested to take care of revenue and yield management, run special promotions, create membership schemes and loyalty programmes. Several respondents also highlight the need for spas to keep up-to-date, for example: Chris Theyer, Training and Development Director of LivingWell Health Clubs mentions "Keeping in tune with customer needs, expectations and trends".

- In terms of environmental sustainability, several suggestions are made, for example, design buildings with natural heating and cooling mechanism; energy efficiency with lighting and use of water (e.g. re-use grey water, solar panels for pre-heating water); eco-friendly cleaning and laundry supplies;

12

control use of paper, e.g. digital spa menus only; get rid of single-use plastic – avoid plastic cups and straws and use large refillable body washes and shampoos; avoid food waste and compost leftovers; buy organic and bio products.

- In terms of social sustainability, staff and customer education are recommended, as well as engagement with local communities. This can include making use of local suppliers and creating a circular economy, as well as attracting more local customers to the spa.

- Look at Green Globe spa benchmarking, Green Spa Network guidelines and good practice examples like Six Senses.

Further reading

There have been a small number of studies on spa experience design. For example, Cohen and Bodeker (2008) emphasised the importance of creating multisensory experiences or 'sense-scapes' in spas. Ferrari, Puczkó and Smith (2014) took this work further and discussed the importance of the environment within spa experiences, including the aesthetics, design and atmosphere. Smith, Ferrari and Puczkó (2016) highlighted the importance of service innovation when creating spa experiences. Hindley and Smith (2017) suggest that cultural differences, expectations and preferences need to be considered in spa experience creation as far as possible. This includes the type of décor (e.g. minimalist or more opulent) and organisation of space (e.g. the separation of genders or guests with different preferences). Smith (2020) provides a broader overview of experience creation in wellness tourism including spas. She uses the Pine and Gilmore (2013) experience model as well as some of the tourism experience design theories of Tussyadiah (2014), as well as discussing service enhancement and sustainability.

There have been a few research papers written about sustainability in spas or wellness environments. Chawla (2017) focuses on eco-spas and provides a discussion of principles and models in sustainability theory and how they have been applied in the spa industry. Strack (2018) examines the challenges of being environmentally sustainable while remaining cost effective in Hungarian thermal medical spa hotels. Chaminé and Gómez-Gesteira (2019) provide an overview of sustainable resource management and water practice issues, including healing waters in spas.

References

Aarts, E. and Marzano, S. (2003) *The New Everyday: Views on Ambient Intelligence*, Rotterdam: 010 Publishers.

Aho, S. (2001) 'Towards a general theory of touristic experiences: Modelling experience process in tourism', *Tourism Review*, **56** (3/4), 33-37, Doi: 10.1108/eb058368

Bali International Spa Academy (2015) 'Building Sustainability into Spas, https://www.balibisa.com/building-sustainability-into-spas/ (accessed 23/09/2019).

Barnes, K. (2016) 'Attracting investment', Spa Business, https://issuu.com/leisuremedia/docs/spa_business_issue_1_2016_digital_e/64 (accessed 10/09/2019).

Boswijk,A. Thijssen, T. and Peelen, E. (2007) *The Experience Economy: A New Perspective*, Harlow: Pearson Education

Businessdictionary (2019) http://www.businessdictionary.com/definition/value-creation.html (accessed 09/09/2019).

Chaminé, H. I. and Gómez-Gesteira, M. (2019) 'Sustainable resource management: water practice issues', *Sustainable Water Resources Management*, 5, 3–9, Doi: 10.1007/s40899-019-00304-7

Chawla, G. (2017) 'Eco-spas: The Sustainability Agenda in the Spa Industry', in S. Rawlinson and T. Heap (eds) International Spa Management: Principles and practice, Goodfellow Publishers Ltd., pp.36-48.

Cohen, M. and Bodeker, G. (2008) Understanding the global spa industry, Oxford: Butterworth Heinemann.

Connor, G. and Cohen, M. (2008) *Understanding the Global Spa Industry*, London: Routledge

Dewey, J. (1934) *Art as Experience*, New York: Perigree.

Ferrari, S., Puczkó, L. and Smith, M. (2014) 'Co-creating Spa Customer Experience', in J. Kandampully (ed.) *Customer Experience Management: Enhancing Experience and Value through Service Management*. Dubuque, USA: Kendall Hunt, pp. 187-203.

Hill, S. (2017) 'The making of a meaningful micro, experience', https://medium.com/@sallyrhill/making-a-meaningful-micro-experience-6b03c6a2ba41 (accessed 10/09/2019).

Hindley, C. and Smith, M. K. (2017) 'Cross-Cultural Issues of Consumer Behaviour in Hospitality and Tourism', in S. K. Dixit (ed.) *Routledge Handbook of Consumer Behaviour in Hospitality and Tourism*, London: Routledge, pp. 86-95.

Larsen, S. (2007) 'Aspects of a psychology on the tourist experience', *Scandinavian Journal of Hospitality and Tourism*, **7** (1), 7-18, Doi: 10.1080/15022250701226014

Market Business News (2019) 'What is a feasibility study? Definitions and examples', https://marketbusinessnews.com/financial-glossary/feasibility-study/ (accessed 10/09/2019).

Pine, J. B. And Gilmore, J. H. (2013) 'The experience economy: past, present and future', in J. Sundbo and F. Sorensen (eds) *Handbook on the Experience Economy*, Edward Elgar Publishing, pp. 21-44.

Smith, M. K., Ferrari, S. and Puczkó, L. (2016) 'Service Innovations and Experience Creation in Spas, Wellness and Medical Tourism', in M. Sotiriadis and D. Gursoy (eds) *Handbook of Managing and Marketing Tourism Experiences*, Bingley: Emerald, pp. 299-318.

12

Smith, M. K. (2020-forthcoming) 'Creating Wellness Tourism Experiences', in Sharpley, R. (ed.) *Routledge Handbook of Experience Creation*, London: Routledge.

Spa Executive (2019) 'How sustainability in spas can improve business', https://spaexecutive.com/2019/04/26/how-sustainability-in-spas-can-improve-business/ (accessed 23/09/2019).

Strack, F. (2018) 'Consuming or overconsuming? Sustainability in Hungarian medical hotels', *International Journal of Spa and Wellness*, **1** (1), 20-38.

Tussyadiah, L. P. (2014) 'Toward a Theoretical Foundation for Experience Design in Tourism', *Journal of Travel Research*, **53** (5), 543-564.

Zátori, A. (2013) 'Tourism experience creation from a business perspective', PhD Thesis, Corvinus University of Budapest, http://phd.lib.uni-corvinus.hu/801/7/Zatori_Anita_den.pdf (accessed 25/09/2019).

C Conclusion

Although this book has mainly provided a pinpointed and practical guide to spa management, the summaries of existing research as well as the interview data from 45 spa practitioners help to position the work in a broader, global context. For a spa manager, it is important to have a clear awareness of international trends and changing lifestyle habits, even if they are working in the same spa for years, even decades. Generational shifts are happening every few years and the cultural background of guests may vary, especially if a location attracts international tourists. Whereas middle aged, professional women used to be the core market for spas, these days, it is just as likely to be couples or families with children. This can create new challenges requiring complex offers that target more than one segment simultaneously. In addition, individuals may wish to receive personalised and co-creative packages and treatments. In this age of social media and consumer reviews, being complacent is not an option. As consumers become more experienced and knowledgeable about spas and wellness, they will be more and more demanding and will benchmark their spa visit against previous experiences. Technology may help or hinder spa development as customers struggle with the dilemma of facilitating their lives through constant connectedness (e.g. lifestyle and wellness Apps to help manage their nutrition or fitness regime), but they may also be in desperate need of disconnecting and experiencing 'digital detox'. People are travelling more than ever at the same time as lamenting about the lack of sustainability of the planet. They may be keen to offset their carbon emissions and assuage guilt in greener spas. At present, veganism is growing at an unprecendented rate, which has implications for spa cuisine. Spa managers must remain alert and responsive to these challenges and contradictions.

This book has provided invaluable advice about how to create excellent customer service in spas through the use of touchpoints and engaging experiences. Spa employees are absolutely central to this process and their attitude and delivery will be the determining factor, regardless of how well the spa is designed physically. However, an holistic approach is essential which begins during the information provision and pre-booking phase and extends long after the visit is over with the creation of loyalty and encouraging repeat visitation. It is clear that research is needed to fully understand the spa's target markets and the motivations and profiles of the guests. More extensive research should be carried out on specific segments as well as on cross-cultural differences. This information is imperative for marketing and promotion of spa services, as well as experience design and creation.

The characteristics of a good spa manager are outlined in depth, highlighting the need to set an example to one's staff at all times. Communication and the ability to gain trust are essential skills, but good organisational skills, a well-groomed appearance and positive attitude can go a long way too. Research on leadership more generally often tries to ascertain which types of leadership work best in different contexts. Spas are highly individual, personal and sensitive environments, so a greater degree of empathy may be required than in some other industries. This was highlighted strongly by the interviewees. Given that it is already challenging in the spa industry to recruit and retain employees with the right qualifications, a spa manager must also work hard on incentivising and motivating his or her staff.

This book has also provided practical guidelines for selling and marketing spas effectively, as well as managing financial issues. A spa manager must have a clear understanding of revenue management, cost control and profit and loss. He or she must also train employees to be aware of how to maximise sales and optimise their own role in the organisation. The sustainability movement has also had a positive impact on many spa businesses, as energy saving initiatives tend to save money in the long term. An increasing number of new technological tools can be used to assist managers in the process of optimising the spa's financial situation. Spa managers and their staff need to be enthusiastic and dynamic when building relationships with guests. It is not advisable to become complacent, even if the spa is attracting a good number of guests. New competition can emerge at any time and it is essential to be aware of the changing needs and expectations of existing and potential guests. Nevertheless, as emphasised by the interviewees, the products must match the promotion and quality of services and treatments is paramount. For this reason, a whole chapter s devoted to quality management.

The process of quality management can be assisted by audits, quality assurance processes, mystery shopping or international accreditation systems. However, simple daily checklists should also be used in the day-to-day running of the spa. Approaches can vary from simply checking the aesthetics and cleanliness of an environment to ensuring that the guest is satisfied (including feedback and reviews) to more serious measures like ensuring that there are no outbreaks of disease. Health and safety is given a special focus in this book, especially those spas that also include medical and healing therapies. Employees must be very clear about correct procedures, including what to do in an emergency. Guests may also need to be properly briefed about the safe and appropriate way to behave in a spa environment.

The latter chapters in this book provide information about the broader context in which spas are operating, which includes lifestyle trends in nutrition, fitness, stress management, sustainability, etc. Different types of spas exist, including those offering balneotherapy or healing waters. However, there is a general consensus among interviewees that the medical and wellness fields are converging and that even wellness guests are asking for evidence-based results from their treatments and therapies. Although the trend at one time was to reduce spa menus, customers may at the same time request a variety of increasingly familiar treatments. As stated by Vladi Kovanic, CEO of Managing Director of VK organisation "Today's spa is much more than the original massage. Consumers expect a variety of massage styles, traditional practices such as reflexology, shaitsu and facials that have an element of cosmetic enhancement using branded product or therapies such as acupuncture". It is also suggested by many respondents that the spa of the future will offer even more integrated and holistic experiences which include relaxation, stress management, mental wellness and mindfulness, healthy and maybe vegan nutrition, fitness and spirituality. At the same time, it is suggested that spas need to become more affordable and to cater to an even wider group of consumers. This is a major challenge for any spa and most certainly for any manager!

Nevertheless, more and more research is emerging in the field of spa and wellness which provides evidence for treatments and therapies, as well as providing valuable information about changing lifestyle trends and characteristics of spa segments. The interviewees in this study were optimistic and excited about the future of spas, but they highlighted the growing competition, increasing knowledge and sophistication of spa consumers and the growth of the 'time poor' consumer who is looking for a quick fix. Health consumers have always been seeking a magic bullet or panacea to ease the challenges of modern living and ideally solutions that eschew the tedium of diets and fitness regimes. However, it is the job of the spa manager and his or her team to educate and awaken the desire in consumers to embrace healthier lifestyles and to enjoy this process. Spas can provide softer and more palatable options to consumers than medical services, combining relaxation and pampering with stress management therapies and suggestions for healthier living. The spa manager is not only a role model for his or her staff, but ideally a role model for his or her customers too. Passion, inspiration, enthusiasm and a desire to be the best that he or she can be. We hope that this book will take existing and potential spa managers closer to this ambitious but achieveable goal.

C

I Index